THE DIVINE COMMUNITY:
TRINITY, CHURCH, AND ETHICS
IN REFORMATION THEOLOGIES

John R. Loeschen

The Sixteenth Century Journal Publishers, Inc.
Northeast Missouri State University
Kirksville, Missouri

Habent sua fata libelli

BT
109
.L62
1981

This book has been brought to publication with the generous support of
Northeast Missouri State University

Copyright © 1981 by Sixteenth Century Journal, Publishers, Kirksville, Missouri. All rights reserved. No part of this work may be reproduced or transmitted in any form or by any means, electronic or mechanical, including photocopying and recording, or by any information storage or retrieval system, without permission in writing from the publisher. Printed in the United States of America.

ISBN 0-940474-01-8

Composed by Julie M. Farrar, NMSU, Kirksville, Missouri
Manufactured by Edwards Brothers, Ann Arbor, Michigan
Text is set in Paladium

This book is dedicated to my teachers:

W.W. SCHROEDER
in partial fulfillment of your courses
and as evidence that your thesis
has been heard

JOHN DILLENBERGER
submitted in evidence of the thesis
that Jackson Pollock is not necessarily
the last word about the possibility
of systematic thought

EDITOR'S PREFACE

With this volume of historical theology, the series "Sixteenth Century Texts and Studies" offers its first publication. Conceived and supported by the editorial board of *The Sixteenth Century Journal*, the new series is intended to provide an outlet for scholarship on all aspects of the sixteenth century.

Dr. John R. Loeschen, in *The Divine Community*, offers a provocative interpretation of interrelations, similarities, and contrasts among some major theological systems of the Reformation. Choosing for analysis the leading figures of three major Protestant traditions, Martin Luther, Menno Simons, and John Calvin, he brings forth some striking similarities and contrasts. But his comparative effort goes even deeper. What he has attempted to demonstrate in each author is that an apparently abstract theological doctrine, the author's conception of the Trinity, had a decisive impact on his conception of the church, and that that conception of the church, in turn, shaped the author's teaching on social and political ethics. Scholarship on the Reformation has had many studies on the social and political doctrines of the reformers, on their ideas of the church, and on various theological questions. Far more rare, however, is what the present author offers, a demonstration of how abstract doctrine was related to the practical issue of the nature of the Christian community and to the even more practical questions of social and political ethics. For good measure, in a concluding chapter as unconventional and challenging as the rest of the book, he analyzes the conclusions of the Council of Trent on these same three areas and shows some striking similarities and contrasts between Tridentine Catholicism and all three Protestant traditions. Not all readers will agree with Dr. Loeschen's interpretations, but no thoughtful reader will put down this book feeling unchallenged.

The Editor wishes to express thanks to the scholars who have evaluated this and several other manuscripts submitted for publication; to the office of the History Department at the University of Missouri-Columbia; to the editorial board of the sponsoring organization, *The Sixteenth Century Journal*; to Northeast Missouri State University for indispensable support; and to the managing editor of the *Journal*, Dr. Robert V. Schnucker of Northeast Missouri State University, whose mastery of the production side of the series and whose financial management are the secret ingredients without which this book, and the whole concept of the new series, could not have come to fruition.

Charles G. Nauert, Jr.
University of Missouri-Columbia
General Editor

CONTENTS

Chapter One   Prologue: Roots and Routes   1

PART I
INTRODUCTION: THE WHEEL   15

Chapter Two   Luther: The Judgment of the Cross   19
- A. Luther's Trinitarian Ascriptions   21
- B. The Church: Conformation to the Word   29
- C. The Church: Life in the Spirit   35

Chapter Three   Luther: Freedom and Order   45
- A. Living and Walking   48
- B. The Keys   53
- C. The Prudence of the Spirit   59

PART II
INTRODUCTION: THE LIVING WORD   67

Chapter Four   Simons: No Other Foundation   73
- A. The Christian Trinity   75
- B. Spirit: The Power of the Word   79
- C. The Word: The Discipline of the Spirit   88

Chapter Five   Simons: The Sign of Tau   97
- A. The Free Church   99
- B. Peace in Strife   107
- C. A Light in the Wilderness   116

PART III
INTRODUCTION: THE SHAKING OF THE FOUNDATIONS   125

Chapter Six   Calvin: Neither Confusion Nor Separation   129
- A. Calvin's Trinitarian Ascriptions   131
- B. A Reasoned Order   138
- C. Justice in Love   146

Chapter Seven   Calvin: Justice and Freedom   159
- A. The Invisible Church: Toward the Image of God   160
- B. The Visible Church: An Ordered Life   170
- C. The Church: Being and Becoming   181

Chapter Eight   Conclusion: The View From Trent   189
- A. Revelation and Trinitarian Functions   191
- B. Justification and Sacrament   198
- C. Church and Spirit   206

Appendix   221
Bibliography   230
Index   235

CHAPTER ONE

Prologue: Roots and Routes

A

It is a good thing that men engaged in the task of transforming the world, often at peril to life and always at peril to reputation, cannot see into the future. Were they cursed with foreknowledge of what later historians would say about them, they would see that their effects on the world were usually quite different from (often opposite to) what they intended. They would see that the issues which most preoccupied them were soon forgotten or transformed beyond recognition. They would see that what to them were at best secondary issues would in the sequel frequently become identified as their whole work of reformation. And finally they would see that the effects of their work, to whatever degree such effects reflected the reforming intention, were slowly transformed by the ongoing course of human life, ever new and ever forgetful. Such a vision, far from stimulating the reformer to redoubled and revised efforts, would surely lead him to heed the wisdom of the sage, that one is best advised to spend his life in the more useful work of tending cabbages.

The Protestant reformers of the sixteenth century would scarcely recognize their religious and intellectual progeny, and with the possible exception of some Anabaptist reformers, would not be generally happy with what they saw. Many issues which meant life or death to Luther and Calvin now would seem quaint, boring, and irrelevant to most of us. The alienation is so great that even a highly-respected historian of the Reformation era—a man writing from *within* the theological tradition—can say at the end of a recent text on the period that the subject is of "antiquarian historical interest—like Alexander's Persian Wars or the agrarian upheavals of the seventeenth century."[1] Except for occasional conflicts over "points of doctrine" which exercise increasingly isolated groups within the self-consciously orthodox Protestant denominations,[2] concern with doctrinal precision is largely a thing of the past.

Yet there is a different area of contemporary thought and life in Europe and the Americas which is still very importantly influenced by the work of the reformers. Technical theological niceties may belong to the past, but the issue of how men seriously concerned to live their religious faith are to res-

---

[1] Hans Hillerbrand, *Christendom Divided* (Philadelphia: The Westminster Press, 1971), p. 306.
[2] The issues between so-called "liberals" and "fundamentalists" were not the concerns of the 16th century reformers. The advocates of "Scripture alone" never identified the written text with Revelation, and the advocates of "Tradition" never intended to supplant the Bible with the results of science or reason.

pond to the institutions, ethics, and events in their society remains very much an existential concern. Is Christian faith effectively relevant in the "real world"? What are the implications of the distinctions characteristic of modern Western institutions, distinctions between private conscience and public responsibility, sacred and secular, church and politics, "moral convictions of church-goers" and "economic realities of modern society"?

Questions like these can be multiplied. If one is afflicted with the penchant for looking at things historically, the bottom-line questions become: why did we develop this way? what decisions in the past contributed not only to the present substance of our problems but even to the very way the issues appear to us and are formulated by our religious consciousness? As soon as the student of the history of Christian thought enters this line of questioning, the Reformation of the sixteenth century immediately becomes relevant as the locus for answers. The western religious man is still a creature of the Reformation and its various settlements.

Luther's teaching, for example, that the Christian as a public man cannot and must not administer society according to the Sermon on the Mount is our living inheritance. The insistence by most Anabaptist groups on the essential independence of the church from the state (and of the state from the church) is in the Bill of Rights to the American Constitution, though it remains a "hard saying" to many a political zealot in our time. And Calvin's belief that the church and the Christian are instruments whereby God transforms the social order has informed generations of civil rights leaders here and abroad.

These three examples all fall into the general category of social ethics, i.e., how the Christian and the church shall exercise worldly responsibility. They are also derivations from decisions made on issues usually considered far more basic to the theological task.[3] But notice the difference of emphasis in the three teachings. To use the terminology supplied by H. R. Niebuhr in his classic work, *Christ and Culture*,[4] the first implies a dualistic, the second a withdrawing or separatist, and the third a transforming position on the issue of the relation between the holy community and the world.

But these teachings are not at all the immediate application to personal existence of doctrines concerning the "higher things" of the divine nature. The teachings, rather, concern God's express will for the world and man's life in the community of that will: they concern the church. Not only do all the reformers, including Menno Simons, agree that *extra ecclesiam nulla salus*, but they all insist that genuine Christian life can happen only as the believer almost literally "receives himself" from that place wherein the Word is preached, the sacraments administered, and the discipline sup-

---

[3]John Calvin's carefully qualified affirmation of the Christian duty to resist and overthrow rulers who unjustly suppress Christian faith—an affirmation about which so much has been written, and which is so important for the history of Calvinism in particular and Protestantism in general—appears only in one single sentence, and that nearly on the last page, of the *Institutes*.

[4]H. Richard Niebuhr, *Christ and Culture* (New York: Harper & Row, 1951).

ported: the church. None of the reformers, when dealing with the issues of Christian ethics, ever considered the individual believer as his primary subject. There are degrees of integration, of course, from Simons' almost complete submersion of the individual into the saved community, to Luther's far more restricted relation. But differences of emphasis aside, the reformers speak as one: the subject of Christian life in the world cannot be adequately considered unless it is begun with a consideration of the church. Christian ethics presupposes ecclesiology.

We have been introduced to the idea that the different social ethics of the reformers can be associated with differences in their understanding of the church and of the individual's relation to the church. But now we are led to the next question: how is one to account for basic differences in Reformation ecclesiology, besides appeal to the cultural, temperamental, and circumstantial differences among the reformers? We experience some difficulty, some unsureness, with regard to the question. It seems to lead us from the more familiar terrain of social ethics into the uncertain and abstruse *terra incognita* of "higher theology." But the way is not so uncertain as we think, for we must remember that for the Protestant reformers the doctrine of the church is itself derived from a still more basic position. For the doctrine of the church does not come first, either to the theologians' thinking or to their pens. The church is understood to be the place, the means, the event, wherein the transcendent, wholly spiritual God makes himself present and effective for the concrete achievement of his will for the world. The church is, as all the reformers would agree, the *corpus Christi*.

The way the theologian understands the church in itself and in its relation to individuals and to the world therefore depends substantially upon the general relationships he sees between God and the world.[5] Ecclesiology reflects both sides of that relationship. On its empirical, sociological thissidedness, the church exhibits all the features characteristic of any basic human institution. On its theoretical, theological yon-sidedness, the church as an object of faith is the perfect society of the elect, the community of God's will, the body of Christ. From both perspectives ecclesiology systematically illustrates the general interrelatedness of God and the world as this is understood by the theologian.

Once again, it is the empirical side of ecclesiology which seems more familiar to us. Yet for the reformers it was the theoretical side which commanded attention. The "general relatedness of God and the world" is not, for the reformers at least, a matter for philosophical speculation, the results of which may then be applied to a constructive and ideal doctrine of the church. If one needs to understand the nature of God and his relation to the world, he must rather go to that place where the matter is discovered and il-

[5]This is as good a place as any to recognize what is, however, a moot question: does the "worldly experience" of the reformer produce his doctrine of God, or does the doctrine of God determine how he views his experience of the world? I will presume the latter view, if for no other reason than that the reformers themselves understood it this way. They were intelligent, trained, articulate men, and I think the burden of evidence is upon those who choose not to take the considered words of the reformers at face value. In any case my object is to discover associations of subjects rather than to promulgate cause-effect theories.

lustrated: to the Word of God, and that means to Christ. We cannot introduce *ecclesi*ology without making continual reference to *christ*ology. If we would make some headway in understanding the nature of the church, even on its empirical side, we must enter into the subject of the reformers' doctrines of Christ. For the reformers agree, though once again with differing emphases: ecclesiology and christology are distinct perspectives on the same matter. God in the fulness of time accomplished salvation in Christ, and thenceforth extends the reality and benefits of Christ to us by means of Christ's body, the church. And we neither ought nor can enter the church for any other purpose than that thereby we may be led to salvation and life in Christ.

If then we want to ask the reformers about the relation of God and the world, we cannot expect them to begin an essay in metaphysics. Rather the reformer will instinctively begin his response with a consideration of Christ, for he believes that it is only in Christ that the reality of God and the world can be usefully discovered. He will assay the matter posed to him, but he will do so from within christology and in theological not metaphysical language. And this means that the reformer will construe the question of the general relatedness of God and the world as a question concerning the Trinity. If we wish to understand the basic pattern of the reformers' social-ethical theory we must proceed, via a consideration of the church and the work of Christ, to a consideration of the trinitarian theology of the Reformation.

To comprehend the trinitarian teachings of the reformers, insofar as they are illustrated in the doctrines of Christ and the church and thereby basically differentiate the reformers' general approach to social ethics: that, and nothing less, is our task in this study.

B

In spite of the apparent massiveness of our theme, limitations of subject emerge as soon as we begin to investigate the christological positions of the reformers. A classical christological presentation usually was developed in three sections: 1) a consideration of the relation between the divine nature incarnated in Jesus and the Second Person of the Trinity; 2) the relationship perceived to exist between Christ's "person" and the two "natures," divine and human, which were actualized in his person at the incarnation; and 3) a presentation of the consequent "work of Christ,"—his accomplishment of salvation and his institution of the church.

We shall not need to be much concerned with the teachings of the reformers about the relation between Christ's person and natures, except where such materials might appear closely relevant to a particular issue under discussion. Just as on the doctrine of the Trinity, so on christology,[6]

[6] It is misleading to separate sharply "christological" from "trinitarian" doctrine, and I cannot do so in this connection. Both matters are in fact concerned with Christ. The so-called "trinitarian controversy" concerns the relation of that which is incarnate in Jesus, to God; with full equality established, the specific issues of the so-called "christological controversy" arise: the full humanity and unity of Jesus.

the church had long since completed its dogmatic clarifications and left precious little room for differences of opinion. On such basic doctrinal matters the Protestant reformers professed and defended their orthodoxy. One of the greatest burdens on the souls of the reformers was the charge of doctrinal novelty. The reformers went to great lengths to refute or evade that charge both before the world and before their own consciences. Usually the defense followed the line that what might appear to be novel teaching was really only the restoration of the ancient doctrines of Christ, or of Paul, or of the early church concerning Christ's person and natures. This line of argument was not, we may safely infer from the sequel, entirely persuasive. But so important in its consequences was the charge of novelty that the reformers extended the greatest effort to avoid occasion for the charge. They had quite enough on their hands without appearing to tamper with the formulas of Nicaea, Constantinople, and Chalcedon.

There is a rather transparent suggestion in the preceding paragraph, that the reformers we are studying really did have different understandings of christology despite their orthodox formulas. Such a view is precisely our thesis, and evidence for it will emerge as we focus attention in the succeeding chapters on two interrelated lines of christological discussion. These lines were indicated above as the first and third sections of christological presentation, the "introduction" and "application" of formal christology. Our interest in the christologies of the reformers will be primarily upon 1) their introductions to christology, i.e., the special meanings and functions of Christ's incarnation, atonement, and teachings insofar as they imply relationship of Christ's divine nature to the Second Person; and 2) the application of christology, i.e., the efficacy or function of Christ with respect to the church as an agency of salvation. The former consideration has trinitarian consequences, and the latter ecclesiological consequences.

Everything said above concerning the reformers' self-conscious abhorrence of novelty concerning christological dogma applies with even greater emphasis (though with less justification!) to trinitarian dogma. I say "with less justification" because while the main technical issues of the relation between the one divine nature and the three persons had been formulated long since, a number of circumstances tended to leave the doctrine somewhat unstable, incomplete, or irrelevant. There were first of all the continuing objections of Judaism and especially of Islam—standing and serious philosophical challenges which no responsible theologian could avoid. Secondly, and more importantly, the Christian tradition had somehow from the beginning got itself into the habit of ignoring the status and function of the Holy Spirit. Trinitarian constructions virtually were confined to the relation of Father and Son. The principles and arguments having first been established, the church fathers, if they remembered, would append the claim that their constructions applied to the Holy Spirit as well. The Holy Spirit is the great afterthought in trinitarian theology. Such an habitual neglect was to cost dearly, in terms of the separation of Orthodox and Roman confessions.[7] Thirdly and most importantly for our purposes,

[7] For a good contemporary survey of the history of trinitarian construction and criticism, see Edmund Fortman, *The Triune God: A Historical Study of the Doctrine of the Trinity* (Philadelphia:TheWestminsterPress,1972).

the church left virtually undeveloped any general "application" of the doctrine, except for some efforts in the areas of the theology of creation and of human psychology, as for example in the writings of Augustine.

It is, however, just this combination of circumstances that makes inquiry into the trinitarian theology of the reformers so fruitful and yet so difficult. For in the broad and virtually undogmatized arena of the application of trinitarian thought to the life of the church—a subject that is nowadays often referred to as the "economic Trinity"—the major reformers developed quite distinct patterns of thought. These distinctive patterns will be the basic focus of our efforts, and our conclusions will go a long way toward structuring the comparative analysis of the social theory of the reformers. What makes the study so difficult and the results so provisional is that the reformers appear to be almost completely unconscious of their own usages, and perforce of the usages of each other. None of the reformers' *de occasione* ascriptions of function to Father, Son, or Holy Spirit seems to exhibit a rigorously maintained line of approach, even though it is possible via more indirect methods of interpretation to uncover distinctive general patterns amid the welter and confusion of data. The limits and qualifications that this situation imposes upon the student will be considered later. But now it is necessary to outline these patterns. To this end we will avail ourselves of the kind of approach to trinitarian issues outlined in the classic little volume by Paul Tillich, *Love, Power, and Justice*.[8] Some metaphysicians and many philosophical theologians such as Tillich see reality as ineluctably trinitarian in character. This view is shared by at least one theologian whose chief empirical interests are in the field of sociology of religion.[9] From the perspective of such thinkers trinitarian theology can be expressed in the way the theologian will develop the meanings and relations among the concepts

power, or freedom;
form, or justice; and
love, or order

within the discussion of God, the church, and the Christian life.

First a *caveat*: we must constantly remember the dictum—one of the few guidelines the theological tradition laid down on the matter—that the Trinity relates functionally *ad extra* as one. Yet it is possible to see the reformers making differential associations between the persons of the Trinity and these concepts, and making commitments as to their degree of importance for various ecclesiological issues. It is also possible to see how these associations influence the various positions taken by the reformers concerning the relationship of the church to the world, and therefore also to the matter of Christian social ethics.

[8] Paul Tillich, *Love, Power, and Justice* (New York: Oxford University Press, 1954).
[9] Cf. the fine work of W. W. Schroeder, *Cognitive Structures and Religious Research: Essays in Sociology and Theology* (East Lansing: Michigan State University Press, 1970).

It is now appropriate to present an outline of the general hypothesis of this study. The hypothesis utilizes the basic definitions and relationships developed in the works of Tillich and Niebuhr referred to earlier.

Since our general hypothesis assays a comparative evaluation of certain relationships as seen by the reformers, it is perforce somewhat complex in appearance. The two following charts, with appended discussion, may therefore be a good way to present our theses.

1. *Patterns of Association Between Certain Concepts and Persons of the Trinity in Three Reformers*

	power, or freedom	**form, or justice**	**love, or order**
Luther[4]	Father	Son[1]: basis of the church[5]	Holy Spirit
Calvin[2]	Holy Spirit	Son[1]	Father: basis of the church[5]
Simons[3] [4]	Spirit of Christ: basis of the church[5]	Word of Christ[1]	Nature of Christ

Note first of all the areas of agreement. 1. All the reformers ascribe the form or justice factor of Christian faith to Christ or the Word of Christ. It may be suggested this is a characteristic Protestant view in contrast to the Catholic ascription of formal priority to the Holy Spirit in terms of his gifts of teaching and sacrament manifest in the apostolic succession. 2. Luther and Calvin, but not Simons, share a reference to the transcendent Trinity. Simons' language is normally restricted to perceived aspects of Jesus. This fact will partially account for the justified sense of common cause between Luther and Calvin over against Simons, in spite of the following. 3. Calvin and Simons, in spite of their differences of "scope," agree against Luther in their trinitarian economy. This fact may partially explain the relatively greater ease with which Calvinism could enter into fruitful dogmatic and ecumenical encounter with some Anabaptists. 4. The Lutheran and Mennonite positions seem farthest apart in terms both of ascription of function and transcendent/immanent referent for that ascription. Calvin thus appears in a mediate position, sharing Luther's transcendental referent but taking Simons' ascriptive pattern. 5. Most importantly, there is a complete difference of opinion concerning the principle or agency in terms of whose establishment the church defines itself as an object of faith. This important contrast in ecclesiology, reflecting as it does all the above trinitarian convergences and divergences of the reformers, in large part accounts for their respective approaches to social theory.

Let us now pick up this important difference in ecclesiological basis, and present the second part of our hypothesis, which concerns how the reformers develop their characteristic positions on social ethics on the basis of their understanding of the church.

2. The Reformers' Understandings of the Church as Influencing Their Approaches to Social Ethics.

	basis of the church	consequent theoretic tensions	characteristic pattern of resolution and application
Luther[1]	Christ (*form*), from which are understood	the relations of *freedom* (Father) and *order* (Holy Spirit) in the interests of	the maintenance of the proper distinctions (*dualist*) among God's orders of creation.
Simons[2]	Jesus' Spirit (*power*), from which are understood	the relations of Jesus' teachings (*form*) and community of his body (*love*) in the interests of	re-establishing the perfect unity with Christ's teaching (*restitutionist*) while sustaining life in the present world of sin.
Calvin[3]	The Father's elective love (*order*), from which are understood	the relations of Christ's Word (*form*) and the agency of the Holy Spirit (*power*) in the interests of	effecting God's will (*transformationist*) in the world by means of the church.

1. Since Luther, like Calvin, adopts a transcendentalist approach to trinitarian ascription, he will have to resolve tensions between the Second Person of the Trinity and Jesus the incarnate savior; between creation and redemption; and between God's free agency in the world and his saving will in the church. Luther assumes the christocetnric or form perspective, and the tensions will tend to be in terms of the resolution of God's power or freedom in the world and the love or order of the Holy Spirit which is characteristic of the life of the church and of faith. The line of solution to the tensions of freedom and order will be in terms of the regimen or orders of creation, among which is the church. The orders must be both distinguished and related according to God's will, and thereby kept in their proper functions. The various issues will be presented in terms of what is to be "bound" and "loosed" before God (the church), before oneself (conscience), and before the world (works of love). In each perspective there are certain areas of freedom and certain areas of order.
2. No transcendental Trinity is effectively present in Simons' theology. He need not therefore deal with the tensions between redemption and creation, the church and the world, etc., as do Luther and Calvin. Rather the problems concern the relation of the present existing church and the perfect unity with Christ as seen in the scripture. The approach to the issue of how perfect love—Christ—is to be realized in the church, will be in terms of the relation of love and justice, since Simons assumes the power or freedom perspective associated with the Spirit. The line of solution will be in terms of the practical resolution of specific questions concerning how the community can achieve likeness to Christ (form or justice) and how the individual can be sustained in the community of faith (love or order). Over-emphasis on conformity to the Word of Christ or on the forgiving love of God will be characteristic problem-producing areas.
3. Calvin is the most complex and subtle among the reformers studied, and is most concerned to preserve the oneness of God and the unity of his operations *ad extra*. Accordingly the trinitarian associations will appear only in carefully qualified shifts of perspective rather than in outright ascriptions. When he is considering the issues from within the perspective of faith in Christ, Calvin associates the Father primarily with love or order, and emphasizes the election of the Father as the final basis for the existence and meaning of the church. The church is manifest in terms of both theory and practice, i.e., in terms of both the maintenance of true doctrine and the disciplined life. Calvin more than Luther will have to resolve the tensions between salvation and creation, since it is most importantly the Creator who establishes salvation. The form the tension takes is how to interrelate the functions of justice (or form) and power (or freedom). Characteristic resolutions will be in terms of the continuity of form and power, of being and becoming, of the indicative and the imperative, in reference to the nature of the church, to the self-understanding of faith, and to the relation of the church to the world. In each of these areas, Calvin will develop the aspects of both freedom and justice.

The following chapters consider Luther, Simons, and Calvin in that order. This sequence has the advantage of reflecting the historical emergence of the positions in all their self-consciousness. Menno Simons developed his position in relation to Lutheranism, and Calvin developed his position relative to both Lutheranism and "the Anabaptists," among whom he included Simons. The sequence allows us to present first what from our point of reference are the "extremes" of the issues—Luther and Simons—and then to portray the more difficult construction of Calvin as the successful effort of a second-generation reformer to achieve an independent and unique, though in effect a mediating, position incorporating the solid contributions of both initiating Protestant views.

The hypothesis breaks naturally into two parts, and accordingly two chapters are devoted to each figure. The first chapter will develop the reformer's trinitarian ascriptions and the expression of these ascriptions in his view of the church. We shall see that this sequence of commitments will issue in quite distinct and characteristic tensions relative to ecclesiastical and ethical theory. The second chapter will examine the manner in which the reformer both reflects and resolves these tensions in the development of a practical theology of the church and of social ethics. Thereby many of the well known specific teachings of the Lutheran, Mennonite, and Calvinist movements will be seen in their patterns of relatedness.

C

To conclude this introductory Prologue, some discussion of the methodological issues involved is required. Once again, in view of the breadth of the subject we are attempting, what is needed are principles of limitation and synthesis.

There is a very large body of scholarly literature available on the social ethics of the Protestant Reformation. Most of it, however, is done in the form of detailed theological examinations of the various doctrines of the reformer or church studied, with little interest given to setting the specific doctrinal commitments within a systematic internal or external pattern. With characteristic late twentieth-century skepticism regarding the use of general models for historical interpretaion, most contemporary students have not sought to use, replace, or go beyond the classic systematic efforts of Ernst Troeltsch[10] and H. Richard Niebuhr.[11] These secondary sources, useful as they might be for specific interpretive problems, do not materially contribute to the general problem we have been discussing. For very little creative work has been done on the trinitarian views of the reformers of the first half of the sixteenth century. Scholars assume that the doctrines of the major reformers are approximately orthodox and agreed on the matter—a not surprising view, since (as indicated earlier) the reformers themselves made the same assumption. There is therefore no important study of the

[10]*The Social Teaching of the Christian Churches* (New York: The Macmillan Co., 1931), especially vol. 2. The first German edition was published in 1912.

[11]*The Social Sources of Denominationalism* (New York: Henry Holt, 1929).

systematic connection between the trinitarian doctrine and the social ethics of the reformers. The present work is thus intended to open a new area of research.

We are interested more in the basic or root perspectives of the reformers than in specific details of their application or alteration. The constructive writings of the seminal figures, writings at once more theoretic and less self-conscious than the works of second-level Protestant leaders, are of fundamental importance. Luther is the beginning of a new approach; Simons and Calvin each so transformed and dominated that inheritance as to virtually recreate it under his own name. These men are therefore the fathers, the sources, for the distinct patterns of socio-trinitarian thought we are seeking. Many other figures will come into our view, of course. But the occasional consideration of their writings well be for the purposes of confirming interpretive decisions made with regard to the three major figures, or for indicating lines of divergence. In order to maintain continuity in the text these supplemental considerations are generally consigned to the notes. Their presence will be indicated by an asterisk following the superscript reference number.

Luther, Simons, and Calvin present very different problems in terms of both selection of materials and interpretive procedure.

Calvin presents us the easier task in this regard. The *Institutes of the Christian Religion*, which Calvin wrote and re-wrote for a quarter of a century, is the second Bible of the Reformed tradition and must be our chief source for study. Materials from the commentaries and other works will be used where relevant, but only if the passages can be confirmed from the *Institutes*. Calvin was very conscious of the power of language, especially in his *magnum opus*. This characteristic allows us the luxury of resting considerable interpretive weight upon his sentences, upon his selection of one word or phrase rather than another to express his meaning, and upon his specific indications of systematic interrelation of his themes.

The writings of Menno Simons are relatively few and generally short, and so our study of the Mennonite position can be based on the entire corpus, excluding only private correspondence. We have in his *Foundation of Christian Doctrine*[12] a basic document which, like the *Institutes*, may function as the standard for assessing the other writings of its author. A small corpus, a basic document—it seems that our interpretive tasks are comparatively easy. Yet Simons proves to be a difficult subject for theological interpretation.

The overwhelming linguistic impression from reading Simons is the degree to which his writings are drenched with the phraseology of the Bible. Simons with unmistakable self-consciousness seeks in his pastoral epistles to reproduce the mood of early, persecuted Christianity. Without suggesting any detraction in meaning, I find his writing to be structured by *theologoumena*: code words, phrases, whose precise or traditional mean-

---

[12]Published in 1539. Citations from Simons are taken from J. C. Wenger, ed., *The Complete Writings of Menno Simons* (Scottdale, Pa.: Herald Press, 1956).

ings are less important than their function of recreating the early Christian mood. Only rarely does Simons define his terms. Explicit trinitarian language, for example, appears almost exclusively in salutations and benedictions, following the model of the New Testament epistles.

In this situation the student must avail himself of other procedures for interpretation than intense analyses of individual passages. To a much greater degree than for the other men considered, our study of Menno Simons' writings makes use, for example, of simple quantitative techniques. The small corpus makes this procedure feasible, and extensive tabulations of his usages have been made. The interpretations are thus to a considerable degree developed from patterns of usage which emerge from a study of the statistical data. Where Simons occasionally argues in traditional academic fashion, where he is writing to "outsiders," and where he is consciously developing credo-like summaries of the faith, I have taken a more direct approach to interpretation. The results of both sorts of procedures qualify each other. I see no more adequate way by which to explicate the simple but rich "theology" of this great pastor and reformer.

Luther's writings are so voluminous, so variable, so complex, as to drive to despair anyone who attempts a consistent method of approach. Though ultimately his theology is simpler and more systematic than Calvin's, Luther's writings are stylistically at the opposite pole from the *Institutes*. For our study the problems of selecting material are variably acute. On the subject of social ethics a large number of relevant smaller tracts exists. Among the more fruitful of these are the famous treatises of 1520, particularly *The Freedom of a Christian*. The treatises *On Monastic Vows, On Good Works*, and *On Worldly Authority* are also valuable. The basic materials on social ethics, as on the subject of trinitarian ascription, must be sought, however, in Luther's commentaries and technical theological tracts. Among the former, the expositions of *Romans, Hebrews, John, Galatians* (1535), and *Genesis*, along with various treatments of individual *Psalms*, are most important. Among the latter, *Contra Latomum, De Servo Arbitrio*, and the treatises on the Lord's Supper are most significant. Documentation will be severely restricted to quotations and to the key interpretive theses. In Luther study it takes tremendous discipline just to keep from drowning oneself in citation and detail. In a programmatic study such as this, we bear, especially for Luther, a particular obligation to achieve adequate, fruitful, and relevant generalization.

Our study of Luther, Simons, and Calvin will not be in the first place overly concerned with the changes in position exemplified in the theological development of the men, nor with their sources. We are not undertaking a genetic study but rather a systematic and thematic one. To a limited extent changes in position will be recognized in the selection of material. Luther's writings on social ethics progressively reveal the essential conservatism of their author during the 1520's and show signs of reactionary currents as the disappointments and frustrations of his reforming work began to take their toll from the 1520's on. In the case of Simons a shift is distinguishable from the more theoretic, adaptable, and liberal views of the young pastor to the more concrete, entrenched, and strict positions of the old man losing sole grip on the tiller of the Mennonite boat. Calvin's progressively greater emphasis on discipline and perseverance can be seen in the sequence of reworkings of the *Institutes*.

On the trinitarian theme less movement is noticeable for reasons discussed earlier. As he gains self-confidence as a theologian, Luther gradually frees himself from reliance on traditional formulae without thereby significantly changing his position. Simons gradually hews closer to orthodox formulation under the pressure of his opponents. Calvin becomes fuller and more careful of expression as a result of what to him was the puzzling and unexpected attack of Servetus.

These changes, which in all cases are no more, really, than changes of emphasis and expression, will be noted where relevant. But the scope of the present study demands that we keep to a relatively low level of analysis. Detailed tracings of subtle shifts, or shades of meaning, would not only result in a text of unwieldy size, but would also work against our goal of grasping a general overview of our subject. We are interested in essentials, not in details.

In conclusion, our study is not concerned with an investigation of the social, economic, political, psychological, or diplomatic circumstances that together conditioned the positions of the reformers. Such an approach may be important for an exhaustive understanding of a more narrowly defined topic but cannot be undertaken in the present work. Moreover, as noted at the beginning of this chapter, the external justification for undertaking the topic of Trinity, Church, and Ethics in Reformation Theologies is the influence of the social theory of the reformers upon subsequent generations, especially on laymen. This influence was not seriously modulated, if at all, by technical and historical scholarship. Rather it arose from study of and meditation upon the relatively straight-forward and simple sense of the popular texts, as these were developed in sermon, hymn, catechesis, and Bible study. What such an approach missed in terms of historical understanding and subtlety of qualification, it gained in terms of achieving a reasonably accurate general understanding of the reformers' views which the average Christian could comprehend and use in attempting to live out of his faith. And it is with a comparison of these main lines of viewpoint that we are concerned. The danger to be avoided is over-refinement of interpretation. Such refinements, while interesting and perhaps true, do not significantly affect the general consequences of the reformers' impact and are therefore basically irrelevant to our purpose.

When one is discovering a new land, a rough, general map of the terrain is the first necessity. That is what this study aims to provide.

PART ONE

Introduction: The Wheel

The initial task in Part One of our study is to attempt to analyze Luther's discourse on God for the purpose of uncovering his distinctive pattern of trinitarian ascription. I say "attempt" because first of all, Luther's text does not permit a completely successful analysis. With few exceptions his writings reveal no overall logical pattern. The form of the presentation, when there is one, is often defined by the sequence of Biblical verses, as in the commentaries, or by the order of points in an opponent's writing, as in many of the treatises. And even when a merely external order is available to him, Luther often wanders very far from the initial text or point, caught up in a chain of associations for which the internal necessity is not apparent to the reader and probably not conscious to the writer.

Secondly, if we give up seeking an overall pattern and concentrate analysis on the very words that Luther uses, we soon end up in a tangle of interconnections from which there is no exit. The method of analysis usually assumes there are precise, stable meanings to the "elements" presumed to constitute the "whole" we are studying. Analysis then is the attempt to differentiate that whole into its constituent elements and in the process to discover the connections the writer used to build the whole.

But Luther does not use language in this "building block" fashion, and his theology is not an "edifice" of some sort. Luther used the terms of his basic vocabulary—"wrath," "grace," "law," "Gospel," "faith," "works," and so forth—as an artist uses colors. Each word-color has a value, but the value-in-itself of the color is relatively insignificant compared to its function in combination with other colors. Luther almost always begins working, moreover, not with an individual word-color but with a pair or axis of oppositely related colors on the wheel: wrath-grace, law-Gospel, faith-works. So his basic values are not the factors, but the dialectical relations of the factors. And as he creates his theological canvas, any given color axis suggests or involves another contrasting axis. "Wrath-grace" suggests "law-Gospel," for example. But as in the color wheel, so on Luther's canvas: the wrath and the grace elements are both constituent in the law-Gospel axis, and the law and Gospel elements are reflexively constituent in the wrath-grace axis. This systematic implication of relationships never ends in Luther's writing. It is a wheel. There is no one axis more primary than any other, and there is no intrinsic reason for beginning with one word-set rather than another. And as Luther finishes his theological canvas, he usually does not refine details, but rather the opposite. He will nearly obliterate details by piling up his elements on, as it were, a light-dark polarity: wrath, law, works, hell, flesh, etc., on one side; grace, Gospel, faith, heaven, spirit, etc., on the other.

Luther thus synthesizes, and so we can reverse his procedure and do analysis, but only to a limited extent, and then only if we observe two conditions. We cannot seek basic elements, but must seek basic relationships. And the ultimate object of the analysis cannot be to get back to the constituent relationships but must rather be to get ahead to the thematic whole in which Luther involves us.

There is a third feature of Luther's thought, however, which further complicates our task. We are seeking his trinitarian theology, and Luther's painting is rather sloppy on this matter, because while it is basic to all his work, trinitarian logic is almost never a conscious subject of his writing, not even a secondary one. Luther was an extraordinarily systematic theologian, and so there is a basic consistency to his understanding of even those subjects, like the Trinity, to which he devoted little effort. But he was anything but a systematic writer, and so, as any scholar who has wrestled with him for a while knows, Luther cannot be pinned down to any given passage. Yet this is not the real difficulty. It is rather that, were Luther to admit us students into his office and hear us ask him to judge our thesis about his trinitarian theology, he would chuck us out, mumbling about our scholastic quest for a "theology of glory." And then in private he would roll the eye of his soul heavenward and demand of God, not altogether rhetorically, what it takes to make students comprehend an evangelical "theology of the cross." And he might be right in his judgment. What we have to do is learn to work *his* way, even though it be for the answers to *our* questions.

Our disastrous if hypothetical audience with Luther is not all that hypothetical, however. As we shall see at the beginning of Chapter Two, Luther very early in his career was well aware of the dangers implicit in merely accepting the conclusions of an old theological achievement such as the "finished" doctrine of the Trinity. Even a doctrine he considered quite evangelical could become in his view the occasion for a "theology of glory"—man's glory—when its use or relevance to the human condition and the existential struggle involved in its formulation got lost behind the finished results. The doctrine then appeared to be merely "out there," "objective" in the worst sense, and the theologians were sorely tempted to play with the teaching as an intellectual or logical game without significant reference to its import for Christian faith. In the late medieval period this perceived distinction between the substance of a teaching and its relevance to us was reflected in the widely applied distinction between considerations of God as he is "in himself" (God's "absolute power") and as he involves himself in the human condition (God's "ordained power" or will).

Luther the reformed theologian rejected all thinking concerned with "God in himself" as the "vain speculations of Reason." Yet he "speculated" rather boldly himself, for example in *The Bondage of the Will* and in the writings of 1527 and 1528 on the Lord's Supper. But he considered these efforts within the arena of God's ordained will for man, and thus felt them to be either evangelically sound or at least not against the Gospel of Christ. Scholars who rather automatically deny any speculative exercise in Luther ought to observe Luther's own discrimination: reason in the service of the

Gospel is good, even if its conclusions occasionally are in error; reason in the service of a "theology of glory" is bad, even where its conclusions are sound. And the inherited doctrine of the Trinity is one major subject where speculation about God as he is in himself could lead to the worst consquences, according to Luther: a bad method, based on wrong tests of truth, issuing in false, indeed spiritually fatal conclusions.

A case can be made[1] for the claim that many late medieval thinkers tended to downplay the existential import of the doctrine of the Trinity, caught up in the logical intricacies of understanding a doctrine they all believed: that God was at once One in the basic sense of the term, and at the same time Three in an equally profound sense of the term. The attraction of interest to the question of God in himself tended to leave undervalued the nature of God's relation to us, even though the truth of this relation had been classically formulated, in reference to trinitarian thought, in the scholastic dictum that as far as his relations with the world are concerned the triune God appeared and functioned wholly as one. By ignoring the demands of considering God according to his relationship to the world, i.e., in terms of salvation history, many late medieval thinkers were liable to drift into a dangerous overemphasis on the otherwise valid distinctions within the Trinity.

Now it is this temptation that is constantly at our elbow as we begin our study of the distinctive trinitarian ascriptions in Luther (and in Simons and Calvin, and among all three men). It will be very easy for us to get carried away by our own analysis, making distinctions where, really, there are none. To the extent we do that, we shall merit Luther's curse on our "theology of Glory."

To avoid that charge, we must, especially in the case of Luther, stick very closely and self-consciously to his insistent perspective and method: we must condition all prospective distinctions by the requirements of considering God only in relation to salvation history—to God's acts in his people.

Theoretically, at least, we are fitted to observe this requirement by investigating the Trinity not in itself but in its functional relationships as they are perceived by our three theologians and as these perceptions influence the basic patterns of their theologies. What in the technical jargon of theology is called the "economic trinity" is especially close to Luther's way of doing things. Almost invariably he approaches the question of the meaning of a subject—the divinity of Christ is the salient example—by considering what that subject does. "This is what Christ accomplished," Luther would say. "No mere man could do this, but only a god; therefore Christ is truly God." The same approach appears in almost all his subjects, as for example on the matter of salvation by merits or by faith. "If you try to work your way into God's favor," Luther might have said, "experience will prove that way to be an utter failure: you will never attain peace of conscience. Therefore salvation by works is a fatally wrong conception—fatal since it is

[1] Cf. for example, Regin Prenter, *Spiritus Creator*, trans. John Jensen (Philadelphia: Muhlenberg Press, 1953), pp. 173ff., 238ff.

a lifelong illusion, and you only live once. Salvation by faith alone, however, is an experienced certainty—an experience of God's certainty—precisely because peace of conscience stands up under the experience of the fiercest onslaughts of the world, the flesh, the Devil, and one's own doubts and sins."

Therefore, let us presume to analyze Luther's trinitarian theology in its social implications, encouraged because we are aware that we must stick close to the rule he lays down for us: to consider God only functionally, in terms of his works in his people. Or, to put it medievally, God in his *operationes ad extra*, in his *potentia ordinata*. Where I make mistakes of interpretation rather than of fact (Luther is too voluminous not to make mistakes of fact), it will likely be due to occasional forgetfulness of the classical rule: God is One God in relation to his saving work in his people.

But we can take some comfort from Luther on the matter of this temptation. Time and again he said that the whole issue in the struggle between God and man was the First Commandment.

Until that one is settled, all the other commandments are relatively beside the point. And, according to Luther, the struggle over the First Commandment is never settled in the world of men. What a Christian theologian has to do, therefore, is constantly repent his arrogance. And trust that God will sustain him in this, his work.

CHAPTER TWO

Luther: The Judgment of the Cross

In his first major theological publication, the *Lectures on the Psalms* of 1513-1515, the young exegete found occasion to apply the tools of Biblical interpretation to what he apparently felt were dangers in a doctrinal system understood as finished; i.e., "merely historical" faith.

> For as the years have passed, so has the relationship grown closer between the letter and the Spirit. For what was a sufficient understanding in times past, has now become the letter to us. Thus at the present time, as we have said, the letter itself is more subtle in nature than before. And this is because of the progress of time. For everyone who travels, what he has left behind and forgotten is the letter, and what he is reaching forward to is the Spirit. For what one already possesses is always the letter, by comparison with what has to be achieved . . . Thus the doctrine of the Trinity, when it was explicitly formulated at the time of Arius, was the Spirit, and only understood by a few; but today it is the letter, because it is something publicly known—unless we add something to it, i.e., a living faith in it. Consequently, we must always pray for understanding, in order not to be frozen by the letter that kills.[1]

The passage is almost more instructive for what is not said than for what is. Luther is very far from asserting a "progressive" theory of doctrinal development, to the effect that old doctrines may need to be expanded, modified, or occasionally discarded in favor of newer ones more representative of our continuing growth in religious and worldly knowledge. The tool he uses here, the distinction between "letter" and "spirit," is not an historian's distinction, i.e., a distinction between past and present, old and new. It is primarily a tool for Biblical interpretation which Luther took over from the fathers, chiefly St. Augustine, and has begun to adapt to his own concerns. In this passage Luther implies a comparison between a Biblical text which an exegete might study objectively or scientifically without reference to its significance for the human condition, and an orthodox Christian doctrine which a believer simply repeats in his confession without feeling or understanding its necessity for faith.

[1] WA 4. 365.5-14. Where possible, references to Luther will be cited from the American Edition by volume and page, or from the *Library of Christian Classics* volumes (LCC). Writings not included in these editions, such as the above, will be cited from the standard German Edition (WA) by volume, page, and inclusive lines.

When this happens, as for example with the doctrine of the Trinity, the doctrine becomes "letter." Not that the teaching is in itself wrong, but rather the otherwise correct teaching, no longer mastered by the controlling appropriation of a living faith, can become an occasion for grave error. Its language may lure a theologian to speculative exercises; its "finished" character may tempt a Christian to confess it merely because it is there to be confessed. It thus can become for both the theologian and the worshipper an occasion for works-righteousness: as Luther puts it, a letter that kills.

To prevent this, Luther says, we must "add" a living faith. The "spirit" does not refer to an actual temporal future, but to the process of working toward a real or existential appreciation of the teaching. In a sense every generation, even every individual Christian, must constantly re-search the achievements of the past generation, and his own past, if his faith is to remain an active, living faith. You must begin all over again all the time, Luther says on innumerable occasions, to "creep into your baptism" every day, lest what once was a live, spiritual faith become a dead letter of doctrine. If this be required for the most basic teaching of the Christian faith, that the Word of God took our flesh and our sins upon himself for our salvation, then it is no less required for those teachings which elucidate salvation in Christ; e.g., the doctrine of the Trinity.

The process of a continous new spiritual appropriation of (for example) the doctrine of the Trinity can often lead the believer to novel emphases, or at least novel language, in his work. As noted in the Prologue, Luther felt a strong compulsion to adhere to the terms of the orthodox trinitarian formulae. Yet as we have seen, Luther felt there were greater dangers in repeating the traditional arguments and words without real understanding than in developing new ways of expressing faith's comprehension of the teaching. In the latter circumstance, Luther felt, the Spirit of Christ working through faith would insure that the essential teaching—that the Father, Son, and Holy Spirit is One God—would be sustained even when our efforts at comprehension fell short.

The young Luther himself made modest attempts in both sermon and commentary to develop new images for speaking of the Trinity. One such effort, in a Christmas sermon of 1514,[2] finds an echo in the commentary passage we have been considering. In the sermon Luther, still really a scholastic thinker, developed an image of the Trinity in terms of *the moving, the moved,* and *rest,* on the distant analogy in created life. What may be unique in this otherwise common form of analogical thinking is that Luther's image is in terms of activity. If we look back from the perspectives of the reformed theologian, it can be seen that Luther is here taking the first steps toward what was to be his characteristic method of viewing all "divine things" in terms of God's saving activity in his people. Something like this appears in the above commentary passage as well. Notice that "letter" and

---

[2] WA 1. 20. 1ff. Regin Prenter summarizes these efforts, *Spiritus Creator,* trans. John Jensen (Philadelphia: Muhlenberg Press, 1953), pp. 173ff. The same view is maintained by David Lofgren, *Die Theologie der Schöpfung bei Luther* (Göttingen: Vandenhoeck & Ruprecht, 1960), p. 35.

"Spirit" are in a sense defined in terms of man's religious exercise: what he has left behind—that is letter; and what he seeks—that is Spirit.

We shall see that Luther's trinitarian language is a bit imprecise by traditional medieval standards. At least part of the reason for this is that Luther insisted on working not out of the technical definitions but out of a more functional approach, or from the perspectives of faith's experience of God's saving activity. Thereby, he felt, wrongheaded speculation could be avoided, the treasure of the Oneness of God be protected, and the comfort of the conscience be sustained.

Such an approach, consistently maintained by Luther, provides us a way into the difficult matter of his understanding of the Trinity. For we can focus our attention on God's operations in his people, as Luther sees them, and thus try to uncover the inner or immanent trinitarian characteristics of the God who is One.

A. *Luther's Trinitarian Ascriptions*

Young Luther's development of the "motion" analogy in the 1514 sermon, and his growing habit of speaking of God in terms of his activity, jointly point to the mature Luther's consistent pattern of considering God primarily in terms of power.

It is a common view, but not a wholly correct one, that the Protestant Reformation reflected a return to a purer Augustinian influence in theology. Many students of the great African saint have concluded with Paul Tillich[3] that the "ontology of love" dominated the considerations of power and justice in Augustine's doctrine of God. In Part Three of our study, however, we shall see as have other students of Reformation theology that the Augustinian influence was more completely represented in Calvin's thought than in Luther's. Scandinavian Luther researchers in particular have demonstrated that Luther advanced to his characteristic theology only as he was able to work himself free of many Augustinian concerns and approaches.[4] On the one hand, Luther was less interested and less well-trained in classical thought than was Calvin, and so was less habituated to a classical ontological or metaphysical approach to theology. On the other hand, and more importantly, however, Luther was increasingly influenced by the Hebraic approach to discourse on God, not only as it appeared in the Old Testament narratives but also as it was manifested in the Hebrew language itself. The Hebraic influence showed itself especially in two interrelated ways: in its consistent preoccupation with Jahweh's will and in its almost equally consistent understanding of Jahweh's will, in fact all God's "attributes," only in terms of God's relations to his people. For Luther (and equally for Calvin, too, it should be noted here) this influence meant that

[3] Paul Tillich, *Love, Power, and Justice* (New York: Oxford University Press, 1954), p. 22.
[4] Cf. in addition to Prenter, *Spiritus Creator*, Anders Nygren, *Agape and Eros*, trans. Philip S. Watson (Philadelphia: The Westminster Press, 1953).

God was to be discussed only as he acted in relation to man, and man discussed only as he responded to God. At the end of *The Bondage of the Will*, Luther noted how profoundly the Hebrew language and the relational thinking it fostered had influenced his basic evangelical discoveries.[5]

1. THE ABOVE REFERENCE to *The Bondage of the Will* of 1525 is significant. For not only was this book (along with the 1535 *Galatians* commentary) the work that Luther himself treasured most highly, but also this is the text that most fully demonstrates Luther's approach to God in terms of relational power.

In the Prologue I postulated as heuristic tools the concepts of power, form, and love, and associated the concept of "power" with that of "freedom." This association is profoundly influential in the argument between Erasmus and Luther.

Erasmus established this thesis: if man has no effective freedom, i.e., no power to do good before God, then God's will must be in part evil, since sin exists in the world. But Luther's response exhibits a subtle reassociation of the emphasized terms. Man is not free to contribute to his salvation, Luther says. It is God who has power, i.e., freedom to act with complete effectiveness in this world in spite of our requirements on him, and it is man's will that is evil, i.e., unfree and in bondage to sinful human nature. Luther's position in *The Bondage of the Will* was developed out of his Hebraic-evangelical habit of considering God's power (as well as all other divine attributes) not as a speculated-upon quality in God himself, but as an active relation to man. Luther took the same approach with regard to man. Man's power and other attributes are only known in terms of how they are actively related to God. If God by definition is absolute in all qualities, then his active power, righteousness, goodness, etc., is without limit in his relation to man and the world. There can then be no other (i.e., competitive) power, righteousness, or goodness in man himself. Thus it is man who is without power, who is unfree and passive. And it is God who has power, who is free and active.[6]*

It is not exactly correct, however, to say that for Luther God "has" power. Luther's functional understanding of God requires that he consider that God is in himself what God does in us. Thus we must say that God *is* active power. Luther did not like to speak of the divine "essence" in itself, but when the issues seemed to compel such discourse he consistently stuck to his own approach by defining the divine essence in terms of God's active presence. This is especially apparent in the writings of 1525-1528: *The Bondage of the Will* of 1525, the *Exposition of Jonah* of 1526, and the great

---

[5] LCC XVII, 309.

[6] Cf. a fuller consideration of this theme in John Loeschen, *Wrestling With Luther* (St. Louis: Concordia Publishing House, 1976), pp. 139ff. The construction of the discussion of free will in terms of power is also the approach of Philipp Melanchthon in the *Loci Communes* of 1555, Library of Christian Classics edition (New York: Oxford University Press, 1965), p. 51, even though Melanchthon's famous "causa concurrens"—that man's will is not wholly inactive or unwilling in God's conversion of him—may represent a moderation of Luther's rather more "either-or" approach.

works of 1527 and 1528 on the Lord's Supper. Throughout the latter works especially, we see Luther identifying God's essence with power; God's omnipotence, therefore, with his active omnipresence. It is on the basis of God's active omnipresence (=omnipotence) that, in Christ, God can be essentially present in the Supper.⁷

So nearly complete is Luther's indentification of the divine essence with power that occasionally, in his emphasis on the Oneness of God, Luther's differential trinitarian ascriptions tend to collapse back into the notion of God as simple power. Thus for example in the 1527 work on the sacrament:

> We know, however, that God's power, arm, hand, nature, face, Spirit, wisdom, etc., are all one thing: for apart from the creation there is nothing but the one simple Deity himself. And thus, if before the creation of the universe there doubtless existed *the power and hand of God, God's nature itself,* then it did not become something else after the creation of the universe. Indeed, he makes and does nothing except through his *Word,* (Gen. 1, John 1) *i.e., his power.* And his power . . . is himself. Then if his *power and Spirit* are present everywhere and in all things . . .then his divine right hand, nature, and majesty must also be everywhere.⁸

It is an apparently unavoidable tendency in the practice of human thought—a tendency any theologian sees in himself and in the theologians of the past—to identify the Father with the divine essence. And it is equally the tendency of human thought to mean "the Father" when one says "God." No orthodox theologian would permit his informal usages to be taken strictly in reference to the doctrine of the Trinity.⁹* But with this strong qualification in mind, the informal usages can suggest to the student how the

---

⁷Cf. particularly 23, 133-149 for the fullest discussion of this matter.

⁸37, 61 (emphases mine). Note also the phrase "for apart from creation there is nothing but the one simple Deity himself." The line suggests that for Luther God is Triune, hence patient of differential ascription, only in terms of his relations to the created world. It would then seem somewhat in tension with the rule that trinitarian ascription properly belongs only to God's internal life.

⁹Both Calvin and Melancthon stubbed their toes on this one. Servetus' accusation of trinitarian irregularities in Calvin bewildered the Geneva reformer, who in subsequent writings watched his language a bit more carefully.

The case of Melanchthon is more serious. While his trinitarian ascriptive pattern follows that of Luther, one cannot escape the impression that Melancthon had difficulty sustaining the orthodox doctrine of the full parity of the person of the Holy Spirit with that of the persons of the Father and the Son. Melanchthon wants to describe the Holy Spirit as a "relation" of the Father and the Son (*Loci communes* XLV, 12f., 16)—a traditional Augustinian approach which by itself gives no occasion for objection. But Melanchthon's ascriptive language exhibits what appears to be a rather self-consciously systematic distinction; the term "eternal" is consistently applied to the Father and the Son, but not to the Holy Spirit (Cf. 12f., 18f., 24f., 39f., 98). Occasionally Melanchthon seems aware of what might be a problem here, and makes a barely

theologian makes his first trinitarian ascription. Thus on the basis of Luther's language, we might surmise that since "God" and "divine essence" normally stand in non-selfconsciously trinitarian discourse for "the Father," and since "divine essence" is understood in terms of power, Luther tends to associate the Father with power.

Our surmise is borne out when we observe the overall pattern of Luther's more or less explicitly trinitarian language. I say "more or less" because many of Luther's passages exhibit the habits and influence of traditional trinitarian thought. Throughout his writings one can find that thought issuing in trinitarian-like phrases on a wide variety of subjects, with no direct reference to God. Luther can speak of "Christian life, righteousness, and freedom," or of "external, personal, and spiritual goods." All this is normal in the orthodox tradition, in which perhaps the Augustinian "trinities" of "body, mind, and soul," and "goodness, truth, and beauty" provide the basic and most frequently occurring images. Secondly, because of the rule that the whole Trinity is active in the work of each person (that God is One in his relation to man), we find Luther often making "trinities" in association with a specific divine person. Thus Christ can be said to be "righteousness, virtue, and wisdom," to "live, work, and reign" in us. And the Holy Spirit can be said to bring "the spirit, faith, and love." Again, these are very common usages.

But Luther occasionally makes self-consciously complete trinitarian ascriptions, and in these we find our surmise confirmed—but also limited and redirected.

In an early sermon, for example, Luther says,

> So the Father wills that we should look to Christ's humanity and love him in return, but yet in such a way as to remember that he did all this at the bidding of [the] Father's supreme good pleasure. Otherwise, it is terrifying to think of Christ. For to the Father is ascribed power, to the Son, wisdom, and to the Holy Spirit, goodness, which we can never attain and of which we must despair.[10]

---

adequate adjustment in his language (Cf. 16) or gives a patristic quotation to the same end (Cf. 28). But in the 1555 *Loci* I could discover only one passage in which there is an explicit mention of the Holy Spirit as eternal. And that passage occurs not in a doctrinal discussion, but in the prayer which closes Ch. 13 (174). Melanchthon's normal phraseology is "eternal Father, Son, and Holy Spirit" with slight variations (Cf. 14, 25, 72, 173). In view of his other patterns of language, however, I do not think the ambiguity in "eternal Father, Son, and Holy Spirit" can be dismissed as unintentional on Melanchthon's part. One is reminded of Servetus' quite similar care with trinitarian expression: his dying prayer went "Jesus, Son of the Eternal God, . . . " not "Jesus, Eternal Son of God, ..."

The matter of Melanchthon's trinitarian position of course requires a lengthy study in itself, which we cannot make here. But Melanchthon was as careful with words, especially in his *magnum opus*, as was Calvin in his. So we can assume the problems are not all illusory.

[10]51,46.

Luther's occasional creedal explanations usually follow this ascriptive pattern, Luther normally associating the articles on the Father, Son, and Holy Spirit with creation, redemption, and sanctification, respectively. And when an occasion arises in commentary on such texts as Gen. 1 and John 1, the mature Luther again roughly follows this pattern, with correlative images borrowed from Augustine and Hilary, for example.[11]* Yet throughout the corpus we find innumerable instances where "power, wisdom, goodness," "creation, redemption, sanctification" and correlate sets of phrases are all applied to either or both Christ and the Holy Spirit. And all these terms, often with the addition of "eternity," "majesty," "glory," etc., are often referred simply to "God," without any further specification—hence, I think, informally to the Father. The force of the rule about the unity of the Triune God's operations makes us leave off any further attempt to pigeonhole Luther's language.

But there is a stronger reason. In the quotation from the early sermon, the trinitarian ascription only came up "masked" (to use Luther's later language) in the "pleasant garb" of Christ's humanity to which Luther would direct our exclusive attention. And in the later *Genesis* commentary Luther is willing to accept the ascriptive patterns of Augustine and Hilary, but he feels he must stress the unity of operations of the Godhead. For he continues, "Nor is it possible in this manner to divide God subjectively, for the Father is not known except in the Son and through the Holy Spirit . . ."[12]

We have chosen to follow Luther's method in discussing God—to view him according to his operations. And now Luther's evangelical message reinforces the way we must travel. For Luther never tired of warning of the dangers to faith, conscience, and theological order, of attempting to contemplate the "naked" God. Instead of this, he constantly directed our attention to God in his work, to God as he wished to be known. That means to God as he is manifest in living Word and Spirit. To Christ.

2. PART OF THE merely apparent confusion in Luther's trinitarian ascriptions noted above is due to the extent to which the systematic assumption of God as act—as free power—dominates Luther's thinking. Throughout the corpus of his writing, Luther constantly describes or defines righteousness, goodness, wisdom, salvation as the power(s) of the One God. The hesitation in the preceding sentence over the plural form is but one symptom of the difficulties we face if we continue to attempt to differentiate Luther's trinitarian ascription regarding the Second and Third Persons of the Trinity, as they are actively manifest in salvation history as Word and Spirit.

---

[11] 1, 49f.; 60f. This pattern of ascription is, in my informal reading, the most frequently occurring pattern in the theological tradition. If this is the case, one of two questions is raised concerning the position and influence of Augustine. Either his own ascriptive pattern is not finally based on the notion of God as love, as is often claimed. Or his influence on the subsequent tradition, especially the Reformation, is less than has been suggested by many students. If the latter is closer to the truth, the view that Calvin was the Augustinian theologian *par excellence* is strengthened. That is my view.

[12] 1, 58.

There is, of course, a basic functional distinction between the Son and the Holy Spirit in Luther's theology. But the distinctions almost always appear only when Luther is combatting opponents, chiefly the "spirits" and Anabaptists. When his writing is not under the pressure of attack, Luther for the most part exhibits the continuation of the ascriptive pattern suggested in the passage from the early sermon quoted in the first section: the Son represents the "formal" or "wisdom" side, the Spirit the "love" or "goodness" side of the Trinity. Yet the plethora of citations we might give does not in the end admit a neat tally in this respect. Luther's assertions that it is the Holy Spirit who is our teacher (formal or wisdom function) and that it is Christ who is the new man living in us (love or goodness function) occur far too frequently for us to conclude that the Son always represents wisdom and the Spirit, love. Once again we feel the effect of the ancient rule that God is One in act.

But in the Prologue we associated the concept "form" with "justice," and "love" with "order." And when Luther feels the pressure of alternative theological positions, two very instructive sharpenings of his trinitarian thought emerge. 1) The insistence on the unity of God's operations becomes very intense. Directing his pen most often against the Anabaptists, but also against Rome,[13]* Luther repeatedly insists that the Holy Spirit has no function, no other or external communication, than to certify in the human heart only that which is revealed in the person and work of Christ. 2) The functions of Christ and the Spirit become sharply differentiated. Luther insists, sometimes actually to the point of "Jesus-idolatry," that Jesus of Nazareth the Christ is the only access we have to knowledge of God; and further, that Christ is "the only God there is" ("for us," let us note well, however). This emphasis often leads Luther to insist, verbally at least, that justice—justification, righteousness, etc.—is a matter of some sort of accord between the Christian and Christ, rather than between the creature and the Creator.[14]

A comparable intensification occurs with regard to the work of the Holy Spirit. Luther's normal emphasis is on the Spirit as instilling the love of Christ in our hearts (Rom. 5:5). But against "spiritual" opponents in particular, Luther stresses the work of the Holy Spirit in terms of order. The "spirits," who seek the teaching of the Holy Spirit outside the Word of Christ, stir up a false external conflict in the church and in society. This is a

---

[13] At the end of the study we will briefly examine the grounds for an argument that the decrees of the Council of Trent, insofar as they suggest a teaching function of the Holy Spirit at least distinct if not supplementary to that of Christ, imply a different conception of the "economic Trinity" than was held by Luther, indeed by any of the three major reformers we are considering.

[14] The tensions between the doctrines of creation and salvation, which many writers have noted, and which I shall discuss later, are fully manifest in Luther's intensification of language. But note also that this intensification exposes the tensions in the trinitarian doctrine itself: Luther stresses the unity of divine operations at the same time as he stresses their distinctiveness.

sure sign that the spirits do not really have the Holy Spirit, though (as he says in his writings against Zwingli) they appear to have "swallowed him, feathers, eggs, and all." The true function of the Holy Spirit, Luther says, is to stir up an internal conflict between the corrupt peace of the old man and the peace which is the indwelling Christ. The true function of the Spirit, therefore, is' to bring God's kingdom, his peace and order, out of man's disorder. But that is a work of *God's* Spirit, not that of the "spirits."

In view of the existence of such fine studies as Regin Prenter's *Spiritus Creator*, there is no need here for a detailed discussion of Luther's doctrine of the Holy Spirit. But one work of Luther's is notable for the profundity and beauty of its treatment of the work of the Holy Spirit. In the 1535 *Lectures on Galatians*, Luther takes occasion at Chs. 3:2-5, 4:6, 5:16, and 5:25 to develop a full, systematic presentation of the work of the Holy Spirit in relation to Christ. Although it is rare to find in the Luther corpus such a rich vein of thematic treatment, it is surprising that more students have not discovered this one.[15]

The beginning theme (Ch 3:2ff.) is that the Holy Spirit is given only through the hearing of the Word or Gospel. Luther insists over and over that our obvious, evident, manifest experience is proof enough of this. Although Luther sometimes speaks of the Holy Spirit as the agent of that which the Christian receives from the Gospel, most often he presents the Holy Spirit as the *gift* brought by means of the preached and heard Word of God.

The Holy Spirit is what the Word brings. But what is that? Certain knowledge of God and of oneself, Luther begins. And that means the forgiveness of sins (26, 213). Luther develops this theme in some detail. Forgiveness of sins, he continues, means that the proper order between man and God is restored. It means that the disordered, false relation to God in terms of works-righteousness is replaced by God's order: the struggle of spirit against flesh, the difficult task of keeping faith and works in their proper relationship and directed to their proper ends (215). The sectarians, who have not accepted the doctrine that the Spirit comes with his gifts only through the hearing of the Word in faith, produce only disorder in the conscience and in worldly relations (221ff.).

Luther then moves to a discussion (Ch. 4:6) of how the Holy Spirit works to achieve this order in men: it is by certifying the promises of Christ and his grace in the heart (375ff.). The argument is directed chiefly against the papal denial that a Christian can know for certain that he is in God's favor. Luther insists toward the end of the passage (387f.) that it is the work of the Holy Spirit that allows us to be sure of God's unfailing love for us.

At Ch. 5:10 Luther again picks up the theme of the Holy Spirit as the love of God, but now develops it in terms of the Christian's love of neighbor (27, 65ff.). And at 5:25 he returns to the theme of the Holy Spirit as the source of peace and order among God's people (100ff.). Here Luther is directing his pen once more against the Anabaptists (103).

---

[15]The material is found at 26, 202-226, 374ff.; 27, 63ff.; 97ff.

The basic theme of Luther's presentation was that the Holy Spirit, operating wholly in and through the preached Word, certifies forgiveness of sins—the love of God—in our hearts, and so insures the ordered harmony of God's love among the community of his people. This work is possible, however, because the Spirit's only concern is to bring the Word of Christ himself into the heart. Luther's discussions of the work of the Holy Spirit are always discussions of the work and Word of Christ, and almost always they are applied against alternate conceptions of the church; i.e., against Anabaptist and Roman Catholic self-understandings. These associations of concerns are of unsurpassed importance for Luther the theologian and churchman, because it is Christ alone who is a) our access to God, and b) the foundation of the Christian Church. I shall briefly discuss the first point below, and pick up the second in Section B.

Luther was often willing to affirm the traditional view that God was present throughout the universe, and that before the fall man could have knowledge of God from creation. He was occasionally even willing to make rather bold speculative ventures along these lines, for example in the *Jonah* commentary.[16] But for Luther this sort of discussion was idle: given the fall into sin, man has no access at all now to true knowledge of God—or perhaps better, to knowledge of the true God—except in Christ.

Over and over again Luther insists that for us God is present, his nature and will made known, only in Christ the Word. His most unguarded and thus potentially misleading statements to this end are passages in which he asserts that "apart from Christ, there is no God"—even "no Godhead."[17] Knowledge of the Triune God is thus only possible through—whom? Not the "Second Person," merely, the form, wisdom, or *logos* aspect of the Trinity, but rather through the incarnated Christ. Most of the passages on this strong identification of Christ with God come up in discussions of the Lord's Supper, the gift or application to us of Christ's atoning work. It is in Christ's body broken for us that God personally reveals himself. And the God revealed there is the Triune God with all his attributes, including omnipresence. It is only because of this that Christ's body can be said to be ubiquitous. Luther's famous, controverted doctrine of the ubiquity of Christ's body does not represent a peculiar quirk of his theology of the Lord's Supper, a stubbornness over the word *est*. It is a matter of basic christological doctrine, and that means it is a matter of basic trinitarian doctrine.[18]

Thus for Luther it is only in Christ that man has connection with the Triune God at all. And even then the connection with God is possible, or rather beneficial, only if it is mediated through the work of the Spirit, i.e., through the reception of faith, the hearing of the Word, and participation in sacrament. Just as Luther understands the nature of God the Father and God the Holy Spirit in terms of activity, so with regard to God the Son: Christ's

---

[16] 19, 44f.
[17] 37, 56 and 61.
[18] 26, 31f.; 37, 296f.

attributes are his works in his people. Thus not only is Christ the only "place" where the transcendently Triune God is immanently "present for us," but God is present for us only where and when there exists the community of faith, formed by Christ's Word and ordered by the Spirit, to receive God as he wished to be received: in the church. For Luther, Christ is absolutely and exclusively the image of God to us, and the basis, the form, and the life of the church of God.

B. *The Church: Conformation to the Word*

> Christ on the cross and all his suffering and death do not avail, even if, as you teach, they are "acknowledged and meditated upon" with the utmost "passion, ardor, heart-feltness." Something else must always be there. What is it? The Word, the Word, the Word. Listen, lying spirit, the Word avails. Even if Christ were given for us and crucified a thousand times, it would all be in vain if the Word of God were absent and were not distributed and given to me with the bidding, this is for you, take what is yours.[19]

Coming through the polemics are two points, both familiar to us. Luther felt that his opponent was working from a "merely historical" faith: the knowledge that Christ had in fact suffered and died on the cross. Such an "inert" doctrine—Luther called it "the letter" in the passage quoted at the beginning of the chapter—induced a speculative error. For Luther's opponent thinks that he must exercise his own religious powers and his own will in order to draw spiritual benefit from his belief in Christ's sacrifice. Thus he offers not an evangelical counsel, but a counsel of works-righteousness.

But secondly, such an understanding, in Luther's opinion, is in fact a denial of God's power and will. It assumes that God is simply there, that Christ and his work is a past, passive fact, and that it is we who can act to conform ourselves to it. Such a view, as we have seen, is wholly at odds with Luther's understanding of God as active and omnipotent, and man as wholly passive and without power. For Luther, no event in salvation history can be anything but "the letter that kills" unless it is seen to make its own way to us and for us. It is the Holy Spirit who accomplishes this understanding in us. Christ without the Spirit's work is but the wrathful, judging God. But the Christ who comes to us and for us via the spirit is the saving Word.

1. SOMETIMES it is easy to be confused by Luther's language. Throughout the corpus of his writings he speaks of "God," "Christ," "law," "Gospel,"—and of "the Word." Often it seems that the last term is used in-

---

[19] 40, 212f. Cf. 37, 193.

terchangeably with the others, but frequently it appears to change the meaning of the others. Thus in the passage quoted above, "Christ" and "Word" appear to be at least distinct entities, even though Luther's normal habit is to identify them.

What we know about Luther's way of speaking of God, however, makes the solution of this difficulty very clear. God, Christ, the Gospel, the things of the Spirit are all useless, in fact, "deadly articles" to us, unless we are led to accept them as God's works to us, for us, and in us. When the Spirit accomplishes this in us, we have God as he really is: wholly active for our salvation in Christ. We have the Word.

There is a strong connection between Luther's trinitarian ascriptions and his concentration on Christ as our only access to God. For in that ascriptive pattern, the formal, justice, or "word" function is consistently associated with the Second Person incarnate, Christ. Since we do not "have" God or his works properly unless we have God in terms of his activity in us, i.e., in and as the Word of God, Luther will normally evaluate all aspects of creation, redemption, and sanctification exclusively through their meaning in Christ. That is why Luther insists on interpreting Old Testament revelation only through the revelation in Christ, and that is why he insists on evaluating the present work of the Holy Spirit only through Christ. We know God properly only in terms of his works in and for us. That means we know him properly only in Christ, for Christ is the work of God for us. Christ is the Gospel, the Word of God. If Luther's theology is more exclusively christocentric than that of Calvin, Simons, or Rome,[20*] I think it is because of the combined effects of Luther's trinitarian ascriptions and his insistence that God is only properly known in terms of his actions in and for us, i.e., in the Word.

[20] I would not wish to press this differentiation too far. But if one compares in order Luther, Calvin, Simons, and the Roman view as expressed in the decrees of Trent, one sees a greater distinction between "Christ" and "Gospel," for example. In Luther Christ simply *is* Gospel. At Trent Christ is but one agent for conveying the Gospel, which exists prior to, concurrently with, and possibly in a subsequent complementary form of, its manifestation in Christ. Calvin and Simons fall somewhere between, the former at least distinguishing if not separating Christ and the Gospel or "doctrine," and the latter rather explicitly following the teaching and example of Jesus as the substance of true religion, but without setting this within any "higher" theological frame of reference.

Melanchthon's position seems to be comparable to Calvin's. Throughout the *Loci* there seems to be a clear, if not functionally operative, distinction between Christ and, for example, "his" Gospel (Cf. 58, 79, 86f., 130, 142 [definition of church], 155, 164f., 267 [definition of church]).

Who is more "christocentric" than whom is of course a matter of some party dispute. Some students of Anabaptist thought assert the greater christocentrism of their traditions. Cf. John H. Yoder, "The Prophetic Dissent of the Anabaptists," in Guy Hershberger, ed., *The Anabaptist Vision* (Scottdale: Herald Press, 1957), p. 100; and William Keeney, *The Development of Dutch Anabaptist Thought and Practice from 1539-1564* (Nieuwkoop: B. de Graaf, 1968), p. 192f. Similarly for Calvin. Cf. François Wendel, *Calvin: The Origins and Development of His Religious Thought*, trans. Philip Mairet (New York: Harper & Row, 1963), pp. 167, 215; and David Willis, *Calvin's Catholic Christology* (Leiden: E. J. Brill, 1966), particularly chapters 3 and 4.

The Word is the Gospel, the Gospel is Christ. And the proper office of Christ, Luther says, is to complete, announce, and "distribute" the forgiveness of sins to his people. In the quotation which opened this section Luther's allusions were to the sacrament of the altar and what happens there. The distinction between "word" and "sacrament" which is often used to structure Luther's theology is really a very deceptive one and ought to be avoided, at least when we are speaking of what is given when Christ the Gospel is given to us. For the Lord's Supper and Baptism are the Word given through physical media; and preaching, though not formally associated with a physical medium, is (because of its dependence on the physical instruments of speaking and hearing) also a form of sacrament. Whether by sermon or sacrament, the whole that is compassed is nothing else than the forgiveness of sins, i.e., Christ. It is Christ who is the basis, the form, and the life of the church.

The Word of God, Luther says, summons us to the place where God wishes to be found; in Christ, in the preaching, and in the sacraments. In the Word alone do we have God, Christ, and the Spirit, and even though Christ is omnipresent, we are not to seek him except in the Word, i.e., except as he is there for us with forgiveness of sins. Only in this active, saving Word do we have proper knowledge of God. And any religious activity which is not wholly founded on the Word is for Luther pure idolatry, even if the doctrines and actions are formally correct. God has no other form than is presented to us in his Word.[21]

As Christ the Word is the sole basis of faith, so Christ the Word alone defines the form in which that faith is received and exercised, and so is Christ alone its life. Luther's insistence that faith comes by hearing, that the ears alone—and not some other organ such as the "eye" of the soul—are the proper organs for receiving Christ, is at least in part intended to reinforce his belief that man is wholly receptive and Christ and the Spirit alone active in this process. We must be made to "lay down our arms," be made obedient or conformed by and to the Word. Only with the oral proclamation of the Word can the full "objectivity" of the Gospel, in Luther's sense of the term, be maintained against man's ceaseless attempt to make himself an active subject in the relationship. Only because of the sole agency of the Spirit in ordering or conforming us to Christ the Word can Luther say of faith that it is the true form of Christ.[22] And only because of this function of the Spirit can the Christian be said to be made truly one with Christ.

Though Luther speaks very often about the conformal unity of the individual Christian with Christ, we must very severely qualify the impression (a not incorrect impression, however) that for Luther becoming conformed to the Word is a strictly private matter. It is true that only individuals hear the Word, only individuals are justified, only individuals saved. But none of this happens except in the controlling, facilitating environment of the divine community, the church, The bulk of Luther's

[21] 16, 109; 17, 138; cf. 27, 87f.
[22] 26, 430; cf. 129. LCC XV, 105.

writing about the functions of the Word and Spirit is directed precisely against the "spirits"—those whom Luther often enough also identified as "individualists" who despised the church as the worldly locus or agency in which faith is not only nurtured but also born.[23]*

Luther's theology of the Word itself forces this severe qualification on us. For his insistence that faith comes by hearing is an insistence that Christian faith is basically social. Neither the creation of faith nor its exercise can be matters merely of private conscience. The hearing of the Word which creates faith takes two; the doing of the Word which exercises it requires the neighbor. The presence of the Word creates the presence of a Christian people. It is not outside the individual soul, but outside the church, that there is no salvation. And it is not the individual, but the church, which is said to be "the body of Christ."

2. AT THIS POINT it might seem appropriate to begin an analysis of Luther's understanding of the church. Instinctively we would first look through the texts for his formal definitions. What we would find is that Luther rarely provides definitions. When he does so, it is almost always in the context of a sermon catechesis, or yet another patient recital of his faith in the teeth of the endless charges leveled against him by opponents. The substance of these definitions would include the notions of the church as a communion or congregation of the faithful; as a spiritual body of Christ adorned by the Holy Spirit; as an assembly formed by the preaching of the Word and the administration of the sacraments; and as the locus of the forgiveness of sins—which phrase, as we know, also defines or includes in itself the whole work and the Word and the sacraments.[24] But this material leaves us unsatisfied. The definitions are fairly traditional and do not either differentiate Luther from other theologians or give insight into the interrelation of Christ and church that we are seeking. Indeed Luther seems as little interested in these required exercises as he is in the similarly-required trinitarian exercises.

But if we turn from this material to texts in which Luther is portraying the life of the Christian people, all of a sudden we feel ourselves on the right track. For here Luther's descriptions are full of the power, excitement, beauty, and paradox which characterize the texts when their author has found his proper subject.

---

[23]Luther's sharp differentiation of his reform work from that of the "radicals" on this point applies in the first instance only to those whom G. H. Williams, *The Radical Reformation* (Philadelphia: Westminster Press, 1962), terms "spiritualists," and not to the later "Anabaptists," such as the Mennonites, for whom the church community was everything. Luther had lost interest in, and knew little directly about, these Anabaptist groups. Yet as we shall see in Part Two, his self-differentiation still has application even to the latter. For conversion of life—which alone gave full access to the Anabaptist church—was largely an individual matter taking place prior to full entrance.

[24]Cf. 51, 167 ; 12, 129; 37, 367; 39, 65-70; 41, 143ff.

> The whole life of the new people, the believing people, the spiritual people, is this: with the sigh of the heart, the cry of the deed, and the toil of the body to ask, seek, and pray only for justification, ever and ever again until the hour of death; never to stand still and never to rest in accomplishment; not to regard any works as if they had ended the search for righteousness, but to wait for this end as if it dwelt somewhere ever beyond one's reach; and to know that as long as one lives, he will have his being in sins . . . .[Christians] confess that they sin and have sinned, but they are sorry for this, hate themselves for it, long to be justified, and under groaning constantly pray to God for righteousness. This is the people of God: it constantly brings the judgment of the cross to bear upon itself.[25]

Such texts can be multiplied, especially out of Luther's early writings. The theme of the Christian people in an ongoing spiritual pilgrimage toward him who has both found and founded it continues to appear in the later writings, but in these another set of themes dominates. Its nucleus lies in the "theology of the cross" of the early Luther, but now it is dilated, transformed, and partly externalized into the "theology of the Word." The true people of God are indeed hidden, the young Luther said, hidden under the opposite. They look like ordinary people, lead ordinary lives, do not even know themselves for something special. Yet there is the greatest possible difference. For it is only in them that—what? Perfection of life and composure of soul may be found? No! Rather it is in the Christian people alone that a real struggle exists, a real dichotomy may be found, between spirit and flesh, law and Gospel, faith and works, things external and things internal. It is from this Christian anthropology, which we will examine more carefully in the next section and in the next chapter, that Luther develops his characteristic language about the church. The sustained contrasts, paradoxes, and dualism which mark Luther's view of the Christian life reappear in his understanding of the church as at once both hidden and revealed, visible and invisible, physical and spiritual, many and one, sinful and holy.

These are the characteristic identifying features of Luther's ecclesiology, features which most sharply conflict with the ecclesiology of the "spirits," and which provide the contrast to the thought of Calvin. But before we enter this part of the study, it is necessary to assess the connection. That is, why does Luther insist on speaking of the church in the way he does? What is the systematic connection between his trinitarian theology and his theology of the church?

In seeking the answer to this question, the first thing we find is that we do not have to establish a connection among Luther's doctrines of the Trinity, of Christ, and of the church. The connection is already there waiting to be discovered. It is already there because the second thing we find is that

[25]LCC XV, 118ff.

these doctrines are not isolated from each other but are in fact patterns of discourse rooted in and emergent from one foundation. That foundation is Christ the Word.

We have already seen how for Luther the Triune God in all his works is known and can only be known as he is revealed in Christ. Thus even when Luther engages in speculative exercises concerning the "divine nature," what he says of God is in a sense only an extension or application of what he sees manifest in Christ. And the Christ who is the basis of Luther's god-talk is not the disembodied Word, the Second Person of the Trinity, but the incarnated, suffering Christ of Galilee. It is because this Christ is both hidden and revealed, both physical and spiritual, that Luther is able, with some qualifications, to speak of "God" in similar fashion. Within limits, what is true of Christ is true of God.

The famous line runs, "What is true in regard to Christ, is true in regard to the sacrament."[26] One can just as well supply alternative forms of the rule: What is true of Christ is true of the Christian; what is true of Christ is true of the church. In his running battles with the "spiritualizers," Luther concluded that the two prominent issues—anthropology and sacramental theory (hence, for Luther, ecclesiology)—involved differences in christology. Zwingli's reliance on what for Luther was a misunderstanding of the Biblical text "the flesh is of no avail" (John 6:63), not only led to a bad anthropology and a bad sacramental theory, but itself reflected a christological heresy, according to Luther.[27] One sacramentarian position, i.e., that the actual body of Christ could be of no spiritual use, suggested to Luther the docetic heresy that Christ only appeared to be human. Another sacramentarian position, that all we have in the Lord's Supper is a human memorial and not really God himself actively present, appeared to Luther an application of the Ebionite heresy that Christ really was only a man. (This view, he thought, also led to the Pelagian anthropological heresy that man can and must contribute to his own salvation.) Incidentally the Roman sacramental theory, which required the elimination of the physical elements for the real presence of Christ, struck Luther as both docetic and Arian, i.e., a denial of the real unity of Christ's two natures.

The point of these illustrations is that for Luther what you must say about Christian life, about the preaching and sacramental activity of Christians-in-community, hence about the church, is systematically defined by what you say of Christ. And the only correct doctrines about Christ are 1) that he is to be known only in and through his saving work; and 2) that Christ known in this way is fully God, fully man, and fully one.

Therefore Luther must strictly apply to the defintions of Christian life and the church all the "dialectical" qualities that obtain with regard to Christ. The Christian and the church are both hidden and revealed, as was Christ; physical and spiritual, as was Christ, etc. And having thus drawn upon the dialectics of christology for the basic patterns of his anthropology,

[26] 36, 35.

[27] 16, 297; 17, 195, 256. Many more numerous references to this connection can be found in the sacramental writings of the late 1520's.

sacramental theory, and ecclesiology, Luther will go on to elaborate more specific teachings in these areas along the lines of the same pattern. Thus Christian love must be both a physical and a spiritual matter. The reception of faith requires both an external word of Christ upon the ear and the internal work of the Spirit upon the heart. The sacraments involve created, natural vehicles for a sign, and the uncreated, supernatural presence of God for the reality. And the church is both a corrupt worldly institution, nevertheless divinely mandated for visible service among men, and a wholly spiritual society, the perfect body of Christ known only to God.

Luther is extraordinarily systematic! When he says that the Christian and the church are to become "conformed to Christ and his cross" by the working of the Holy Spirit, that sentiment is much more than a pious phrase. It is the reality of the church as Luther sees it, and it structures from top to bottom everything he would say about the church.

C. *The Church: Life in the Spirit*

> . . . The Christian life does not consist in things comprehended by reason. For the Christian lives and has his existence from his first to his last breath solely in the Holy Spirit, not in reason or in good works but only in the will of God and the Holy Spirit. It is the Holy Spirit, not reason, who teaches me to be baptized and believe. Consequently, my life must consist in the Holy Spirit, who blows where he wills.[28]

It was noted in the last section that while Luther's formal definitions of the church leave us a little unsatisfied, we are amply rewarded if we seek the answers under the rubric of "Christian life." This is the case, I think, because Luther's formal definitions are *theologomena*, finished, distilled summaries or sign-language for a much richer content. The hiddenness, growth, and tensions which comprise Christian life are not apparent to reason or experience. The work of the Spirit is always a living, inward act, never dead and externalized achievements which can be toted up into a definition of the church.

It is not hard to provide a typically Lutheran definition of the church which is easy to understand. 1) The church truly exists where the Word of God is truly preached and the sacraments truly administered. 2) That church is manifest externally where correct doctrine is maintained and where properly-called and ordained churchmen exercise their offices within the orders established by God.

The hook in these defintions is of course the presence of such terms as "truly," "correct," and "properly." These are the doors into the richer discussion of Luther's understanding of Christian life in the Spirit. For the

---

[28] Comment on John 3:8, 22, 302f.

true proclamation of the Word in sermon or sacrament, says Luther over and over, occurs only as the Spirit inwardly establishes the right distinctions between law and Gospel, faith and works, etc. And the new creature which the Spirit accomplishes in the people of Christ is an object of faith and hope. It is secret; it is not a new me, but is Christ in me. Therefore works of love and correct doctrine, though necessary, are never even trustworthy analogs to true faith but are always ambiguous, always riddled with sin and error. That is why, as Luther says in the introductory passage, the Christian life is not patient of comprehension by reason but is known only in the Spirit, who is free of the evidentiary obligations we would like to place on him. When we have discovered dialectical tensions such as these, we have a sure sign that we have discovered where Luther lives.

1. THE FUNCTION of the Holy Spirit, according to Luther, is to conform our hearts, minds, and indeed our bodies to obedience to the form of Christ. The Holy Spirit who presided over the Word becoming flesh is the same Spirit who works to turn us creatures of flesh into a form of the Word.[29] Alternately put, the function of the Holy Spirit is to certify, increase, and bring to fulness the living presence of Christ himself in those whom God has called with his grace.

Menno Simons would have nothing but praise for this view as developed to this point. But Luther continues. The becoming of the new creature is a processs which 1) is hidden both from the world and from the Christian himself, in the sense that the Christian never can find any good in himself sufficiently unalloyed with evil to seize upon as evidence of his sanctification. And as far as the Christian is concerned, his experience is that of 2) having to begin from scratch all over again every moment, to creep into his baptism daily. (The Holy Spirit *"teaches* me *to be* baptized"—note the tense!). His life is a constant seeking, an ever-new beginning. There is never any "accumulation" of holiness he can call his own. The Christian is just as much a sinner on the day of his death as on the day of his (first) baptism. Indeed, if there has been any "progress" in Christian faith and living at all, the Christian at his final death (we all must die daily, Luther said) is more aware of his sinfulness than he was at the beginning. (If one imagines Simons listening and reacting to Luther's words, at this point Simons would become uneasy, though he might grant a particular sense in which this description is true.)

But Luther goes on. To the extent he is successful in ordering our Christian faith to the form of Christ, the Holy Spirit stirs up a mighty conflict in the Christian life. The unredeemed world is alone at one and at "peace" with itself: everything is well ordered in terms of its own values, its own egocentricity. When the Word of God comes, however, the world is thrown into confusion and disorder. The function of the Spirit is now to fight against

---

[29] LCC XV, 188.

our settled unfaith, to change our mind. We resist. Thereby a fierce, intimate, private war is created within the soul whom Christ has touched with his Spirit. Christ and the Spirit invert all our normal, natural values.[30] Only in the Christian, and not in the unredeemed man, can be found two selves: the self of the Old Adam, for the first time self-conscious of its sinfulness and active opposition to God; and the self which is the indwelling Christ, the New Adam, who struggles with and overcomes the Old Adam daily and anew as he overcame it once for all on the cross. Only the true Christian really experiences, knows, and believes himself to be a sinner, says Luther. (Menno Simons would now be packing his bags against the sequel.) Luther continues. The coming of the Word of God to us increases our sinfulness, our sense of it. Sinfulness and faith are not mutually exclusive acts. They are in a sense correlative, almost interdependent. Christ saves only real sinners; the Spirit intercedes for us in our weakness. "Therefore," says Luther, "sin boldly . . . ." (Menno Simons would by now have left town.) And Luther continues, ". . . but believe more boldly still."

This kind of dialectic, so characteristic of Luther, forms the pattern of discourse for most of his themes. Where Menno Simons, as we shall see in Part Two, describes the subjects which make up Christian existence in basically univocal or direct terms, Luther almost invariably distinguishes these subjects into a brace of interdependent dialectical contrasts. Thus in the proclamation of the Gospel there is both an outward and an inward word, each necessary. The Word of God is only properly received as it is distinguished into law and Gospel. The law itself must be distinguished into prescriptive and "theological" uses. The benefits of Christ appear in terms of justification and sanctification—benefits which from Christian perspectives are quite distinct, since there can be no human equation of righteousness and holiness, faith and works of love. And we have already seen the dialectics involved in Luther's descriptions of the church.

This theological approach is too well known to belabor futher. The important question is, why does Luther speak this way? The track our pursuit of the answers will describe is a circuit. We shall quickly follow it back to its source and then try to sketch its applications to what thereby become characteristic tensions in Luther's social ethics.

The dialectical patterns illustrated above exhibit the situation in which man is placed by conversion. Unlike Simons' understanding of conversion as a change from the life of sin to the life of holiness, conversion to Luther means a change from the life of sin to the life of faith.[31] The difference here is not so much one of ideals: the Lutheran is as much under obligation to struggle against the sin in his flesh as the Mennonite is bound to recognize its continued existence. The difference is rather one of the scope and form in which the Christian life is to be lived. Sin and perfection are by themselves as mutually exclusive as the righteous God and evil man. But they are en-

---

[30] LCC XV, 225f.; cf. 34f.
[31] Among the myriad of possible citations the following, closely associating baptism with faith, are most relevant: 36, 58f.; 25, 286; 1, 30, 42, 82; 10[1a]. 231.16f.

compassed, joined together, in faith. It is faith (=repentance), Luther says over and over, which is the link or the glue joining the heart of man with the Word of God.[32]

But now we must push further. Why is faith, according to Luther, a union of opposites, a dialectical reality in which the believer is both wholly a sinner and wholly righteous, for the first time? Quite simply, because faith is for Luther the form of *Christ*, as we have seen.[33] And it is Christ and Christ alone upon whom Christian life and the church are founded, from whom they take their form, and to whom they direct their hope.

Yet now we must ask again: though faith be the form of Christ, why is it on that account a dialectical contrast? The answer is again ready to hand: because Christ in his atoning work shows himself to be both God and man.

Here we are led to the heart of Luther's theology. Many writers have observed that it is Luther's approach to christology, via what Aulen calls the "classical" theory of atonement, that differentiates Luther's theology from that of others. Luther's presentations of Christ's struggle on the cross, the best examples of which are found in the 1535 *Galatians* commentary, are among the most powerful, beautiful, troubling and intensely dialectical passages in the entire Luther corpus. On the cross Christ became more human, more sinful, more abandoned by God than is humanly possible. It is in these superhuman depths that Christ reveals himself as fully God and as the locus of a cosmic death-struggle between the Good and the Evil he has become.

> Therefore Paul would like to draw us away completely from looking at the Law, sin, death, and other evil things, and to transfer us to Christ, in order that there we might see this very joyous duel: the Law battling against the Law, in order to become liberty to me; sin battling against sin, in order to become righteousness to me; death battling against death, in order that I might have life. For Christ is my devil against the devil, that I might be a son of God; He destroys hell, that I might have the kingdom of heaven.[34]

Christian faith is a dialectical contrast or tension because the work, hence for Luther the person of Christ, from whom Christian faith takes its form is a dialectical contrast.

---

[32]LCC XVI, 89. Cf. LCC XV, 322; 14, 343; 9, 93. That is why Luther will describe faith, as all his other subjects, in dialectical form.

[33]We need not repeat that discussion here, but might only add the note that the equation of "Christ" with "faith" was originally a hermeneutical connection made by Luther early in his career. Not only did he not abandon it later, but he generalized the connection into the basic dialectical contrast of his theology.

[34]26, 164; cf. similar passages elsewhere in the comments on 2:19 and 3:13.

Now one last transitional question emerges: why does Luther raise his presentation of the work of Christ to this cosmic or transcendent scale? Again the answer is clear: because Christ is not merely Jesus of Nazareth; he is first of all the Word of God. He is the Second Person of the Holy Trinity.

2. AS SUGGESTED in the Prologue, the basic difference between the trinitarian theologies of Luther and Calvin and that of Simons is that the former sustain a "transcendent" basis for their trinitarian ascriptive patterns, while Simons does not. Every theologian feels the difference between his apprehension of the Christian message and the unspeakable reality he "knows" it to be. This difference is one of the creative tensions driving the theologian, and it is the always partially failed attempts to overcome this tension that often differentiate one theologian's work from another's.

The tension in Simons is, as we shall see in Part Two, expressed, so to speak, in an historical or "horizontal" dimension. It is the difference between the actual, ideal life of Jesus of Nazareth and his New Testament church on the one hand, and on the other hand, our latter-day attempt to reproduce it. For Luther and Calvin this tension is included as a feature within a much more basic, "vertical" or metaphysical dimension of tension: that between God and world, eternity and change, infinity and limit, the One and the Many.

Since they share this metaphysical tension it is more difficult to differentiate Luther from Calvin than either of them from Simons. Yet a clear distinction exists even if we are not able to uncover it fully! In a sense the argument here is a circular or "bootstrap" hypothesis. It was suggested that for Calvin the ultimate "point of contact" between the transcendent Trinity and worldly Christian existence is the person of God the Father, while for Luther it is God the Son. Now this hypothesized difference, if true, may be either the cause or the consequence of what is, however, a very clear difference in the reformers' theological constructions. Without getting into the subject at this point, let me simply assert that Calvin's overriding concern is to stress the oneness and transcendence of God. Luther's theology by contrast is marked by a very strong dialectical tension which often appears close to a dualism in his doctrines, including the doctrine of God. And Luther attempts to overcome this dualism by his stress on the presence of God, both hidden and revealed in Christ and in the world. His exclusive concentration on Christ, in whom the tensions between God and the world are revealed most sharply, is what makes Luther's theology so consistently dialectical.

These dualistic tensions in Luther's theology must now be summarized. The summary can thus function as a reprise of the chapter and as an introduction to the characteristic patterns of "immanence relationships" which will be the subject of the next chapter.

Luther, while seeing indications of the Triune God in the natural world, sustains a fully transcendent reference in his trinitarian theology. This transcendent reference he shares with Calvin but not with Simons. But Luther's exclusive concentration on Christ and his work as the sole locus wherein the pattern of God-world relationships can be known distinguishes the form of his theology from that of both Calvin and Simons, and gives it its characteristic features.

The main effect of his combination of transcendental trinitarian reference and epistemological concentration on Christ is that Luther becomes systematically inclined toward a fusion of the transcendent God and the natural world. Because his theology is dominated by the doctrine of Christ, who is the one incarnation of God and man, Luther de-emphasizes, at the very least, the more traditional, metaphysical distinctions of God from the world. Where the metaphysical distinction of God and world was basic, the main burden in traditional theology was that of adequately expressing the connection of God and world. In the doctrine of creation, this often meant a carefully adjusted schema of transcendent-immanent relationships; in the doctrine of redemption, a felt need to stress the oneness of Christ's person; in the doctrine of sanctification, the sacramental unity of church and world, by means of such concepts as a hierarchically-ordered Christendom.

But for Luther it is the unity of God-world relationships, as seen in Christ, that is metaphysically basic. And so Luther is constantly preoccupied with developing and sustaining the proper distinctions in this relationship. It is the systematic need to properly distinguish, within the metaphysical unity he assumes, that gives Luther's theology its thoroughly dialectical character. And his concentration upon Christ as the sole ground or locus of our Christian knowledge means that Luther's dialectics are essentially epistemological, not metaphysical. This characteristic is most clearly and generally evident in Luther's preference for speaking of God, not in terms of "transcendence/immanence," "absence/presence," "spirit/matter," or similar dualisms, but in terms of God as both a hidden and a revealed presence.

It is the epistemological dialectics of God's presence as hidden and revealed that gives Luther's teachings on creation, redemption, and sanctification their characteristic patterns of tension.

a) For Luther, God the Creator is best conceived as an active presence. This means that the Creator alone has absolute freedom and power. But in Christ our normal understanding of God's power and freedom is severely altered. For Christ's atoning struggle reveals to Luther that God's power is divided against itself. On the cross God's grace struggles to the death with God's wrath, the God of Love with the God of Judgment; the Holy Trinity with the unholy Tyrants. Luther believed that in some literal sense of the term, God became powerless in this atonement, that he had to suffer evils, to empty himself of his power in order to achieve—by his power!—salvation for man.[35*] The verse "My power is perfected in

---

[35]Melanchthon's position seems somewhat shy of Luther's on this matter, perhaps because he, like Calvin, wishes to give no occasion for the notion that God could actually be weak in something like human sense. Thus Melanchthon stresses that it was Christ's human nature that suffered, that the divine nature "held back" its powers—or "forsook" Christ on the cross. Cf. in the *Loci*, 23, 31, 35. In these passages, at least, Luther's dialectics are broken.

weakness" always stimulated Luther's dialectical pen. And the incarnation of Christ reveals to Luther that God's freedom is not to be understood to result from a divine spiritual self-exemption, so to speak, from the natural world. Rather it is manifest precisely in God's act of binding himself to the conditons of flesh and worldly institutions. "This very baby, chubby-cheeked, lying helplessly and dirty of diaper in a box of straw," Luther might have sermonized, "—he it is who is the Creator of the universe and free master over it."

The dialectics of God's power-in-weakness, of his freedom-in-bondage, have consequences for the relationship of the Christian to Christ and for that of the church to the world. The Christian must be passive in relation to the salvation accomplished by Christ in him; and the church must enter fully into the physical institutions of worldly life in order to act in God's service.

b) For Luther, God the Redeemer is clearly, definitively manifest only in Christ the Word. As we heard Luther say earlier, God has no other form in which to be found than in the form of his Word, i.e., in Christ who thus reveals the justice, the righteousness, the glory of God. Yet to Luther the glory of God is anything but obvious in Christ. Christ has "no form nor comeliness, that we should behold him"; he "empties himself, taking the form of a servant." Christ's humble birth, unenviable life, and ignominious death all point Luther to the truth that the divine glory cannot be like man's glory. It is not "a thing to be grasped," but is rather a hiddenness of form, indeed often a hiddenness under the opposite appearance. Accordingly the will of God as manifest in the teachings and example of Christ very severely alters our normal sense of God's righteousness or justice. Luther took endless delight in the way Christ's parables of God's kingdom outrage our sense of justice, how Christ's radicalization of God's law in the Sermon on the Mount destroys our comfortable assumptions about God's righteousness, and how Christ's refusal to supply a new law of God disappoints our religious expectancies. And Luther seldom got more outraged than when confronted with the natural (sinful) religious desire to take Christ's words and life as a literal example which the Christian must simply follow in order to gain or express the righteousness of God. The justice, the righteousness of God, according to Luther, always appear to us as unrighteousness. Therein is the true glory of God manifest.

Again, the dialectics of God's form expressed only in hiddenness, of God's justice manifest in what to us is unrighteousness, have applications in the doctrines of creation and sanctification. Christian faith is a hiddenness. And the true church, itself hidden from the world, must take its external form from whatever worldly circumstance in which it finds itself. Similarly Christian works of love cannot be dictated by absolute prescriptive rules but must be free, finite responses relevant to the situation or need close at hand.

c) For Luther, God the Sanctifier is definitively experienced by Christian faith as the God of love. In Christ's incarnation and atonement we have the ultimate expression of God's love for us. And the goal of that divine love is the restoration of the harmony or order between God and man which obtained before the Fall.

But in Christ, Luther sees what appears to be the opposite of God's love. He sees the personal indifference, the soulless impartiality, of God's action. Jesus himself is personally innocent. Luther's extreme linguistic intensification of Christ's suffering in terms of the "tyrant" language exposes the metaphysical, impersonal character of the atonement battle. It is no longer the individual man Christ, but it is the evil human condition embodied, that is the object of divine wrath. And it is not now the Heavenly Father who is testing a dearly beloved son, but it is Righteousness itself, the all-consuming Fire which annihilates all opposed to it. God is the impersonal killer.

—Yet, for Luther, all this takes place only for *me*; and it takes place only so that I might have life.

In the same way, Luther sees in Christ what appears to be the opposite of order or harmony. He sees disunity or separation. God's hatred of sin is so profound that Christ, who has become Sin incarnate, experiences on the cross what no mere man, however sinful, ever has or can experience: total abandonment by God. Jesus' confession of faith and trust, "My God, my God . . . ," is addressed to the One who, at only that one moment in creation history, is not present; ". . . why have you forsaken me?" Similarly, the phenomenon of Christ throws the settled world into disorder and self-destruction. Christ's birth forces the death of a generation of male children; his life, the undercutting of all social values; his teachings, riots in the streets; his death, fissures in the heavens, the earth, and the temple; his resurrection, foolishness in the Greek, scandal in the Jew, and in each increased hatred of the other; his church, the contempt and opposition of the world.

—Yet it is in these circumstances, according to Luther, that God comes to me and conforms me into the unity of the divine life in Christ.

Once more there are applications of these dialectics in Luther's understanding of creation and redemption. God the Holy Spirit, who "blows where he wills," and who "has nothing to do with slow enterprises (W.A. 27,32)," forces us to give up our own personal life and interests and directs us forthwith and exclusively to the tasks which need to be done. And it is just in this forced giving up of our own selves in works of love for the other that the Spirit creates in us our true self, i.e., the self of Christ. It is the Holy Spirit who, secondly, teaches us to take responsibly the multiplicity of circumstances to which the various aspects of our spiritual lives are to be directed. And it is in just this way that the Holy Spirit makes us one with the form of Christ.

****

God is power and freedom, yet he acts through weakness and bondage;

God is *logos* and just, but he is manifest in hiddenness and what to the world is unrighteousness;

God is personal, spiritual love and ordered unity, yet he completes himself in objective physical embodiment and in the autonomous multiplicities of creation.

These are the characteristic dialectical tensions in Luther's trinitarian theology. In a sense all are expressions of the basic tension in trinitarian doctrine between God as One and God as Many. Luther approaches these tensions from the assumption of their unity in Christ, the Second Person of the Trinity, the expression of God's form, of divine justice. Thus it is in Christ that the resolution of the conflicts of power and love, freedom and order, will be sought.[36] The social-ethical expression and resolution of these dialectical issues in the life of the Christian-in-community, the church, is the subject of the next chapter.

---

[36]Tillich, *Love, Power, and Justice*, p. 49, also sees the matter this way.

CHAPTER THREE

Luther: Freedom and Order

Introduction: After the Fall

This study began by postulating the terms "power," "form," and "love" as tools for discovering the contrasts in Reformation theological ethics. These terms received no *a priori* definitions, for such a discussion would have led us away from our subject, a fault that often occurs in critical studies in the field of intellectual history. Our object, after all, ought not to be to celebrate those great thinkers of the past who agree with our philosophy, nor to disparage those who do not by labelling them "illogical," "pre-scientific," or "merely religious." The object is rather to find out what they thought on their own terms. This tiny pinch of humility in our attitude toward the past enabled us to sit still for a discussion of the Trinity conducted on the reformer's terms and not necessarily on our own—a theological rather than a metaphysical discussion.

A second demand then faced us. Luther—and as we shall see, he shared this stubbornness with Simons and Calvin—was not willing to talk of the persons of the Trinity in such bare terms as "power," "form," and "love." To do so would have been to practice what Luther called a "theology of glory," i.e., no theology at all, but merely human reason cloaked with pretensions to divinity, Instead, the reformers insist that in order to answer our questions we must consider what man has in fact done with God and what God has in fact done with man, as Holy Scripture reveals these matters. We are led out of metaphysics and into *Heilsgeschichte*.

But once we have allowed ourselves to be led this far we find that our related concepts, "freedom," "justice," and "order," come into their own as fertile instruments of analysis. There is no need for a lengthy excursus rehearsing the particular (but by no means exclusive) association of the concepts of freedom, justice, and order with those of power, form, and love, respectively. There is quite sufficient warrant for these associations in the western intellectual tradition which we (no less than the reformers) have inherited. The theological tradition has its own favored cognate forms for expressing these concepts. Thus the theologian prefers to speak not so much in terms of "freedom, justice, and order," as in terms, for example, of "salvation, conversion, and sanctification." The mutual interrelatedness of these cognates also has its cognate theological language. The active expression of God's free power and his reuniting love can be called "grace"; of his power with his form or righteousness, "wrath" or "judgment"; and of his righteousness with his love, "forgiveness." Christ's incarnation is the expression of God's love; his death, of God's righteousness; his resurrection, of God's power.

But the particular theological warrants for our transition to the concepts of freedom, justice, and order are two. The circumstances they reflect are related, perhaps in a causal way, but the question, "which produced which?" is a question of basic principle demanding a commitment as nondemonstrable as it is necessary for further thought. In a theological nutshell: did man discover his own discrete autonomy and then as a consequence abandon God, or conversely? Most theologians have maintained that the scriptures insist that the rupture between man and God produced the ruptures among men. It is in a discussion of these disharmonies, theological and ethical, that the concepts "freedom, justice, and order" emerge as effective tools of analysis.

Almost the entire tradition agrees that the events proclaimed in the Christian Gospel would not have been necessary except for the fall. It is only with the fall that, for better and worse, human being and society in any form recognizable to us begins. And so it is only in this context that the terms "Christian," "social," and "ethics" gain their meaning.

Although they differ over emphases, theologians generally see in the story of the fall and its consequences a presentation of 1) the perfect, ideal unity of God's love, power, and form; 2) the apparent negation of these qualities in the world as a consequence of the fall; and 3) the beginning of the Christian—and human—task of re-establishing at least an analog to the divine unity.

In or before the beginning only the perfection of God's love, power, and form obtained. The temptation was, as Luther in particular emphasizes, a temptation for man to take for himself what belonged to God. The temptation appears as a grab for divine power and glory. Perhaps God Himself tempted man. He asked Adam to give names, i.e., create identities for the creatures. The grab for divine power ("you shall be as gods"), expressed itself in the lure for divine form or truth ("knowing good and evil"), and took as its occasion the ordered beauty of God's creation (the tree of knowledge was in the *center* of the garden, and *pleasing* to the eye). The fall has already taken place. Otherwise the temptation could not have been serious. The power play is for a fake goal ("you shall be *as* gods"); the quest for truth is spurious (why could man assume as meaningful the claim that there was both good and evil to be known?); and the desire for beauty already perverted, disordered (the tree was pleasing "to the eye"—and forget other considerations).

As a reward for his attempt to gain divine qualities, man received their opposites. He became powerless, a victim to both the fact of his physical being (he had to die) and to the conditions for even its temporary existence (he had to work). Man became clouded with ignorant fear (he hid from God, and he covered his own nakedness). And his world became an ugly chaos (he was thrown out of the garden, and into weeds). The real, and personally innocent inheritor of the effects of these disasters was that first "son of man." The founder of the human "community," as we know it, was Cain: he did the first murder and built the first city.

It is in the Biblical context of the separation from God and the consequent separation from self and other men that theologians speak of freedom, justice, and order. The concepts gain their meaning only as they presuppose and express the brokenness that exists between God and man, and among men; and they both affirm and look toward the overcoming of that brokenness. The concepts are social concepts because they reflect the multiplicity, after the fall, of divine and human interests. They are ethical because they reflect the fact that these many interests, after the fall, are often mutually competitive and at the same time possess rights to self-achievement. They become Christian to the extent men see that, after the fall, the resolution of the conflicts among them is achieved, clarified, and extended to men in God's deeds in Christ.

Toward the end of the preceding chapter we began to see how Luther gave expression to these tensions in his trinitarian theology. Luther so intimately associated thoughts of God with thoughts of man that he could not limit to the sphere of human life his discussion of the worldly tensions which clearly exist among and within love, power, and form. These tensions and their resolutions had to be seen in the divine life as well. In fact it is only as the tensions among love, power, and form in the divine life are revealed through the Word, according to Luther, that the Christian is enabled to see their existence in human life.

Luther, as we saw, approached the issues of Trinity and society from the point of view of Christ, who is the form or justice of God. This means that Luther's discussion of the human level will be shaped by his views on christology and justice. Therefore the issues of Christian ethics will be seen by him as issues of dueness, of the just apportionment, of the areas in which power and love, freedom and order, are each to be exercised in this world. Because of the distinction of Christ's two natures, the areas of freedom and order must be cleanly distinguished. Because of the personal oneness of Christ, they cannot be separated. Thus Luther's ethics, like every other area of his thought, will be expressed in dialectical form.

Paul Tillich concluded, perhaps on different principles than I, that the basic ethical circumstance for Luther was the question of the relationship of love and power.[1] Again from his own principles Tillich asserted that the tension between divine love and power basically refers to the subject of creation rather than salvation.[2] Though he may not have had any historical figure in mind, Tillich's assertion, I believe, is correct for Luther. The relation of love and power, order and freedom, is exclusively a creation issue for Luther, and not at all an issue of salvation. That is why Luther so sharply differentiates ethical considerations from the matter of justification before God. And that is why Luther's ethics are directed exclusively to life in the creation and among men. That the issues of the relation of freedom and order are issues of "creation ethics" in Luther is further indicated by the characteristic terms in which his discussion is couched. For when one begins to speak on Luther's ethics he finds himself very quickly speaking of "orders of creation," "mandates," "veils," and especially the "two realms." Lutheran ethics involves the recognition, the due apportioning, of what belongs to each realm. The dialectical issues of freedom and order in each realm can be expressed as issues of "binding" and "loosing"—the "two keys." This chapter is about what Luther means by "the two keys."

[1] Paul Tillich, *Love, Power, and Justice* (New York: Oxford University Press, 1954), p. 49f.
[2] Ibid., p. 113.

A. *Living and Walking*

They gave no thorough instruction about sin, nor did they teach anything about Christ, our Mediator, or the consolation attained by the keys. Teaching nothing about faith but only about the unbearable and futile torments of penance, confession, satisfaction, and our own human endeavor, they represented Christ as a cruel judge whom we had to appease, not only with our penance, confession, and works of satisfaction, but with the intercession of his mother and of all the saints. We had to placate Christ with every priest's mass and with every monk's and nun's merit, yet without avail. Nothing remained but a troubled conscience, a fearful heart, despair, and the beginning of the pangs of hell. Is it not so? Who can deny it? Are not the bulls and documents at hand? When I tried to rebuke such manner of penance, I merited the distinction of being condemned as a heretic through Pope Leo and his jackasses. Their harmful and blasphemous abominations had to stand as true articles of faith.[3]

The above autobiographical fragment from the 1530 treatise *The Keys* can be appreciated for its brass and irony. But because of its subject, the statement brought no smile to Luther's face as it might to ours. We have not had to endure the onslaughts of conscience he suffered because of the situation he describes. Of the hosts of specific issues that stirred Luther's tongue and pen, none was more critical to him, none more personal, none more instrumental in driving him to the work of reformation than the issue he speaks of here: the torment of conscience produced by a corrupt penitential system which had lost its Christian rationale.

Although the passage is not intended as a substantive analysis of the problem, it does contain a number of points which we can utilize to begin our discussion of Luther's ethics.

The intended purpose of the penitential praxis—the way "the keys" are used in the church—is to bring the troubled conscience into the peace of Christ, to rejoin the sinner with the Savior. The knowledge of Christ as the Savior of sinners is the foundation of Christian penitential life and thus[4]* of

---

[3] 40, 376f.

[4] The relationship, as specified here, between penitential life and ethical life in Luther's theology is a relationship which to one familiar with Luther's writing is as persuasively obvious—once it has been called attention to—as it is overlooked as a subject for detailed study. Once the terms of the connection are noted, any Luther scholar's mind will race with relevant quotations and arguments. Luther's ethics, at least the specific conclusions of Luther's ethics, are well known and often discussed. Similarly with the importance Luther attached to the (almost) sacrament of penance. The main pattern of linkage is also clear: what Luther calls the "Christian life." One brings to mind immediately the theme, expressed over and over in the

Christian ethics, according to Luther. But that foundation having been lost sight of, the penitential system worked the opposite of what its Founder intended. First of all, the vision of the loving Christ—note how Luther easily translated that into "faith" in the second sentence— was lost. In place of the union of Christ and faith, secondly, there come the separations. Led to concentrate on "our own human endeavor," Christians found themselves trapped in a host of distinctions and practices whose multiple use still could not undo what had now been done: Christ made into an implacable tyrant, faith into reflexive, compulsive acts of a terrorized conscience.

Besides the important "misuse" of the saints, the mass, church vocations, and the penitential system itself, the result which most stirred Luther's wrath was that, Christ having been lost, the freedom of the Christian conscience was lost. And hence its peace. As we shall see, the issue is not one of freedom versus order. It is rather one of the proper arenas in which Christ directs freedom be exercised and order or discipline maintained. The penitential praxis Luther scores here seems to him to confuse, in fact reverse Christ's direction. It binds the conscience before God and permits the illusion that therefore the body may be free before the world. As a consequence nothing remains but bondage.

The argument introduced in the above paragraph is not explicit in the quoted passage. But no one familiar with Luther's writings can fail to see that this autobiographical passage, as well as the topic of the 1530 treatise in which it occurs, is but a specific language for, and application of, basic principles worked out years earlier. If we are looking for one particularly good vehicle for exposing these basic principles and arguments, we can hardly make a better selection than *The Freedom of a Christian*.

1. LUTHER'S FAMOUS 1520 treatise, *The Freedom of a Christian*, like all classics both justifies its fame in many different ways and is often esteemed as something it is not. The treatise is sometimes taken as Luther's first major evangelical writing on Christian social ethics. It is not that, at least not directly. The text is basically a theological work concerning a central issue of Christian religion: how does man stand, and how shall he stand, before God? As Luther reiterates throughout the treatise, the issue of what a man *is* (i.e., what he is before God) must be settled before one can properly evaluate what he *does* (i.e., what he is before men). The treatise, therefore, is not itself a work on Christian ethics. But it can and must be taken as a treatise on the *foundation* of ethics. That is how we shall approach it now. In a brief analysis of the text we shall discover all the basic themes we are pursuing in this chapter.

The famous opening paradox, that the Christian is at once perfectly free and perfectly bound, is approached by Luther from a consideration of

---

corpus, most famously in the first of the 95 theses: the nature of Christian life can be expressed in one word: repentance. I believe Luther's decision to refuse sacramental status to penance was the single most agonizing technical judgment the theologian, the churchman, and the pastor had to make. Which *persona* won out?

man's twofold nature as spiritual and physical (31, 344). But the paradox is not relaxed in the obvious way: that man is free in spirit, bound in body. Rather the subject of the treatise, as Luther insisted right at the beginning, is the issue of the freedom and the bondage of the spirit. The first major section, on how the spiritual man becomes what he is, confirms the order of discussion noted in the above paragraph. Only when the matter of man bound and free before God (in the spirit) is determined can Luther in his second major section (358ff.) speak of man's actions (in the body) as bound and free before both God and man.

Nothing "external" is relevant to the matter of the spirit's status as bound and free. The whole matter is one of righteousness or justification. That is a matter exclusively between the conscience and God, and a matter whose resolution accordingly is exclusively achieved and revealed in Christ the Word, and therefore also in faith (345f.).

Luther's entire discussion of justification in this section is a discussion of power and love as these relationships are illustrated in Christ and in faith. Utilizing an approach which will be authoritatively illustrated in his later work, *The Bondage of the Will*, Luther construes the issue of man's justification before God as an issue of ability or power. Both theoretically and effectively man is unable, powerless, to achieve justification by his spiritual or bodily works. Faith and faith alone is this power, since faith is the gift and the very presence of Christ himself (348f.). Before God, therefore, man is free of works and of law, bound to faith and to Christ. And it is only as he is bound to Christ that the Christian is able to be truly (i.e., freely) obedient to the law (349f.).

The image of being "freely bound" to Christ suggests to Luther the image of love or union as explicating the meaning of the power of faith (351). Because of the loving union of the believer and Christ, the struggle over the First Commandment is won in the Christian breast as it was won on the cross. Christ reigns in both the spiritual and the physical order, and accordingly so does the Christian. He is a lordly king. He rules in worldly life not by physical power—Luther here quotes the passage, "My power is made perfect in weakness"—but by spiritual power. And he is an omnipotent priest, although this does not mean that in ecclesiastical life all distinctions of function are abolished (354f.).

The summary construction of the issues of justifying power in terms of love provides Luther the way of transition to his second section, the binding and loosing of the "outer" man in the area of sanctification. In the first section, when the theme of the discussion was power, Luther spoke of freedom resulting from the loving union with Christ. In the second section the theme is love, and Luther approaches it in terms of the order by which God establishes unity among men.

In the outer man, Luther begins his second section, the only thing that is relevant is works—works of love, of course, and that means for Luther only works done freely, i.e., works of faith. Only because of the freedom of Christian faith can the necessary disciplines upon one's own rebellious flesh for the purpose of serving the neighbor avoid the extremes of disorder produced by bondage to the law of works-righteousness (358f.). The Christian, who is the form of Christ, i.e., a servant (366), is free of bondage to disruptive ideologies, bound to respond freely to what the moment requires in order to maximize the possibility of concord among men. This means conforming to the cultural environment in which one finds oneself when its particular demands are not perceived as ultimately inimical to the Gospel of Christ (368f.). And it means taking the opposite pole when extreme demands in the social environment threaten to break the balanced social harmony to which the Gospel of Christ looks, whether those demands come from programmatic antinomians or from instinctive legalists (372ff.).

There is no real mystery in this foundation of Luther's ethics. The principles are dialectical but clear. Before God, one is free of bondage to one's own works, bound only to Christ's free gift of himself to faith. Therefore one can be free of bondage to religious ideologies, and one is bound to respond freely, i.e., relevantly, to Christ's requirements for our life before men.

2. THE THEMES of *The Freedom of a Christian*, perhaps Luther's best known small treatise, illustrate the foundations of his ethics. For those not thoroughly drenched in Luther's writings, the foundations outlined above may not be persuasive. If not, one or two impressions may be responsible for the lack of enthusiasm. The object of Luther's ethics seems to be that of preserving the given social order. In other words, it appears to be a literally conservative ethics. And while conservation is of course a good, it may or may not be necessarily the last or even the most important word one would wish to say about the proper object of Christian ethics. Secondly, Luther's discussion seems based upon a very sharp, settled distinction between "flesh" and "spirit" or between "what belongs" to God-man relations and what to man-man relations. Again, while grounds for the distinction can be recognized, the sharpness of the distinction—culminating occasionally in the implication that opposite attitudes and behaviors are required in each realm—can be taken as artificial and spurious.

These impressions are not necessarily incorrect for any given circumstance, but they cannot be generalized into an overall sketch of the purposes of Luther's ethical principles. Both impressions, as suggested above, suffer from insufficient study of Luther. In this sub-section we shall discuss the matter of Luther's supposed conservatism. In the following section the question of the distinction of the realms will be considered.

To put it quite simply: the object of Luther's ethical principles is not conservation of the past, but harmony in the present. The christological or "justice" base from which he works requires that his chief concern be the dueness, the proper relationship or balance, between the exercise of freedom and the requirements of order. The proper relationship is one that Luther feels is revealed in the Gospel, and accordingly one which will maximize the possibility of social harmony, the spiritual circumstance in which the Gospel may best grow among men: peace.

Most importantly, peace of conscience. The title of the treatise is *The Freedom of a Christian*. And its chief concern is that the conscience (man before God) be free of the unbearable and false burdens of feeling itself responsible for its own salvation. One is either finally saved or not saved; there is no more or less. Were the issue of the "is" or "is not" made conditional upon even the tiniest bit of human spiritual quality or ethical achievement, the conscience even then—especially then, perhaps—would be bound to roast on the spit of "scruples," as Luther called them from long personal acquaintance. The Christian conscience is free, and Christ and his Gospel of salvation faithfully commended, only when that salvation is preached as an unconditionally free gift, an absolute, completed achievement. The one "scruple" Luther maintained, one he felt did good service in behalf of the free Christian conscience, was that of preventing the demands of order—law—from entering the relationship of God and man. For Luther knew, as he expressed this truth often in his writings, that law cannot exist at all unless it reign. That is why it must not be permitted to poke even its nose into the conscience.

And it also is on behalf of the effective reign of law, in its proper arena, that Luther insists on the freedom of the conscience before God. For were the demands of law to be applied to the spirit, the reign of law itself would be destroyed. One aspect of Luther's basic approach to the supposed "ethical-religious" teachings of Jesus in the gospels was his argument that the radicalized demands of law drive men to despair. "You must be perfect" says the law, "in order to be [on *your* terms, at least] saved." Man cannot achieve that status. He hears that it is the premise for gaining salvation. He might then remember Anselm's argument that even perfection of life would fall short! So man ends up hating and rebelling against the law, even in its proper sphere. Luther's greatest social objection to the religious legalists of his time was that the bondage of conscience they effected by a mistaken application of God's law ended up producing not peace, love, and order, but revolution, indifference, and chaos. For the good of order in the body and in the body politic the conscience must be free before God.

Comparable, reversed arguments hold with respect to the proper limits of the freedom of a Christian.

Although Luther insisted that there was no real freedom unless first the conscience was free before God, he emphatically rejected the notion that, therefore, there ought to be complete freedom in the body. As we have seen, Luther insisted that discipline upon one's own flesh—not for its own sake but that we might better serve the neighbor—is a proper use of the law. Bodily discipline purposed in this way is the natural (gracious!) consequence of the free conscience which is the gift of Christ. "Since we live by faith, let us walk by faith," said Paul. Luther insisted upon the imperative as a necessary consequence as much as he did upon the indicative as premise.

Besides the Biblical warrant demanding order, Luther felt that such a requirement also served the interests of freedom of conscience. For if man had unrestricted freedom in the physical realm, the result would not be the utopia finally achieved but rather a chaos. Luther's strong, dark sense of the human condition riddled with original sin led him to insist on "law and order" in the physical and social world. Only in this way could that savage animal, man, be kept from destroying himself and everything he held dear, including his spiritual freedom.

The intent of Luther's ethical principles, then, is the maintenance of the proper balance of freedom and order, for the benefit of each and for the spiritual environment in which the Gospel might best flourish. As we noted in the analysis of *The Freedom of a Christian*, Luther advised the Christian to take an opposite course when confronted by an extreme demand. The ability to do this is also a mark of Christian faith and freedom. Both "living" and "walking" are "by faith," not by conscience or body, and not by principles of freedom or order. For Luther argued that Christian existence is a life of love which "stands above" all law, whether the principles of freedom or the law of order. Thus the Christian, bound in love to respond to the needs of the ethical moment rather than to the requirements of abstract principles, might choose to violate social order in the interests of spiritual peace. Luther did this in the case of the bigamy of Philip of Hesse, and in his own life with the decision to marry. And the Christian might choose to sacrifice freedom in the same interests. Luther did this in his rejection of the rapid changes in worship effected in his absence by Carlstadt and others. He also did this with respect to church organization in Germany.

Both Luther and the church bearing his name tended to opt for order at the sacrifice of freedom when the circumstances forced a choice. This tendency, I believe, is more significantly attributable to the massive social disorders produced by the Reformation than to the personal constitution of Luther. Had he lived in a modern totalitarian society, Luther would have taken the opposite course. In both the actual and the hypothetical situation Luther's ethics of "freedom in love"' have the same ultimate object: peace of conscience before God and thus before men.

B. *The Keys*

[Christ says:] When you use the keys, I will also. Indeed, if you do it, it shall be done, and it is not necessary that I do it after you. What you bind and loose (I say) I will neither bind and loose, but it shall be bound and loosed without my doing so. It shall be one single action, mine and yours, not a twofold one . . . But such ideas regarding two kinds of keys ["heavenly" and "earthly" keys] originate in the mistaken notion that God's Word is not his Word. Because it is spoken through men it is regarded as the word of men. And God is thought of as way up there in heaven, very, very far removed from his Word here below. So we stand there and with open mouths stare heavenward and invent still other keys . . . Rely on the words of Christ and be assured that God has no other way to forgive sins than through the spoken word, as he has commanded us. If you do not look for forgiveness through the Word, you will gape toward heaven in vain for grace, or (as they say), for a sense of inner forgiveness.[5]

To distinguish the perfect work of God from the imperfect works of man seems an exercise in good Christian humility. And so it is, Luther agreed, when the distinction is properly done and when the distinctions made are the right ones. But distinguishing correctly is a task Luther acknowledged time and again to be as difficult as it is vital for Christian theology, faith, and life.

If a man sets about the task "under his own recognizance," so to speak, he invariably botches the job, to the grave injury of the Christian conscience. This is the situation Luther is addressing in the above passage. Assuming a spuriously pious separation of God and man, the Roman Church according to Luther practiced a serious abuse of its ministry, mocked the promising Word of God, and destroyed Christian faith. The church's two keys of binding and loosing were considered "earthly" keys which, because of the "truth" that God's ways are not man's ways, cannot be said to work in perfect correspondence with the "heavenly" binding and loosing. Much of the polemics in Luther's 1530 work, *The Keys*, is directed against the political abuses this false distinction permitted. But his real anger was stirred because the effect of the distinction was to deprive the conscience of all faith, hope, and trust in God's Word in Christ.

To counter this fake human distinction and its disastrous effects on the Christian conscience, Luther drew attention exclusively to Christ the Word, and in fact overemphasized the togetherness of God and man with regard to the church's ministry of that Word. This does not mean, however, that Luther was not equally insistent upon the proper distinction of God's from man's works. But in order to learn what belongs where, how freedom and order are exercised in God's two realms, and what is bound and loosed in each, Luther insisted we must go to that place where the proper distinctions are revealed to us: to Christ.

As soon as we encounter Christ the Word, we encounter the distinctions that the Word both reveals and produces. Luther's language for these distinctions varied with his purpose. Thus, for example, he spoke of a twofold "clarity" of Scripture: an external ministry and an internal knowledge of the heart. The words of God are composed of both law and Gospel. There is an "inner word" inseparable from Christ's body, and an "outer word" which can be separated. And the Word sharply distinguishes an external or physical realm, ruled by Christ's humanity, from an internal or spiritual realm, ruled by Christ's divinity.[6] "External-internal," "law and

[5] 40, 365f.
[6] LCC XVII, 112, 172; 37, 133; 30, 20; 26, 174; 27, 171.

Gospel," "spirit and flesh," and the "kingdom of Christ's divinity and humanity" are each languages with nuances useful to investigate. In the preceding section the distinctions "spirit-flesh," and to a certain extent "external-internal," informed our discussion. In this section the "kingdoms" of language and (to an extent) "law-Gospel" will be important.

Throughout his writings Luther constantly urged that we must properly distinguish between what belongs in the spiritual and what in the physical realm. Such a continuing emphasis is necessary because men constantly "confuse" the realms. The confusion, according to Luther, is not due to human ignorance, since God's Word is quite clear on the matter. The circumstance giving rise to the confusion is that both realms refer to the same reality: the created world. We would go off course in our pursuit of Luther's social ethics were we to construe the two realms as referring to different realities. Thus it is not gratuitous to state again: the two realms refer to aspects or perspectives on the same reality, the world. Yet it is very easy to make the error, and Luther's terminology can reinforce the temptation. His most frequent usages are "heavenly" and "earthly" kingdoms, or the "Kingdom of God" and the "kingdom of the world." These designations have nothing to do with real estate. Rather they define the judgments and the perspectives from which the single fact of life in the world is to be viewed. Thus we should try to keep the temptation to error minimal by using alternate forms of Luther's designations of realm. We shall speak of the "theological" and "social" realms, or of the realms of "faith" and "love." These designations are themselves far from perfect, but at least they do not immediately suggest that one realm is "God's," as though the other was—therefore—"man's." The fact is, of course, that both realms are God's. And both man's!

The confusion of realms is not a matter of human ignorance, but is the expression of a power struggle over who, God or man, is to exercise his judgment in both realms. It represents, as Luther puts it, the eternal struggle over the First Commandment: whose righteousness or justice shall be recognized, that of man or that of God? The struggle over justice is a struggle over the distribution of freedom and order, as we saw in the preceding section. Man tries to be master of both realms first by confusing them, and then by reversing the ways and areas in which freedom and order are exercised.[7] The treatise *The Freedom of a Christian* can just as well be directed against churchmen as against secular politicians. Some churchmen, for example, wish to bind the conscience and body when it comes to "religion" and to free conscience and body when it comes to "life." Others, most often politicians, wish the converse. God, however, insists on quite different ways of construing things, according to Luther; ways which neither churchmen nor politicians find to their liking. So the power struggle is on. Since all men try to confuse the realms, the true preaching of the Word and the Kingdom of God, according to Luther, is at the same time the proclamation of the proper distinction of the realms.

[7] Luther argued that both the papacy and the fanatics confused and inverted the spiritual and physical realms. Cf. WA 18, 18.30-36; 40, 147f., 191f.

The proper distinction, unity, and relationship of the realms, Luther insisted, is made known only through the Word. That means it is made known only in Christ, and only in faith. For Luther the divinity and humanity of Christ is the basis for the distinction between what pertains to faith and what to law, or as he can put it alternatively, between faith's "internal nature" (justification) and "external nature" (works of love).[8]

Perhaps Luther's most frequently occurring language concerning the realms, however, is that of law and Gospel. We need not enter into a full presentation of this rich theme in Luther's theology, but will confine attention to one or two notes particularly relevant to our topic. Perhaps because of the "confusion" of realms discussed earlier, Luther's texts are dominated by the need to distinguish sharply between what pertains to the law and what to the Gospel. He will use every image he can conjure up to expose the distinction, since the proper distinction of law and Gospel is the summary of all Christian doctrine.[9*] Yet he is also quite concerned that law and Gospel not be falsely separated. The Word of God is both law and Gospel. Law and Gospel cannot be separated and are not contradictory (though we are contrary to both!). Perhaps Luther's most profound, troubling attempt to express the relationship is his construction of law and Gospel as the "alien" and "proper" works of God.[10]

However the relation be expressed, it is clear that the two realms do not correspond to one reality which is "good" and one which is evil. As noted earlier, God and Christ rule in both realms. Luther also claims that the Devil inhabits both realms; the worldly realm, for example, in the form of bad politicians, the spiritual realm in the form of bad teachers of theology.[11]

Law and Gospel include all reality, as do the two realms, and are best defined by function. The whole *summa* of scripture, Luther states in the *Isaiah* commentary, is the revelation of the work of law to humble us bodily and spiritually, and the revelation of the work of the Gospel to comfort us bodily and spiritually.[12] Those are also the functions of the two keys.

Just as Luther preferred to define law and Gospel functionally, he defined the related concept of the two realms functionally. The "realms"

---

[8] 27, 30; 171; 26, 272f.

[9] 26, 117. Luther's most concentrated writing on this matter is found in the *Galatians* lectures of 1535. Among the more frequently occurring images are:

Law	Gospel
teaches us the ought	teaches us the how
is on earth	is in heaven
does not bring the Holy Spirit	brings the Holy Spirit
is comparable to an active life	is comparable to a contemplative life
is the voice of a servant	is the voice of a lord
pertains to the flesh	pertains to the spirit
veils God	unveils God

[10] 12, 340, WA 39¹, 416.8-14; 566.1-11; 14, 335; 16, 234; WA 46, 672, 24f.
[11] 26, 455.
[12] 16, 327.

language, as has been noted by some students, connotes not only power but also the competitive aspect of a power struggle between God and man.[13] This connotation is most classically illustrated throughout Luther's *Bondage of the Will*, even though the "realms" language itself is not explicit in the text. A key thesis in the treatise is that the question of freedom and bondage is spurious unless we define the issues not only in terms of God's power or ability, but also in terms of man's power to act vis-à-vis God. The distinction which carries his argument in this text is the same one which occurs in the treatise *The Freedom of a Christian*, the same one which he uses to differentiate the realms, the same one he uses to distinguish faith and love, and in a sense law and Gospel: the Christian's relationship to "things above himself," i.e., to God, and his relationship to "things below," i.e., to men and life in the world. As one should expect by now, Luther's assertions concerning the "directions" in which freedom or bondage obtain are not univocal but dialectical. There is a proper freedom and bondage, a real peace and order, in each direction or realm. To give only a very few illustrations: on the one hand Christian freedom means the forgiveness of sins; Christians have the freedom of the Gospel only with respect to their relationship to God.[14] Yet Christians, like all other men, are bound in will or ability to act in regard to their salvation. This is the major thesis of *The Bondage of the Will*. On the other hand Christians are, as we have already seen, free to respond beyond the demands of law in worldly life, and are—again, this is a theme in *Bondage*—metaphysically free in all ordinary worldly choices. If there is "compulsion" in external matters, Luther insists, faith is lost. Yet by the same token, Christians are bound by God's commandment regarding life among men, bound to respond to the demands of love, bound to achieve order. For in this area, as Luther put it in a comment on the Sermon on the Mount, we are speaking not about one's status as Christian, but about the "Christian-in-relation," i.e., about his life and obligation to other men.[15]

Though these judgments appear confusing, in fact the distinction allowing them is clear. In the theological realm Christians are free from obligation to save themselves, bound to fail if they try. In the social realm they are free from the absoluteness of the law's demands, and bound to respond in love, that is, relevantly to the need at hand.

Clean though this distinction appears in theory, one might object that the clarity is either spurious or impossible to achieve in practice. Luther would agree, as far as that opinion goes. In fact he would intensify it. The distinctions are impossible to realize—*unless!* Unless and only as Christ the Word indwells the heart. And that means only as the Holy Spirit is present as grace and as gift, turning us poor sinners into God's new creature. For Luther insists that it is not we who make the right distinctions, but rather

---

[13]Cf. Gerhard Ebeling, *Word and Faith*, trans. J. W. Leitch (Philadelphia: Fortress Press, 1963), pp. 386ff.; John Loeschen, *Wrestling With Luther* (St. Louis: Concordia Publishing House, 1976), pp. 159ff.

[14]44, 313; 40, 303.

[15]44, 313; 26, 119; 21, 291.

the Holy Spirit, the Spirit whose function it is to bring God's grace in Christ to us, to certify our hearts into conformity with Christ, and to renew our minds with the Word and the wisdom of Christ.

The unity and distinction of the realms which Luther expresses in his dialectical language about the Father, about the Son, and about the relation of Father and Son, thus reappears in his language about the Holy Spirit and about the relation of Son and Holy Spirit. The language of the realms is, as we have noted, a language about power—the power of God (God the Father). So Luther's discussion of the realms, the powers, of God, is developed in terms of the dialectical relationship between Son (form, justice) and Holy Spirit (order, love).

As Regin Prenter among others has observed in his study of Luther,[16] there is especially evident in the young Luther what we might call a continuing oscillation between two foci in the presentation of the work of the Holy Spirit. Prenter describes this oscillation as that between the Holy Spirit conceived as the "gift" itself of faith (the indwelling Christ), and conceived as "grace" as the source of the gift of faith. From our perspectives this oscillation appears as a dialectical contrast between the Holy Spirit, who is both grace and gift, functioning to define and realize *both* realms for the Christian.

On the one hand Luther often describes the establishing of the theological relationship (man before God) in terms of the Holy Spirit's work. The Holy Spirit convicts of sin, persuades us of our inability and our need for Christ. The Spirit is grace—and that means that the Spirit is forgiveness of sins. The chief function of the Spirit is the revelation or knowledge of God's gracious disposition to us, i.e., it is the Spirit who sets us into faith, into Christ.[17] On the other hand Luther can describe the establishing of the social relationship (man before men) also in terms of the Holy Spirit's work. Thus the Holy Spirit (= grace) is the agent effecting the realization of obedience to the commandments, the realization of righteousness, the realization of love.[18]

The Holy Spirit, therefore, both defines the realms and achieves their realization in Christian faith and love, according to Luther. In the preceding chapter it was noted that Luther never completely isolated his ascriptive patterns vis-à-vis the Holy Spirit from his patterns vis-à-vis the Son. Especially in Luther's earlier writing the Holy Spirit often appears in the "form" or "justice" function—that is, as instructor. In our present discussion, this function reappears in terms of the Holy Spirit as definer of the two realms. The object of this discussion is to lead the reader into Luther's understanding of Christian social ethics, i.e., into the worldly realm. In this connection, the Holy Spirit is the teacher of what structures God has

---

[16]Regin Prenter, *Spiritus Creator*, trans. John Jensen (Philadelphia: Muhlenberg Press, 1953), pp. 31ff.

[17]Cf. LCC 16, 270; 315ff.; 327; 348; LCC 15, 126ff.

[18]LCC 16, 317; 329; 339f.; Cf. also Luther's frequent comments upon Galatians 5:22 and Romans 5:5.

created in and for the world. It is from the interior testimony of the Holy Spirit, in other words, that we learn about the "orders" of creation.

As is well known, Luther maintained that there are three orders. His language varies somewhat, but in general the orders are those of the church, the government, and social / economic life.[19] At this point only one observation is necessary in preparation for the concluding section of this chapter. The three orders are all orders in the worldly or social realm—including the order of the church. The inclusion of the church as a worldly order sharply differentiated Luther's understanding of the church from that of Calvin, Simons, and the Roman Catholics, and produces, as should be obvious, very significant consequences for Luther's social ethics. As we turn now to a more detailed overview of Luther's social ethics, we shall see that it is in the context of the three orders that the issues of the relationship between faith and love, justice and order—the relationship of the keys of binding and loosing—come to expression.

C. *The Prudence of the Spirit*

At the end of the preceding section the profound implications of Luther's view that the church is a worldly order were noted. While many things are ingredient in this position—chief among them the controverted distinction between the "visible" and "invisible" church[20]*—Luther's affirmation of the church as a divinely-instituted worldly order is what most basically distinguishes the Lutheran ecclesiology and ethics from many Anabaptist traditions. Says Luther in a 1537 exposition of the Gospel of John:

> Whatever goal these hypocrites may want to attain with their "Spirit," I do not choose to share it with them. May a merciful God preserve me from a Christian Church in which everyone is a saint! I want to be and remain in the church and little flock of the faint-hearted, the feeble, and the ailing, who feel and recognize the wretchedness of their sins, who sigh and cry to God incessantly for comfort and help, who believe in the forgiveness of sin, and who suffer persecution for the sake of the Word, which they confess and teach purely and without adulteration.[21]

[19]Cf. 26. 504; 37, 364f.; 41, 177; 43, 30; 50, 652; WA 46, 616; WA 39^2, 42. for examples of Luther's varying terminology.

[20]In this section the discussion of the church as a worldly order presupposes the senses in which the church as an object of faith is understood by Luther to be "a people of God," "a society of the elect," and so on. There are senses in which the church does bear a special relationship to God not manifest in the orders of marriage or government. But because of the dangers of misconstruing the church as "the spiritual realm" or "the kingdom of God" (cf. note 36), I do not want to introduce consideration of the special status of the church in the context of a discussion of the orders. The special status of the church has been considered in the preceding chapter.

[21]22, 55.

Passages like this have been used earlier for the purpose of beginning or ending a discussion with a moving, lovely thematic sketch from the "treasury of Luther's art." But such descriptions, whatever their emotional effect, are intended primarily to be exact and serious theological presentations of their subjects. And there is no way we can take seriously such passages as the above—beginning with its astonishing second sentence—unless we realize that the church of which Luther is speaking is an order in the worldly realm, hence an order bearing the corruptions, errors, and moral failures characteristic of all worldly orders. For centuries theologians have misinterpreted St. Augustine's theoretic distinction between the "City of God" and the "City of Man" to mean "the church" and "the world," with connotative adjectives assigned accordingly. Luther's distinction of the two realms, though by no means identical to Augustine's construction, is at least as misleading if it is interpreted in terms of "church" and "world." Such an interpretation is, to put it in a visual metaphor, just the wrong angle to cut the cake. The orders of economic life or marriage, church, and government are all orders in the worldly realm, and all are equally instruments of the kingdom of God. The orders are differentiated by function, not by holiness quotient. They are in a sense God's "extension," "masks" or "*larvae*" of himself in the world, and as such are impure.[22] They may be misused by the Devil through evil men, and even at best, as God's instruments, they are clumsy, dull tools wielded by us, his unprofitable servants. Nevertheless, the orders are God's will incarnate, and his will is accomplished through them.

Before we sketch the tasks or mandates which define the orders, one other stray thought must be probed. Do the three orders bear any systematic relationship—as immanent expressions, perhaps—to the Trinity as Luther understands it? One or two students have made suggestions along these lines.[23] Luther finds the three orders in scripture, and for him that is the end of it. He does not consciously derive them from trinitarian logic, and would reject as useless speculation any attempt to do so. Yet Luther insists on only three mandates, and has to stretch the order of marriage somewhat beyond its natural sense in order to encompass the reality of economic life and labor.[24*] It is even possible to see something like analogs of function in the orders corresponding to Luther's trinitarian ascriptive pattern. Thus the order of marriage, which Luther considers the basis of the other orders, may be seen analogously to the function of the Father as

---

[22]For documentation and further discussion of Luther's images of "extension," masks, and so on, see John Loeschen, *Wrestling With Luther*, pp. 95ff., 138ff.

[23]Cf. J. Lawrence Burkholder, "The Anabaptist Vision of Discipleship," in *The Recovery of the Anabaptist Vision*, ed. Guy F. Hershberger (Scottdale, Pa.: Herald Press, 1957), p. 139.

[24]Some justification for this may be found in the original sense of the Greek *oikonomia* as "household management." But Luther usually bends, expands, or compresses his borrowed terms only when he needs to in order to use them in other than their natural meaning contexts. Dietrich Bonhoeffer, here (as in so many other places) a sensitive developer of Luther's theology, breaks the tension by positing labor as the fourth Christian mandate. Cf. his *Ethics*, trans. Neville Horton Smith, ed. Eberhard Bethge (New York: The Macmillan Co., 1962), pp. 73ff.

creative power. The order of government, whose function it is to sustain order, would then reflect the work of the Holy Spirit. The church is of course the form of Christ. And it is in fact from the Word of Christ proclaimed in the church that all the orders find their exposure and definition. For whatever it is worth in the interests of our speculative question, Luther did produce a creed-like summary of his faith at the end of his 1528 treatise on the Lord's Supper, in the "second article" of which, on God the Son, he introduced his understanding of the three orders.[25]

We need not go into great detail concerning the orders and the social, personal, and religious ethics that Luther sees implied in each. The work by Gustaf Wingren, *Luther on Vocation*,[26] remains unsurpassed as a general study. Our tasks here are rather to see how the three orders interrelate, how they mutually qualify, govern, and assist each other in God's task, and how in each particular order (as also among the orders), the Christian meets the "binding and loosing," the "freedom and order" themes we have been investigating.

As with most else in Luther study, it is an error to separate what he but distinguishes. The three orders are not isolated cells of responsibility. As Luther indicated in one of his first Reformation tracts, the orders are the common responsibility of all Christians, even though we are severally called to exercise particular care in different areas.[27] There is just no way we can secularize, i.e., avoid joint responsibility for God's will. As Luther put it in his commentary on the Sermon on the Mount, God's requirement of perfect love and obedience falls upon all Christians and upon all aspects of life.[28] Thus holiness—dedication to God's service—must characterize public service and personal/economic life from Monday through Saturday in the streets at least as much as it should characterize worship in church on Sunday. And churchmen have no unique obligation to assume the role of embodying the goodness of the community. Legislators, businessmen, laborers, and householders are equally under the obligation.

The mutuality of the orders is expressed in other ways as well. Every Christian lives in many vocations at once. He wears many hats: lover, parent, laborer, businessman, public servant, churchman. Especially is it the case in the modern complex world that the exercise of all orders is required in each. The parent is a citizen, and also a teacher of faith to his children. The legislator must deal with profound moral and religious issues. The minister is a parent, a public servant, a businessman, and most of all, perhaps, a laborer and a lover!

Because of this interrelatedness of orders—each rooted in God's command and each exercised by the Christian—each order functions both to assist the special task of the others and to limit the exercise of the others.

---

[25] 37, 364.
[26] Trans. Carl C. Rasmussen (Philadelphia: Fortress Press, 1957).
[27] *Open Letter to the German Nobility*, 16, 45, 98, 202f.
[28] 21, 129.

There is therefore a general sense of binding and loosing, freedom nd order, which emerges from a consideration of the three orders. Each order is free of improper demands from the others and is bound by the limits set by the others. Each order is free to elaborate its structure in accordance with the particular need for which the order is established, and each is bound to support the other orders in their own proper elaborations.

Luther considered marriage and parenthood the foundation and source of the other orders, whose joint obligation it is to support family life and maintain an environment in which it might flourish in accordance with God's will. Luther's views on family life ("a school for character") are too well known to require elaboration here. We might only note some senses in which the order of marriage supports and in a sense transforms the other orders, and is in turn supported by them. It is in family life that the child learns respect for authority, obedience, and the necessity of limiting his own demands for the sake of others. And it is in the family that parents learn the burdens of decision, the necessity for compromise, and the value of mercy over justice in the face of human weakness. These qualities reinforce the proper exercise of government, whose task it is in turn to protect and extend the sanctity of family life. The eminent consequence for the church of Luther's views of married life is of course the parsonage, an invention which, excepting possibly only the catechetical instruction and hymn-singing, is the greatest single institution for religious education to emerge from the Protestant Reformation. By the same token the parsonage serves as a model home from which Christian laymen can draw direction and ideals for their own home life. This is a personal responsibility which many a minister and his family have prayed be taken from them. Much grief has indeed been generated because a congregation or community has demanded, against Luther's own principles, that the minister's house be more perfect than their own in morality and propriety. Yet the obligation remains a just one. The minister should not avoid it, but rather should take the lead in transforming the morals of the religious community by his example, as did Luther.

Of greater historical and scholarly interest is the relationship, as Luther sees it, between the orders of church and government. Again we need not rehearse well known material in detail. In general Luther insists that the church is utterly bound to the preaching of the Word and the ministry of the sacraments as these are articulated in scripture and doctrine. In one of his fullest accounts of the nature and function of the church, Luther insists that, besides the positive signs indicative of the binding of the church to the Word, the church not only has no power or authority to elaborate new doctrines or practices, but also must exercise its task of condemning all new inventions of belief.[29] On the other hand the church is free to elaborate its own internal shape and operations according to the dictates of reason and common sense, since, as Luther put it, the Holy Spirit has better things to do than decide matters of internal church organization.[30] In its exercise of judg-

---

[29]*On the Councils of the Church*, 41, 123-174.
[30]41, 60.

ment and discipline, the church must exhibit "the prudence of the Spirit," which is to choose the common good for the common life.[31] The ban must be used scripturally and sparingly, only in cases of open sin or heresy. The church must not rush ahead with even justified reforms such as the abolition of the Mass and images when such efforts bruise consciences and upset public tranquility. In these ways also we see the exercise of the church's proper office benefitting the family, just as the strictures against novel, extended claims of ecclesiastical authority serve to support civil concord and promote the effective ministry of the governmental office.

As for government itself, its task, in a word, is peace.[32] Luther's somber estimate of the human mass, barely harnessed and protected from itself by the thin filaments of civilization and law, produced an essentially negative estimation of the peace-sustaining mandate of the governmental order. While for many the distance of time and intervening political philosophy permits us to study Luther's views on the function of government with the curious dispassion we give to quaint old teachings, what he has to say about the nature of and authorization for government, especially in reference to religion, remains for us "hard sayings."

When Luther argues that it is the just function of the government to compel outward piety, for example,[33] we feel he has gone too far, even though such compulsion be in the interests of civil peace. Why is this not an improper intrusion, according to Luther? His answers can be marshalled in a row, each one a shock, a concussion upon all our Anabaptist-bred souls: 1) Because temporal power is no "lower" than spiritual power. 2) Because the "flesh" is "of avail"—hence the governmental order. 3) Because government, though an outward or bodily order, binds our faith because it is mandated in the Word of God. 4) Because, as something mandated in God's Word, government is a religious institution.[34]

And it is no consolation to hear Luther claim that this "concern" of the governmental order for the order of the church works the other way around as well: that the Third Commandment contains a bodily, i.e., a civil mandate,[35] that the church bears responsibility not only for certain common legal functions but more importantly, responsibility to defend all proper governmental actions such as a just war and to publicly criticize and actively oppose governments which do not live up to the mandates that the Word of God discloses.

The Anabaptist in us must wait until Part Two of our study to find satisfaction, however. For Luther's positions flow naturally and systematically from the balanced dialectical relationships he sees among the issues of freedom, justice, and order, issues which themselves systematically derive from Luther's understanding of the Trinity.

It is necessary to stress the close interrelationship of the orders because of the popular misimpression, too often reinforced by scholarly works on

[31]LCC XV, 226.
[32]13, 45; 30, 74.
[33]40, 83.
[34]40, 83; 37, 137, 365; 16, 13f.
[35]44, 72f.

Luther's theology, that Luther's "ethical creature" is a person of multiple unrelated personalities, a person who lives his life in sealed chambers, his actions in one often radically opposed to those in another.[36]* We shall close this chapter with one further matter, not only relative to this misunderstanding, but also relevant to our general consideration of Luther's social ethics.

Each order is defined by the need to which it is called to minister, and not by the standards or methods by which it responds to the need. Presuming continued recognition by the order of the basic need to which it is called (this is the "binding" of the order), the order is free to develop what it feels to be the most effective and efficient ways of response to the need of the moment (this is the "loosing" of the order). Luther was usually uninterested, very reluctant, or like the Holy Spirit (!), just too busy with important matters to develop specific standards or structures for the orders. His is indeed a

---

[36]Such can be the effect of the writings of even the most careful of Luther's interpreters. Consider Paul Althaus, *The Ethics of Martin Luther*, trans. Robert Schultz (Philadelphia: Fortress Press, 1972), for example. Althaus' discussion of Luther's ethics, like much else in his work, is excellent in detail but suffers a lack of organizational and thematic unity. In the case of the *Ethics*, the discussion of Luther's view of the orders is made deceptive because Althaus combines these themes with a discussion of Luther's doctrine of the "two realms." Althaus confuses the issue officially by speaking of the "two governments," worldly and spiritual (p. 43ff.). It is almost impossible, given the fusion of interest and the terminology, to avoid construing the order of the church as the "spiritual realm" (= government). Althaus has said earlier (p. 37 *et alibi*) that all the orders have the same validity and evoke the same respect. He says (p. 46) that the Lordship of Christ cannot be identified with a worldly institution or order. But, having included all the orders, save that of the church, as part of the "secular government" (p. 45), he then is led to assert that the "spiritual government" (= church?) is "higher" (pp. 56ff.). Evidence of difficulty here is that his citations do not relate to his thesis. Nevertheless, his position is reinforced at p. 79, where he says that the secular kingdom does not stand under the Lordship of Christ in the same way the "kingdom of Christ or Christendom does. On this, Jesus and the New Testament agree with Luther." [*sic!*] Anachronisms aside, it is Althaus' ill-conceived connection of the "realms" with the "orders" that finally produces a justified conclusion in the reader that Althaus' Lutheran "ethical person" is schizophrenic. He argues that the "two persons"—public and private—cannot be harmonized because of the opposition of the two kingdoms (p. 66f.); that diametrically opposed behaviors are sometimes required (p. 68). But then he goes on to try to assert that nevertheless the persons are compatible (p. 78).

Comparably to the solution St. Thomas proposed to the troubling question about the degree of Jesus' worldy knowledge, Althaus makes distinctions which look good theoretically but fall apart when one realizes that he is presumably talking about a single, concrete individual. The "self" of sin and the "self" of righteousness are indeed opposed; but this is a theological consideration involving the realms, and Luther's ethical person acting in the orders does not exercise opposed ethical warrants.

As in the case of St. Thomas, the difficulty with Althaus' work lies not in the solution but somewhere in the construction of the problem. In this case, I think that the difficulty is the way he joins the theme of the two realms with that of the orders, as though the "kingdom of God" is a parallel form of "church," and the "kingdom of the world" parallel to "government and marriage." Because of this, the legitimate dialectical tensions *coram deo* are transmitted to the consideration of man *coram mundo*, with the corresponding deleterious effects on the presentation of the teachings of Luther about the church, the orders, and ethical behavior.

"situation ethics," a situation ethics, however, more radical than has so far been suggested in our study. For even though each order is mandated to respond creatively in the moment to the need for which the order exists, even *this* general rationale is transcended now and again. God is free over his Word, Luther says; Christ is not the servant of the church, but its Lord; the Holy Spirit blows where he wills. Above all orders, Luther says, above all the specific tasks of the orders, stands the *order of Christian love*.[37] Not really a distinct fourth order, of course, Christian love in the context of the orders should also not be taken as a pious "addition" to the ethical requirement. It does not mean a relaxation of the ordinary worldly demands of vocation, stimulated by a misty intuition of some "higher" utopic kingdom. Love is "the prudence of the Spirit." In Luther's description, love "gets down" and becomes incarnate.

In the ethical realm, the requirement of love is a requirement to act not "above" but "through" or "beyond" the strictures of order. The need for love beyond order arises precisely because the orders are worldly orders, and as such are shot through and through with all the consequences of sin. All the orders are "masks" of God's will; hence they are that will made effective, incarnate. But they are also therefore partially corrupted. The structures of marriage, church, and government are never perfectly suited to the need. Again and again we see, as did Luther, the chief failure endemic to what is nevertheless the necessary institutionalization of service: focus and energy constantly shifting away from the need to be served to the needs, structures, and processes of the serving agency. In modern parlance, the order of government, for example, tends to become "inner-directed" rather than to remain "outer-directed." In consequence the work of the order tends to become dissociated from that of the other orders. The one in need becomes first the "client," then inexorably finds he exists—and is encouraged to maintain his "existence-in-need"—for the sake of the order. And even when this reversal of need and service has not yet taken place, the order tends to absolutize its procedures, with the result that the need is not really served in fact, but only in theory. The order becomes a mindless machine, its processes cranking automatically, a surrealistic nightmare of endless lines, files, punch cards, offices, all doing their proper jobs, of course. We all know about this. Change but the terms, and the same applies to the orders of church and marriage.

The task of Christian love in the context of the orders is then clear. When the orders "separate," when they become inner-directed, when the real need is not served because the order orients itself to the theoretical need, to the law rather than the life—then love comes in to break through the structure of law. Luther's discussions of Christian love rolling up its sleeves to get down to work, moving, shaking, upsetting what is "in place," are clearly intended to indicate how the orders are to be kept relativized and open to each other and to the needs of life. There are circumstances when the Christian magistrate must suspend law, bend it, even break it, in order

---

[37] 37, 365, *et alibi*.

that the primary task of government be met. Mercy must counsel civil justice in order that civil justice, itself only a means to an end, may achieve that end. There are circumstances when the Christian church must bear the weakness, the failure, the sinfulness in itself, and temporarily forgo or forestall the reforms which are necessary—again for the sake of its primary task, for which the church too is but an instrument. And Luther's own experience, in particular of that character-building school, marriage, indicates how often the internal structures of that order must be modified for the sake of the end. For there will come times (all the time, it seems!) when the spouse must deny his own just rights for the sake of the other. There must come a time when to be good parents, the parents must not only accept but even encourage, and if need be force the disobedience and independence of the hopefully no-longer-child.

Luther's own history, and that of the church bearing his name, is full of examples of love beyond order. Often mistakes were made. Often too much was sacrificed, when "love" and "the prudence of the Spirit" were mistaken as "expediency for the sake of survival." Love, too, is a worldly power. Yet it was Luther's firm belief that God acts through our vocations and is able to accomplish his will even by means of our failures. "My power is perfected in weakness." We are to work, leaving final judgment to God. Our ethical task is always the same: whether in orders or beyond them in love, to maintain and extend peace, the circumstance in which Word and faith may flourish.

PART TWO

Introduction: The Living Word

He was Frisian, of a psychic constitution that even Germans range before Polish, Bavarian, and Swiss as the preferred butt of liquored jokes, and that even his partisan biographer calls "slow moving . . . not easily stirred and changed." His formal education in religion was what an early sixteenth-century back-country Franciscan house could provide toward the making of a local parish priest. He was self-taught in scripture beyond that. The movement of which he was a part was a sea of what to an historian are nonentities, the "ordinary citizens." He was only one among the myriad putative leaders of the movement: a name, a character, who re-exists for most of us only during the moment when a specialist historian's light illumines him. He would not acknowledge the "doctors and preachers" of his day and was in fact deeply suspicious of any highly-educated and well-bred thinker. He rejected the long-pedigreed theologies around him, mostly without learning much about them; rejected theology itself as a professional and academic discipline, choosing instead the ministry. His one conscious attempt in theology—a theory of the incarnation—was ill-borrowed, ill-developed, and thankfully ill-received by his church. Apart from a very rare ironic phrase there is not a cool breeze of humor in his writings, although the circumstances of his ministry make the absence understandable. His biographer and editor admit that even his small corpus of writings is often boringly repetitious. And except for articles in the scholarly journal of the church that took his name, his thought has stimulated comparatively little historical research outside the Netherlands.

And yet if subsequent influence on religious consciousness be a measure of a churchman's greatness, Menno Simons (c.1496-1561) must rank with Martin Luther, John Calvin, and Ignatius Loyola as a key figure of the Reformation century. The comparisons with Calvin and Loyola are particularly apt. As did they, Simons became absolutely single-minded of purpose once he was committed. As did they, Simons entered the lists when it looked as though his church's cause was foundering, and by his steady discipline greatly assisted its recovery. But unlike Calvin and Loyola, Simons' faith was universally ridiculed and hunted down. There was no political or military support, no intellectual and cultural respectability, no money, no above-ground organizational network. In the sixteenth century there was no question, for Simons and his friends, of victory. Only survival. And what survived organizationally was a remnant: a loose federation of small conventicles in northern Europe, some like-minded brethren among the Swiss, and at farther remove, a sequestered commune in Eastern Europe.

And also some convictions regarding the practice of the Christian religion. Let me list a few:

1) That Christian faith is a matter of living experience and daily commitment, not of theory once learned. In other words, it is caught, not taught;

2) that before the Lord and this assembly, all men—and women—rich and poor, learned and simple, are equal;

3) that the Bible is by itself a sufficient guide for life, and that the teachings of Jesus were meant to be taken as they read;

4) that entrance into the church must be by personal, free decision, and that continued membership in it must be verified by firm belief in its principles and by a changed lifestyle;

5) and that the church, as a private organization, must neither attempt to wield political authority, nor permit political authority to determine its internal life.

If these ideas seem self-evident and beyond serious dispute, that is because against Luther, Calvin, Rome , and all the centuries of contrary opinion behind those men, these ideas have, for the most part and up to now, won the upper hand. And that is why, as the most responsible spokesman for what with a certain irony is now called the "radical" reformation, Menno Simons is the subject of Part Two of this study.

****

There are many reasons for the underdeveloped character of historical research on Anabaptist thought: the relative lack of interest in historical theology in the Anabaptist traditions themselves; general antipathy toward Anabaptist thought in the Lutheran and Reformed traditions, which *are* interested in historical theology; and the scarcity of critically edited primary sources, combined with a formidable linguistic barrier in most cases. But when these difficulties are overcome, another looms in the way.

The writings of a sixteenth-century main-line Anabaptist such as Menno Simons are unmistakable. Only the roughest thematic outline structures the text, and often that is changed, abandoned, or suspended in mid-subtopic. Whatever the particular topic, the same words, phrases, concepts, and Biblical references recur so monotonously that one is tempted to speculate that the writers had a large but fixed anthology of phrases and sentences upon which they drew, as from a linguistic matrix, for any and all needs. But such speculation is unnecessary, for the anthology actually existed: the Bible. The substance of Simons' writings is almost a continuous stream of Biblical quotations, paraphrases, allusions, phrases, and words. It would be difficult to make an accurate quantitative judgment, but from my own multiple readings of the corpus, I would conservatively estimate that sixty per cent of the total physical text of Simons is made up of directly Biblical language! It washes over you endlessly, in every permutation of phrasing, without apparent choice of sequence: Judges and John and

Jeremiah and Joshua and James and Jonah all jumbled together and flooding your brain until it is drowned in the world of the Bible. And that is the point: total immersion.

The style of Simons' writings reinforces the impression. His works are in all senses "pastoral epistles." They begin with a variably lengthy salutation in the style and language of Paul, and usually close with a lengthy Pauline-like coda. His self-defenses, criticisms of opponents, and admonitions to his congregations are in the best style of II Corinthians 12 and Galatians 1. An early autobiographical treatise strikes the reader as though the twenty-fifth Psalm were being uttered for the first time in front of him, not merely used as the titled occasion for a meditation. And in a number of writings Simons composes series of biographical synopses of Biblical characters for the edification of his readers, as though the Bible had not been opened to them until then. That, too, is the point: it had not.

And all of this—the themes, the style, the language, the contents—is repeated over and over again, often enough in the same work, as though Simons, by following an Aristotelian educational method, were determined to make New Testament reality your second nature. And that, too, is the point: he was.

The Anabaptist writers, of whom Menno Simons was typical, tried to reproduce, or better, reconstitute, New Testament Christianity in the lives of people in sixteenth-century Europe whom the current Christian churches either had hardly touched or had betrayed. They accomplished this by taking the principle of *sola scriptura* not merely as the standard for doctrine, but also for life—and as we have just noted, for writing as well. The text of Menno Simons is the Living Word.

Then why the difficulty mentioned above? Because to many academic theologians this kind of writing is boring. Because in order to make any headway with the study he has in mind, the scholar has to fight constantly against the inertia of the text itself. And because the text is intentionally evasive, unclear, non-technical, informal, or just plain void of the kinds of issues that professional historical theologians like to investigate. Simons' criticism of the profession of theology, justified or not, falls upon us very intimately as we open his text for study.

How then are we to pursue our study, a complex and subtle one even though it is but an introductory overview? Our object is the systematic connection among the subjects of trinitarian ascription, the church, and social ethics. Simons is voluminous and reasonably precise on the third subject, adequate on the second, and all but unaware of the first.

As suggested in the introductory chapter, the fact that a writer is unaware of a subject is potentially a rewarding circumstance for a student interested in that subject. Calvin's extreme self-consciousness regarding trinitarian language will make him a very difficult subject for analysis. Menno Simons seems conscious of his trinitarian usage in only two circumstances: when occasionally he responds to an opponent's claim that he is heterodox on the doctrine of the Trinity, and in the somewhat formalized openings and closings of his pastoral epistles. Nevertheless his "ordinary language" is at least as trinitarian in character as that of Calvin, and much more so than that of Luther.

The differences between Simons' formal and ordinary usages will be of considerable interest, assuming that the latter more accurately reflect the reformer's mind. But because of the nature of Simons' writings, we must utilize a different method than would be appropriate for Luther and Calvin in order to uncover Simons' trinitarian ascriptive pattern. We shall assume that the maelstrom of biblical allusions in his text reflects a more or less conscious selection among the possible choices, and that the relative frequency of various word choices reflects Simons' own emphases. An exhaustive statistical tabulation of his usages therefore seems a useful approach.

Fortunately Simons composed a basic doctrinal instrument which, like Calvin's *Institutes*, its author used as a touchstone for all other writings, and which his church subsequently took as the foundation for religious teaching. Menno Simons' *The Foundation of Christian Doctrine* (1539, 1558), usually referred to as the "Foundation Book," thus provides a manageable and valid locus for statistical analysis.

Included in the next chapter are interpretations based upon that analysis. The six tabulations reflect a statistical study of the relationship among 1) nouns referring to the Trinity or to various persons of the Trinity; 2) nouns referring to or theologically cognate with the concepts of love, power, and justice; and 3) the relationship between the above associations and nouns referring to or cognate with the church and its functions as Simons understands them. The tabulations were made upon the standard English translation of the *Foundation Book* done by Leonard Verduin (in *The Complete Writings of Menno Simons* [1956]). A thorough comparison with the *Opera Omnia Theologica* of 1681 revealed, as expected, no variability in the translation of what after all are very frequently-occurring and usually proper nouns in any theological text.

The results of this analysis structure the present interpretation of Simons' theology. Even though the *Foundation Book* is just that—the foundation of Menno's and Mennonite thought—a somewhat less rigorous check of the patterns which appeared in this text with those occurring in the rest of the corpus was undertaken. While there is the expected variability in frequency of noun usage, depending upon the main subject of Simons' treatise, the relationships among the terms as discovered in the *Foundation Book* did not vary significantly throughout the rest of the corpus.

The quantitative study has been kept to a very low level of refinement. The subtle, complex meaning-relationships in a theological mind render spurious any results of more sophisticated statistical analysis of a theologian's language. Secondly, to the best of my knowledge quantitative methods heretofore have been applied to texts only in order to shed light on authorship, as for example with the text of Shakespeare or the *Federalist Papers*. In the present case, authorship is no problem: the object is to ascertain Simons' meaning-associations. While I think the results are valid, the low-level statistical analyses are offered only as an early experiment in what might be a useful approach to the study of some subjects in the field of historical theology.

These qualifications recognized, it still is an exciting possibility that computers might give the scholar-theologian a chance to glimpse the Word as it actually lived in the soul of one of his fathers.

CHAPTER FOUR

Simons: No Other Foundation

Menno Simons, like Luther and Calvin, assumed the doctrine of the Trinity as it had been confessed by the church for 1500 years. The trinitarian pattern of his writings is nearly as pervasive as that of St. Augustine and Calvin, and much more so than Luther's. Yet formally trinitarian theology is almost nonexistent in Simons' writings. It is not used to structure thought, as it is in Calvin. Although there are trinitarian passages in the *Foundation Book*, the Trinity does not appear as a doctrine to be treated in this most basic document. Only three times in the entire corpus does the Trinity come in for serious discussion: once to counter the influence of Adam Pastor,[1] once indirectly in response to the Calvinist Gellius Faber's critique,[2] and once in response to criticism by John à Lasco, also a Calvinist.[3] In all cases, moreover, the Trinity itself is not at issue, but is brought in to illustrate implications of certain christological teachings.

Apart from rare quasi-trinitarian passages in the main body of Simons' writings,[4] the only other significant usage comes in the openings and closings of his epistles, following the style of Paul.[5] It therefore seems as though Simons volunteers formally trinitarian language only as a means of evoking the mood of the New Testament, but that otherwise it is at best peripheral to the pastoral issues that stir his pen.

Terms referring to the First, and especially to the Second, Person of the Trinity occur repeatedly on nearly every page of the corpus. References to "Spirit" are even more voluminous. But as we shall see, the direct association of the term "Spirit" in Simons' thought is with Christ, as in "Spirit and Word of Christ," or, less frequently, "Spirit of Christ." The more traditional and explicitly trinitarian term "Holy Spirit" is used sparingly by Simons, and then only in specific associations. There is a burst of forty references to the Holy Spirit in his short 1539 work *Christian Baptism*;[6] twenty-eight in the 1550 *Confession of the Triune God*, against Adam Pastor;[7] twenty-seven in the 1550 *A Clear Account of Excommunication*;[8]

---

[1] CW 496f. All references to the writings of Menno Simons will be taken from *The Complete Writings of Menno Simons*, trans. Leonard Verduin, ed. John C. Wenger (Scottdale, Pennsylvania: Herald Press, 1956), and indicated by the prefix "CW" and page. Titles and dates of individual works will not normally be cited in the references. However, a rough chronology can be discerned in the pagination, since in this edition Menno Simons' major writings from 1535 to 1560 are in order (pp. 31-1018). Letters and minor works from 1542 to 1558 are also in order (pp. 1019-1070).

[2] CW 759-772.   [3] CW 810.

[5] Fully trinitarian salutations occur at CW 105, 422, 489, 535, 581, 625, 917, 947, and 1030; benedictions, at 226, 485, 522, 577, 622, 913, 952, 998, 1015, and 1036f. As noted in the introductory Prologue, the Holy Spirit is the "great afterthought" in Christian theology. Simons' usages reflect the New Testament in this regard. Salutations at 66, 235, 324, 409, 457, 501, 525, 786, 1021, 1046, and benedictions at 86, 287, 418, 454, 530, 540, 1049, 1059, and 1063 omit reference to the Holy Spirit. A salutation at 89 and benedictions at 102 and 405 omit reference to the Father.   [6] CW 229-287.

and many references in those portions of the corpus dealing with the incarnation as Simons understood it.⁹ There are other occasional references to the Third Person when Simons' subject is the calling of ministers, or conversion.¹⁰ The gist of this informal check of Simons' usages is that reference to the "Holy Spirit" occurs in association with 1) formally trinitarian language, 2) Simons' theory of incarnation, 3) the sacrament of Baptism—but *not* that of the Lord's Supper, 4) initial conversion to Christianity or call to ministry, and 5) excommunication. The impression is that a fully developed trinitarian pattern occurs only when the subject is, so to speak, a formal or official action regarding Christianity or the Christian Church. In all other matters, Simons utilizes a significantly different trinitarian language.

Even a superficial reading of any one of Simons' writings will reveal some senses in which he is more rigorously and exclusively christocentric than Luther or Calvin. As we shall see, Simons has no time for philosophy or what we would call "natural theology." He is not interested in history, Biblical or otherwise, for its own sake. He interprets the entire scriptural text exclusively through Christ. In regard to the Bible, Simons appears unaware of any serious epistemological gap between the text and existential truth. Hence there is no conscious hermeneutical procedure, no linguistic study, and precious little exegesis in Simons' text.¹¹ Menno Simons simply identifies the printed text with the Word of Christ¹² and seeks to obey it.

Thus the trinitarian ascriptive pattern we are seeking in the writings of Simons will be developed in almost exclusive reference to Christ. Faber's suggestion that Simons' teachings led to questionable trinitarian views prompted Simons to a responsive essay, not on the Trinity, but on christology.¹³ In another revealing example of his real center of attention in the *Foundation Book*, Simons begins a short paragraph with reference to ". . . our eternal Father. . . . His Son Jesus Christ, . . . His Holy Spirit, . . . ," but then in the next paragraph moves quickly to a statement about "Christ . . . His Holy Spirit and Word, . . . ," and then to ". . . the Spirit, nature, and love of Christ. . . ."¹⁴

The Trinity that we must investigate is that of Christ (or Christ's nature, life, etc.), Christ's Word, and Christ's Spirit. To those based in other theological traditions, this might not seem like "Trinity" at all. But for Simons it is the one that matters. As it says at I Corinthians 3:11, the verse

⁹Cf. for example CW 422-454.

¹⁰Cf. for example CW 71, 160f., 329. For the most part, I have not considered references to the Holy Spirit in the *Foundation Book*, since these will be treated individually in this chapter.

¹¹George H. Williams, *The Radical Reformation* (Philadelphia: The Westminster Press, 1962), pp. 816ff., does summarize differences among the various groups on this matter.

¹² CW 525. Cf. also CW 308, 328, 528, 797. William E. Keeney, *The Development of Dutch Anabaptist Thought and Practice from 1539 to 1564* (Niewkoop: B. de Graaf, 1968), pp. 39ff., denies this identity in Simons. Franklin H. Littell, in *A Tribute to Menno Simons* (Scottdale, Pa.: Herald Press, 1961), pp. 55f., 59, shares this view. But others, for example, Simons' editor, John C. Wenger, "The Biblicism of the Anabaptists," in Guy Hershberger, ed., *The Recovery of the Anabaptist Vision* (Scottdale, Pa.: Herald Press, 1957), pp. 173f., affirm it.

¹³CW 759-772. ¹⁴CW 185.

which appears on the title page of all his writings, for Simons there is no other foundation than Christ. Or as he puts it in a trinitarian reference in the *Foundation Book*: "We must be in Christ, and Christ in us; we must be moved by His Spirit, and abide in His holy Word outwardly and inwardly. Otherwise we have no God."[15]

A. The Christian Trinity

The only sustained discussion of the Trinity in the writings of Simons occurs in the small treatise *Confession of the Triune God* of 1550 (CW 489-498), written to counteract the influence of Adam Pastor, a Mennonite bishop who in 1547 had in effect denied the divinity of Christ, and whom Simons and his colleague, Dirk Philips, excommunicated in that year. As the title indicates, the treatise is a Bible-based confession defending the "full" divinity of the Second and Third Persons, with Simons exhibiting a rare exercise in theo-logic in his discussion of the functional divinity and unity of the Second and Third Persons with God (493, 496f.). The above quotation marks around "full" are due in part to certain problematic features of Simons' understanding of the incarnation which are not explicit in this text. Simons' understanding of the relation of the Second Person to God the Father is somewhat ambiguous, as some students have noted.[16] Occasionally he will assert, for example, that the Father is changeless but that the Son was "diminished" ("*verkleynt*") and suffered for us in his divine nature.[17] On the other hand he denies any change in the Word, asserting that it is God's will, purpose, etc., which is changeless.[18]

But we ought not press Simons' formally trinitarian language very far because (for one thing) his language in this matter is no more rigorous than that of other reformers.[19] More importantly, however, such an attempt on our part would be misdirected, for Simons' trinitarian ascriptive pattern does not derive from what we might call the "transcendental" Trinity, as it does in the cases of Luther and Calvin, but rather from the "immanent" trinity of Christ's nature, Word, and Spirit.

---

[15]CW 191, cf. 144. The same sentiments occur in other Anabaptist writers related to the Mennonites. Cf., for example, the Hutterite Ulrich Stadler, *Cherished Instructions*, excerpted in George H. Williams, ed., *Spiritual and Anabaptist Writers*, Library of Christian Classics, XXV (Philadelphia: The Westminster Press, 1957), p. 275.

This language, while also discoverable here and there in non-Anabaptist writers, can be taken more seriously in the Mennonites. I shall have occassion to discuss this at greater length on the subjects of Simons' understanding of sanctification and the incarnation.

[16]Keeney, p. 96; Williams, *Radical Reformation*, pp. 394ff., 833. For a general discussion of the relationship of Mennonites to anti-trinitarian thought, cf. Robert Friedmann, "The Encounter of Anabaptists and Mennonites with Anti-Trinitarianism," MQR 25 (July 1961): 139-162.

[17]CW 437f., 771, 797, 799.

[18]CW 810, 811, 815ff.

[19]For example, Simons occasionally says that it is the *Creator* who suffered for us (CW 145, 428). Such assertions can be found in writers throughout the theological tradition, but one would not conclude from such an assertion that its author is therefore a patripassionist.

A preliminary assessment of Simons' emphases can be gained if we consider Tables 1 and 2 in the Appendix. (Note the introduction to these tables, which describes the method of data collection and the statistical treatment employed.) Apart from references to "Christ" in the *Foundation Book*, it is references to "Word" and "Spirit" that massively dominate the text. Although Simons had perhaps the most fully developed doctrine of the Holy Spirit among the reformers,[20] even the significantly large number of references to "Spirit" are nearly doubled by the number of references to "Word." Secondly there are very few references to the Trinity in the text, and among these, none in which "Word" is associated with the Second Person. This seems to suggest that Simons did not usually think of "Word" or "Spirit" in connection with the Trinity, and that in particular, as Franklin Littell has pointed out,[21] Simons never identified the indwelling Word with the Second Person of the Trinity. If these conclusions are valid, the question then becomes, with what *did* Simons associate "Word" and "Spirit"?

The analysis in Table 1 concerns the association of "Word." Again as Littell points out,[22] Simons used the phrase "Word of Christ," "Word of God," "Word of the Lord," and "Holy Scriptures" interchangeably. This fact precludes rigorously maintained classifications, but it also gives a very definite character to Simons' usages taken together.

Simons speaks of the "Word of God" most frequently (proportions 1 and 3). But in no case is either this phrase, or simply "Word," used as a formal designation for Christ. Hence its usage suggests no trinitarian association. In almost every instance where a specific association was made, "Word of God" was Simons' term for the scriptures. One can assume that Simons held God the Father as the Author of scripture. But if we combine references to the "Word of Christ" and "Word of the Lord"—taking the latter phrase as a reference to Christ when it is not specifically associated with God (proportions 2 and 4)—then Simons is shown to associate "Word" significantly more often with Christ than with God the Father. The dominance of "Christ," "Lord," over "God" also holds when other important terms such as "grace," "love," "faith," and "church" are brought into the comparison.

In Table 2 the analysis concerns Simons' associations with "Spirit." Even when "Spirit" and its cognates are brought into consideration, thereby maximizing the possibility of trinitarian language, trinitarian phrasing is significantly absent (proportion 1). Simons very clearly associates "Spirit" with "Christ" rather than "God," even when the otherwise non-associated term "Lord" is ascribed to God (proportion 2). The most interesting feature of Table 2, however, is Simons' differential use of cognates. He quite clearly prefers the term "Spirit," which he has associated with Christ, to "Holy Spirit" (proportion 3). Though there are too few instances to generalize, the raw figures suggest that Simons tended to prefer the phrase "Holy Spirit" for trinitarian association, most likely because that is the usage in the missionary/baptismal formula in Matthew 28:19f. "Holy Spirit" occurs in

---

[20]Littell, pp. 55ff.
[21]Ibid., p. 56.
[22]Ibid., p. 12f.

association with "Christ" only on those few occasions in the text when Simons refers to Christ's incarnation or baptism by John.

The basic conclusion from this preliminary analysis is that while of course Simons holds the orthodox doctrine of the Trinity, the doctrine has little if any significant function in his theology, and occurs in his writings almost always in somewhat "formalized" contexts. His entire focus is upon the message of the scriptures, and for Simons that means focus upon Christ. Even specifically trinitarian terms are largely absent from Simons' text. "Father" occurs rarely; "Holy Spirit" somewhat more often, but almost always in a direct New Testament quotation; and "Logos" does not occur at all.[23] In place of these terms Simons employs what was called an "immanent" trinitarian linguistic pattern: he speaks of Christ, Christ's Word, and Christ's Spirit. It is this christological trinity which provides the nucleus of and the structure for Simons' writing. Hence our further analysis will focus on the associative patterns in this trinity rather than on the orthodox doctrine.

While "Word" and "Spirit" are almost exclusively the terms used by Simons throughout the corpus to indicate two aspects of the trinity of Christ, his terms for its third aspect are considerably more variable. Most frequently, of course, he simply mentions "Christ" or other proper names and titles without further specification. Occasionally he will refer, in trinitarian context, to Christ's "disposition" or "example." His most frequently occurring specifications are Christ's "life" and "nature."[24] Because of this diversity, we shall begin with the associations Simons makes with the terms "Word" and "Spirit."

Table 3, in which Simons' uses of the terms for "Spirit" are considered by themselves, indicates no significant difference in frequency of association with the concepts "power," "form," and their cognates. Each association, however, occurs with significantly greater frequency than association of "Spirit" with "love" and cognates (proportions 1 and 2). Thus it seems that Simons tends to associate the Spirit of Christ with concepts other than love. Our hypothesis is that "Spirit" is associated by Simons with the concept "power" rather than "form." The fact that the tabulation does not show a significant difference in relation here may be due to the fact that the term "Spirit" in Simons' text occurs regularly in close association with "Word," as in "Spirit and Word of Christ." Therefore an "overflow" of meaning, from "Word" to "Spirit," might be expected.

That this direction of possible overflow can be specified is clear from Table 4. The "Word" phrases occur much more frequently than the "Spirit" phrases, both absolutely (see Tables 1 and 2) and relative to the concepts

---

[23]Williams, *Radical Reformation*, p. 25, suggests the rendering of the Vulgate "verbum" as "sermo" in the translations of Ficino and Erasmus made it very difficult to sustain, at least on Biblical grounds, the conception of Christ as the *logos* of God.

[24]For "life," cf. CW 119, 150, 156, 158, 163, 166, 173f., 180, 181f., 186f., 190, and 209 in the *Foundation Book*; for "nature," cf. CW 55ff., 92, 268, 409f., 416, 423, 439, 507, 553, and 600f.

love, power, and justice or form. Thus it is possible to make an analysis of the "Word" associations significantly free of possible meaning overflow from the "Spirit" associations. This analysis produced the strongest associative pattern in the entire study (proportions 1, 2, and 3). Simons, like his fellow Protestant reformers Luther and Calvin, associates "Word" predominantly with the concept of form or justice. But unlike the latter theologians, Simons' association is much more exclusive.

Let us conclude this statistical introduction to Simons' ascriptive pattern by considering Tables 5 and 6, which concern 1) Simons' associations with "Christ," his "life," and most importantly, his "nature," and 2) the connection of the above with the church. We have seen that Simons clearly associates Christ's Word with the concept of form or justice. His associations of Christ's Spirit with power are also reasonably clear. Part of the reason for the lower confidence level with regard to the latter pattern, as suggested above, is the fact that Simons uses the phrase "Word and Spirit" as a theologoumenon. Another reason may be the variety of cognates used for "Spirit." As we saw in Table 2, "Spirit" almost always was used in relation to Christ, so that we could take "Spirit" as meaning "Spirit of Christ" unless clearly specified otherwise. "Holy Spirit," however, is used consistently in what we might term a "formal," legitimating, or official sense. Specifically, these terms appear in formally trinitarian invocations and benedictions, in references to the initiation of Christianity (Christ's incarnation and baptism), and in references to the initiation of the church (Pentecost) or to entrance into and exclusion from the congregation (baptism and excommunication).

If the (Holy) Spirit, as power, is seen by Simons in a legitimating, initiating function, especially relative to the sacrament of baptism, it is the love of Christ which is the substance of the church's life. Table 5 indicates that the concept "love" occurs significantly more often than the phrase "Holy Spirit" (proportion 1). It is significant that references to love are extremely dense in a brief (10-page) section of the *Foundation Book* on the Lord's Supper. A lesser but still noticeable concentration occurs at the end of the text, in a song to the church that is modelled on the Song of Solomon.[25]*

The Lord's Supper, according to Simons, is an institution by which Christ in his love extends himself to his church, so that it may participate in his life. The association of "Christ—love—church" in Simons is very strong (Proportion 2). In a very large majority of these associations, it is Christ's

---

[25]The preferred association of love with the sacrament of the Lord's Supper is characteristic of many Anabaptist writers. This preference reflects a theology of the sacrament which Luther embraced early in his reforming career (the sacrament as a symbol of Christian unity), but later set aside. It might also be noted at this point that the mature Luther tended to associate love with the sacrament of baptism, while for Simons, baptism reflects the power of Christ's Spirit. Notice in Table 5 that "power" is clearly not associated by Simons either with the Lord's Supper or with love.

suffering, atonement, humility (i.e., Christ's life as Simons views it) which is the first term in the association. Table 6 links Christ's life of love with the church. Simons' clearly preferred terms "church," "Christians" (proportion 2) are associated very strongly with "Christ"—and not with any or all combinations of other terms, including "Christ's Word and Spirit" (proportion 1).

It is our thesis that in Simons it is the power of the Spirit rather than the love of Christ which achieves the connection between God and man. The results of Tables 5 and 6 should not be taken to suggest otherwise. In fact they tend to confirm the thesis—by a very significant omission. As easy as it would have been for Simons to use the term in discussing the love and unity of Christians with Christ, "Christ's nature" does not occur at all in the text, in connection either with the Lord's Supper or with the concept of love. Yet as we shall see, union with Christ's divine nature is a key concept in Simons' theology.

To anticipate the discussion in the remainder of the chapter: it is conversion of life by the sanctifying power of the Spirit, who conforms us to Christ's Word and example, that at baptism initiates us into union with Christ's nature—a union which is nourished, reflected upon, and communally shared in the life of the church.[26]

B. *Spirit: the Power of the Word*

"O reader, precious reader, it is a fearful thing to fall into the hands of the living God!" (*Foundation Book*, p. 115)

Simons' theological understanding of human nature is an interesting contrast to that of Luther. Like Luther, Simons normally used the terms "flesh" and "spirit" to characterize human reality, rather than the tripartite psychology of "body, spirit, and soul," or variations of this common to the tradition and utilized by other Anabaptists such as Balthasar Hubmaier.[27] Again like Luther, Simons contrasted "flesh" and "spirit" very sharply, almost to the point of mutual exclusiveness. But while Luther's language consistently referred to the attitudes which man as a whole entity takes in relation to God, rather than to constituent parts of the human being itself (a difference of meaning that caused grave communications breakdowns among the reformers), Simons like Zwingli and others normally used these

---

[26] The functional trinity of Father= love, Son= justice, Holy Spirit= power is shared by Dirk Phillips, *Enchiridion*, in Williams, *Spiritual and Anabaptist Writers*, pp. 234f., 237ff.; also by Peter Ridemann, in his *Account of Our Religion, Doctrine, and Faith*, trans. Kathleen Hasenberg (London, 1950), pp. 9, 15, 24, 36, 78, 165, 187. For a good discussion of "power" and its basic importance in Simons' theology, cf. the excellent article by Willis M. Stoesz, "The New Creature: Menno Simons' Understanding of the Christian Faith" *MQR* 25 (January 1965): 5-24.

[27] Cf., for example, CW 55, 439. For Hubmaier, cf. *On Free Will*, in Williams, *Spiritual and Anabaptist Writers*, p. 116f.

terms in their ordinary senses.[28] His understanding of "nature"—a matter that will come up in our study time and again—is elusive only if we look for too much philosophical subtlety. Simons rarely defined "nature." His fullest exercise in definition comes, most significantly, in a discussion with Martin Micron on the christological union, where "nature" is defined as a "property possessed" by a person.[29] Simons was aware of *verbal* distinctions between "person" or "Son" and "nature" in christological discussion, but he consistently refused to acknowledge or use the *ontological* distinction.[30] His refusal to differentiate (such distinctions are not scriptural, after all) has major consequences for his view of the incarnation. But *the absence, or rejection by Simons, of any significant ontological meanings is perhaps the most eminent single characteristic of all his positions.*

His text is full of Biblical language reflecting the transcendence of God and Christ, of course. But Simons just did not think philosophically in terms of a vertical, "two-level" universe, of a "really real" above or under "mere appearance." In spite of the unavoidable habits of linguistic convention, all of Simons' teachings exist in a "one-level" universe, a plane of discrete actual existences,[31*] the horizontal axis of which runs from Simons' reality back to that of Jesus. Thus while in Simons we occasionally find such distinctions as Original Sin/actual sins, Human Nature/human beings, The Church/churches, and Word of God/words of the scripture, to name but a few of the more important traditional *differentiae*, the distinctions are never used ontologically by Simons. In every case, Simons' theological world is that of the lower case plurals and not that of the upper case singulars. The consequences of this position are omnipresent. We have already considered

[28]Occasionally Simons does approach Luther's way of speaking, as for example when Simons speaks of sinful human nature as a "native disposition" (CW 949), or refers to the "depraved human heart" as the source of wickedness (CW 655). But these usages are common enough in the tradition, and verbal similarity should not by itself be taken to indicate real similarity.

[29]CW 901.

[30]Cf. CW 792f., 804, 807, 812f., 821f., 825ff., 855f., 866, 871, 876ff., 900f.

[31]It would, of course, be misleading to term Simons an "existentialist," even though that is a designation which readily comes to mind, and is one which, taken informally, is not incorrect. Simons did not know himself as a philosopher. For that reason, among others, it is of no great value to be more historically proper in our designation and call him a "terminist" or "nominalist." Simons clung to the simple Biblical language and ordinary usage. He most probably shared the indomitable, if quiet and usually unreflected-upon skepticism of nearly every ordinary citizen concerning the abstract philosophical complexities, the real existence of which is asserted by the learned (in order to bamboozle good men?).

The absence of an explicit ontological dimension in Simons' thought is one reason why his views, like those of other like-minded Anabaptists, have long been ignored, dismissed as superficial or boring, or worse, suspected of heresy by scholars and theologians in other traditions. No further comment is needed on that point. But that same characteristic of Simons' thought, and Anabaptist thought generally, is a reason why sympathetic students must resist the temptation to over-intellectualize Anabaptist theology in response. This *caveat* remains in force even though the denial of "metaphysics" is itself a metaphysical position, and though an apparent absence of explicit metaphysical position in a writer by no means indicates a real absence.

one: that Simons' effective trinity is an actual historical trinity of Christ's Word, Spirit, and life, and not the transcendental, philosophical Trinity of Father, Logos, and Holy Spirit. Now, following this necessary digression in our presentation, we turn to another consequence: Simons' understanding of sin.

Simons maintained that Adam and Eve fell because of their act of disobedience against God's commandment.[32] While for some reformed theologians such as Luther the disobedient act was but an exterior consequence of the fall already accomplished in man's prideful, jealous, and egocentric heart, Simons' views were not at all extraordinary in either Reformed or Catholic thought. As strongly as Simons, like Luther, might contrast man's first nature with his nature after the fall, Simons sided with the more liberal Protestant tradition and with the Catholic position against Luther by insisting that 1) the fall did not eliminate all the virtues by which man might approach unto God, and that 2) baptism does not by itself effect, reflect, or guarantee a restored relationship to God which cannot be altered by subsequent human acts.[33]

Although Simons often described the condition in other terms, the phrase "original sin" rarely occurs in his text, and then usually in connection with a discussion of the practice of infant baptism.[34] Simons' descriptions are traditional, and the distinctions he maintains about kinds or classes of sin are suprisingly Roman Catholic.[35] But Simons' positions on a number of topics relevant to the subject of the nature of sin lead one to the inference that he did not sustain a "strong" doctrine of original sin as a corrupted ontological state, as did Luther and Calvin. Instead, Simons consistently understands sin in terms of acts, and his functioning distinction is between premeditated, intentional or mortal acts of sin ("lying down in sin") and unpremeditated or venial acts of sin ("falling into it by surprise").[36] Sometimes it appears that even what Simons means by "original sin" is a reality whose power, at least, can be broken by a healthy fear of God and knowledge of his just wrath.[37]

Simons' view concerning the "sinlessness" of the people of God, a view which we shall consider later, and his beliefs concerning the status of children, reinforce the impression that for Simons "sin" is purely "acts of sin." His major argument against infant baptism, besides its lack of scriptural warrant, was that children do not share the curse of "original" sin. They are in grace, do not sin since they have no understanding, are covered

---

[32]CW 503 contains a typical description. Cf. Ridemann, pp. 20, 54, 56 for the same view. Cf. Williams, *Radical Reformation*, p. 428, Keeney, p. 67, and Richard E. Weingart, "The Meaning of Sin in the Theology of Menno Simons," *MQR* 44 (January 1970): 25-39.

[33]CW 961, 245.

[34]CW 130, 134, 244, 563ff.

[35]CW 563ff., 447, 269, 982. Cf. Keeney, pp. 68, 158.

[36]CW 982ff. So completely is Simons' understanding devoid of ontological reference that his explanation of Matt. 18:15 and Luke 17:4 appears extraordinarily simplistic. Cf. CW 979ff.

[37]CW 949. The initial underassessment of the power of original sin became problematic for second-generation Anabaptists. Cf. Williams, *Radical Reformation*, p. 798; Keeney, p. 68.

over by Christ's promises prior to the age of discretionary baptism, and are included in God's election to salvation should they die before that time.[38]

One's status before God (according to Simons, one's religion) is quite simply one's behavior.[39] It might be suspected that this view of things might lead to the Pelagian heresy, and we wonder whether Simons precluded this possibility by asserting a strong doctrine of divine election. Once again the references in his text are few, and in no case technically theological. He seems to accept pre-creation election to salvation and to deny election to damnation.[40] Here and there in his writings are indications that Simons accepted Luther's view that the proclamation of Old Testament law served a function of revealing to man his sinful nature.[41] But nowhere do we find the view that God's giving of the law served to increase human opposition to faith among the non-elect, and nowhere is it suggested that the law is or must be given first in order to break down human arrogant insensitivity to the Gospel—interpretations which are basic to the views of Luther and Calvin. Menno Simons took the law and the Gospel in their most obvious sense: they are given to be followed straightaway, and those who choose to obey will be saved. Simons clearly does not share Luther's conviction that a healthy (albeit wrongly-placed) fear of God and his wrath is an impediment to the making of a true evangelical Christian. The fear of God and his wrath can be learned and is a prerequisite to conversion. It precedes the gift of grace, is the first fruit of faith, and is a primary characteristic of those who make up the true church.[42]

In this section, the task is to discover how, according to Simons, the church is created out of the world, and which divine agency he sees as particularly instrumental in its creation. The directions of study pursued in the preceding paragraphs do not get us very far. For Luther, it is the proclamation of God's Word (law and Gospel) that hardens the hearts of the lost, creates faith in the saved, and thereby defines the existence of the church. But in Simons, there is no evidence to suggest this function for the Word. The law does not "harden"; the preaching of the Gospel does not create faith in its hearers.[43] God's Word, the scriptures, is simply the clear revelation of God's positive ordinances and his will for man, and is therefore the vehicle unto salvation for any man who avails himself of it, even though only those who are first converted to Christ can fully realize God's will.

---

[38]Cf., among many other passages, CW 122, 126f., 131, 134f., 137, 240, 248, 271, 278, 570.

[39]CW 77, 91, 96f., 505, 508; Keeney, p. 44.

[40]CW 75f.; cf. also CW 132f., 249, 262f., 688, 692, 705; cf. Alvin J. Beachy, "The Grace of God in Christ as Understood by Five Major Anabaptist Writers," *MQR* 37 (January 1963): 5-33.

[41]CW 818f.; 718.

[42]CW 115, 182f.; 187, 192f., 195ff., 202, 207f., 329, 337, 339, 445f., 497, 511, 527, 967.

[43]Dirk Phillips *may* hold a different view. Cf. his *Enchiridon*, in Williams, *Spiritual and Anabaptist Writers*, p. 234; cf. also Ridemann, p. 47.

Neither is God's elective love the precipitator of the distinction between the church and the world, as we shall see is the position of Calvin. Simons frequently speaks of "the elect" in reference to the church, but the term is used only in its Biblical and traditional senses, and never in the developed technical or doctrinal sense we find in Calvin or Luther. God in his love manifest in Christ wills all men to salvation, and in Christ's death offers the means by which that object may be won. All those who die before the age of discretionary choice—and, it might be added, those good men who die without ever having had the opportunity of choice—are firmly believed to rest in God's loving care.

Thus neither the Word (= form, justice) nor God's elective love (=order, harmony) appears a likely avenue of approach to Simons' understanding of the creation of the church. Each avenue is blocked in large part because of the same fact: Simon's understanding of sin and righteousness wholly in terms of acts. But it is just this fact that will take us to our goal. For *act* means for Simons, as it does for Luther, the power and freedom to act. But unlike Luther, Simons, as we have seen, associates power and freedom primarily with the Spirit. It is the Spirit of God in Christ that creates the church.

Our statistical analysis of Simons' usages in the *Foundation Book* indicated that Simons associated "Spirit" with "power" consistently. We also found that while the "Word" aspect of the christological trinity was very sharply delineated, and the "Spirit" aspect less so, the third aspect was somewhat vague. Simons had a variety of terms for Christ's "person" (= ? "nature"). None was directly asssociated with function, and so the assertion that Simons associated "love" with Christ's nature was based on less direct considerations.

It may be possible, however, to discern a rough systematic pattern in this apparent diffusion with regard to the references of "Spirit" and "Christ." The fuller meaning of "Christ" in Simons' thought will be the focus of the next section and of Chapter Five. For now, "Spirit" and the creation of the church command attention.

Throughout the corpus, Simons is quite clear that faith must be present before the process of conversion to Christ can begin. The faith of which he speaks is an intellectual assent to the truth of the scripture. Simons does not appear to have considered the question of the origin of this faith. In his first writing as a reformer, *The Spiritual Resurrection* of 1536, Simons appears unclear: the "new man" originates from a "seed" of God's Word[44] planted in the elect. At the same time one gets an unmistakable impression from the text that the "elect" are only those who themselves have "grasped" the seed of the Word and made it sure.[45]

[44]CW 57f. This is a theme emphasized by Keeney, pp. 43ff.
[45]CW 59, 61. It should be recalled that Simons did not believe the Fall removed all the theological virtues from the human race. This view was shared by other Anabaptists, of course. Cf. Balthasar Hubmaier, *On Free Will*, in Williams, *Spiritual and Anabaptist Writers*, p. 120f.

The term most consistently used by Simons in referring to the source of faith is not "seed," however, but "grace." Like most other theologians, Simons makes very abundant use of this term but never gives it a clear, single meaning. There are some occasions when "grace" refers to God's favorable disposition, but usually the *favor dei* is indicated by adjectival or adverbial forms of the word. Simons' basic usages fall into two broad, interrelated categories: grace as God's power, and as the presence of Christ. The most interesting aspect of these usages is that in Simons' text they roughly parallel his associations with "Spirit" and cognates.

In many contexts Simons very clearly associates "grace" with the major "Spirit"-cognate forms "Spirit of God" or "Holy Spirit." He speaks very often of the "spirit of [God's] grace," for example.[46] The basis of this close association of grace with the cognate forms of "Spirit" is power. More precisely, grace as power is associated with those official, facilitating, or initiating functions which Simons consistently ascribes to the Holy Spirit, as we saw in the earlier statistical tabulations. Conversion of the man who has in faith accepted the truth of scripture is by far the most important of these functions. Among the many references listed in the above footnote, Simons' autobiographical report of his own conversion process (CW 668-674) is most revealing: "grace" and "God's Spirit" are mentioned significantly more often than either "Word" or "Spirit."

Simons is, not surprisingly, full and explicit in his description of the process of conversion. God's work ". . . is a heavenly power, a vital moving of the Holy Ghost which ignites the hearts and minds *of believers*. . . ." (CW 149, emphasis mine).

> [Faith] firmly believes and lays hold upon and acknowledges every word of God, the threatening Law as well as the comforting Gospel, to be dependable and true. Whereby in turn the heart is pierced and moved through the Holy Ghost with an unusual regenerating, renewing, vivifying power, which produces first of all the fear of God. (CW 329)

The "fear of God," a fruit of faith, is a power which slays the sins of believers and is the first part of true repentance, as the baptismal ordinance teaches. (CW 337) From this fear of God springs a second fruit of faith: "For love which is sincere is a noble, precious fruit, it is a branch and plant of faith from which the second part of true repentance issues, namely, the unblamable new life, represented to us by baptism, as related above, out of the fear of the Lord." (CW 338f.)

The point of our concentration on the association of grace as power with the acts of the Holy Spirit in the conversion process is that all of this process takes place outside of, prior to, and without specific reference to life

---

[46]CW 70, 82, 108, 113, 132, 249, 262f., 266, 315, 318, 326, 341, 372, 504ff., 564, 668ff., 688, 692, 696, 705f.

in the church or union with Christ. Conversion is not a mark of the church—it is a prerequisite for entrance. And it is not the church's act of baptism which effects or communicates the grace of conversion—it is rather the promissory Word of God, independent of the baptismal act.[47] Simons consistently uses the term "Spirit" and not its cognates when he is speaking of life within the community of Christ. And in this context the term "grace" is consistently *dis*sociated from the term "Spirit."

As noted earlier, a favorite communicative device of Simons is that of piling up in series a number of "Christian" or generally "religious" words, the intended effect of which is to carry the reader off into the ambience of the New Testament. His different combinations of these words, with and without connective terms, allowed us the kind of study we have pursued in this chapter. We have just seen that one frequently occurring combination is the association of "grace" with "Holy Spirit," the connective term or concept being power. What was consistently missing from this combination, however, was explicit reference to Christ.

When one concentrates on those series in which "Christ" is associated with "grace," a different picture emerges. Although Simons occasionally does mention "Spirit" in close connection with "grace" in these christological series,[48] usually the "Spirit" reference is omitted and the basis of the association between Christ and grace is other than power—often it is love.[49] Finally there is a multitude of cases in which the terms "grace," "Spirit" (or "Holy Spirit"), "Word" (or "Christ") occur in series, without apparent grounds for association. In these cases the key to Simons' usage is that the series is always a series of three terms or phrases.[50] They represent the major variations of Simons' christological trinitarian pattern! The term "grace" replaces reference to Christ, Christ's nature, life, sufferings, etc. And as suggested above, the concept *love* then becomes unusually frequent in the association.

In order to see the pattern in this variety of linguistic association, we must remember that the presence of explicit reference to Christ—and the strictly correlative choice of "Spirit" rather than its cognates—indicates that Simons in such contexts is speaking from within the "circle of faith," within the church and its life. "Grace" in this context is therefore not used as a term for power (the functional attribute of the Spirit of Christ), but as a term for Christ's nature, life, love, etc., as it indwells the believer and the believing community. It is a term for Christ's real presence.

[47]Cf. CW 94f., 101, 234ff., 734ff., for the most important descriptions of the church. Cf. CW 240, 245, 685f., 693 for instances of Menno's dissociation of conversion grace from the baptismal rite. Cf. Stoesz, pp. 8ff.

[48]Cf., for example, CW 148, 150, 167, 315, 336, 397, 448f., 633.

[49]Cf. CW 89, 96, 116, 125, 129, 144, 233, 241, 244, 307, 315, 329, 336, 340, 397f., 445, 633, 984, 989, 995. CW 506f. is a good example of the exception proving the rule. In a series of vigorous associations of "grace" with "Christ," the connection being the efficacy, or power, aspect of grace, it is the Holy Spirit, and not Christ's Spirit, that is mentioned.

[50]Cf., for example, CW 68, 71, 73, 81, 107, 115, 148, 189, 201, 224, 226, 341, 349, 372, 396, 399, 448, 582, 605, 631.

It is now time to bring together the results of our study of the function of "Spirit" in Simons' thought. In doing so we might also gain a new perspective on the related issues of election, free will, and the charge of Pelagianism with which this section began.

Menno Simons' understanding of the Spirit is richer, more varied, and more important to his theology than is the case with any other major Protestant reformer of the sixteenth century. As our interest in this study is rather narrow—Simons' trinitarian ascriptive pattern as it influences his understanding of the church and Christian ethics—we have sketched only a basic outline of those features of his Spirit-theology relevant to our theme. But already we have before us a range of usages which, whether Simons was himself fully aware of it or not, indicates a consistently maintained pattern of theological expression, a range of systematic expression which on this subject at least surpasses that of his better-trained colleagues Luther and Calvin.

The eminent—not exclusive, but eminent—function Simons associates with the Third Person is power. But this association, as dominant and omnipresent as it is in Simons' writings, is refracted through a spiritual prism of greater import: the basic distinction between that reality which is within the true church, and that which is still without. This basic distinction is reflected in Simons' understanding of the Spirit as power.

When Simons must speak about the general relationships of God and the world, matters which are more philosophical (= technically theological) and less explicitly expressive of committed Chrsitian life, Simons' language and meanings are correspondingly general, indeed traditional. It would be appropriate from Simons' perspective to term this reality "pre-Christian" reality. This reality itself can be looked at from two angles. The world considered by itself, internally, naturally, is of very little interest to Simons, even though if asked he would insist that the "Holy Spirit" is effective with his "power" in controlling all creation in the interests of the Creator's will. Of much greater interest to Simons is the power of God's Spirit acting in the world to bring natural man to the true fellowship of Christ. In this pre-Christian evaluative perspective, it is the Holy Spirit who is the moving force effecting those official, formal, "signpost" decisions and acts which signal either the beginning of the Christian fact (e.g., the incarnation, the baptism of Christ, Pentecost, the Great Commission), or the beginning of man's entrance into that fact (e.g., the stirring of the heart of the faithful to repentance, desire to conform to Christ's teachings, and baptism). The terms for the functions of the Holy Spirit are now more intimate. Instead of "power," we have "an urging," a "vital moving," "piercing," "unusual regenerating, renewing, vivifying" action. (Cf. the material quoted earlier on the sequence of conversion). Simons' own theological term for power, "grace," is correspondingly modulated in meaning.

And now, the subject shifting from the preparatory work of the Spirit to his agency within the committed Christian life-in-community, Simons' language changes again. Now it is the "Spirit of Christ" who effects, sustains, and re-establishes the full union of the Christian with the nature and the life of his Lord. The Spirit certifies to and persuades our hearts regarding Christ's teachings. He strengthens our bodies and wills against the sins and temptations that would separate us from Christ. He humbles and chastises us when we have separated ourselves from Christ, so that we might return to fellowship. He effects the elimination, via the ban and shunning, of those whose retrogression endangers our unity with Christ. He nurtures the bonds of union, via the Lord's Supper, family life, and persecution from "the outside." The Spirit is power in the interests of unity with Christ. Now the term "power" achieves its most intimate Christian expression. What the Spirit does is effect the presence of Christ. He makes Christ present to us and brings us into the presence of Christ. Simons has a theological word for the living, actual presence of Christ, Christ's being, nature, life, suffering, and most of all Christ's love. It is Christ's grace. Grace is God's power become Christ's presence in Christian life.

Inevitably, irresistibly, we are getting ahead of ourselves as we follow Simons' presentation. Let us do a necessary if artificial reprise.

Suppose one is a Lutheran, or perhaps wears Calvin's spectacles. He hears that Simons 1) has no metaphysical base, 2) believes sin is an act, 3) believes man did not lose all theological virtues in the fall, 4) holds that God's words of law and Gospel are meant to be taken simply—read, learned, and obeyed as they appear in the text, 5) insists that faith is assent to the truth of those clear words of the Bible, and 6) maintains that this faith, a possibility for any man, can produce a fear of God which is the first step in genuine repentance.

One's reaction?—"Pelagianism!!!"

This charge has been levelled at many Anabaptists for four hundred years. Unfortunately most of those who have sought to exonerate Anabaptists of the charge have also accepted the presumptions of the critics. Once that is done, the case is lost.

For introit, one might note that it has been a habit of "orthodox" Protestantism to arrive, after a quick pass at study, at the name "Pelagianism," and therefore to condemn the Anabaptists as enemies of Christ's Gospel. May we presume, however, that it is theologically more important to find out the degree to which a position is true than it is to recall who was its first well-known advocate?

The important presumptions made by the critics are that 1) one is saved wholly by faith, which is a "gift of God, not of works, lest any man should boast"; and 2) that this faith-gift by which one is saved is present in the heart as a simple, absolute trust in the efficacious truth of Christ's atonement and his promising words. Therefore, since Simons understands "faith" as an assent which any man who reads the Bible is capable of making even apart from divine grace, election, etc., Simons is a Pelagian worksmonger, one of the "Schwermerei" who, in Luther's words, outmonked even the pope himself in merit-peddling.

The only trouble is that those presuppositions are not shared by Simons! In their place, instead of a pre-eminent doctrine of the Word as the effecting, quasi-sacramental agency by which faith is created in the elect, and the existence of which is then declared by God to be sufficient grounds for salvation, stands Menno Simons' doctrine of the Spirit and of the transforming power of Christ's presence. The Spirit makes the church, not the assent of faith.[51]

Yet the *Spiritus Creator* who "over the bent world broods with warm breast and, ah! bright wings" (GMH) is none other than the Holy Spirit who effects conversion to Christ. And the Holy Spirit is none other than the Holy Spirit who effects our conforming, saving union with Christ. Menno Simons knows this. His differential names designate functions, but it is still one agency doing the one will of the one God. Simons is an orthodox trinitarian, after all, and we should not forget that. What we termed his "immanent," or "christological" trinity is not in conflict with the traditional doctrine, which he would have died for.

But Simons, the persecuted minister and churchman, did not waste his time trying to solve the merely insoluble theological problem of the relation between theology and christology, between creation and redemption. And that is the real yet sterile issue behind the disputes over election, free will, the extent of original sin and its effects, Pelagianism, etc. Simons made his own commitments, and on his presuppositions cannot be accused of Pelagianism (even if the position be right). Faith as he defines it is a human possibility but is not by itself grounds for salvation. It can issue into the "fear of God," but it is the Holy Spirit, who "blows where he wills," who effects the conversion. And conversion is not the same as salvation. Even conversion plus baptism (a subsequent work of the Holy Spirit) is not the same as salvation. They are not even effecting sacraments indicating salvation. They are but the preliminary works of the Holy Spirit, who blows where he wills. When—if—they happen, they bring one into that place where salvation becomes possible, into that place where it is possible to become conformed to Christ's words, life, and Spirit. Hence into that place where the Spirit, who blows where he wills, effects salvation in those whom he elects.

Into the living church of Christ.

C. *The Word: The Discipline of the Spirit*

> Let Gellius put it as he pleases, and let him give it whatever color he likes; the Word of Christ remains and is the word of the cross; all who accept it in power and truth must be prepared for the cross. This both Scriptures and experience teach abundantly. (*Reply to Gellius Faber*, 1554: CW 656f.)

As indicated in the preceding section, the presence of faith is not for Simons the marker dividing those within the church from those without. In general there are two basic differences in the understanding of faith separating Luther and Simons. Of lesser importance, from Simons' perspective, is his greater emphasis on faith as acceptance of the content of

---

[51] A view insisted upon by Ridemann also; cf. *Account*, pp. 9, 38f., 92.

the Bible. A corollary to this is his belief that this faith is a human possibility. Of greater importance is Simons' belief that justification is much more than a formal, forensic declaration by God in relation to the presence of faith, whether that faith be understood either as belief or as trust.

Simons insists very strongly that faith is an utterly free gift of God's grace, and that it is the basis for God's justification. But the faith he is talking about, the faith which justifies, is the *entire process* of sanctification, the process of which only the beginning is belief in the scripture. In the very brief section of the *Foundation Book* dealing with faith (CW 115-120), and in the shorter but richer passage in the treatise *True Christian Faith* of 1541 specifically dealing with it (CW 328f.), Simons' understanding of faith as the process of sanctification is quite clear.

> And God's Word knows of no other faith than that which has power and fruit, that which regenerates the heart, converts and renews, as the Scriptures say: "The just shall *live* by faith." . . .Nor is it only a boasted *formulation* as we find among the great and persecution-free sects. It is an *effective* gift, the *power* of God; a living heavenly *calling* in a heart or conscience that has been opened. (CW 328, emphases mine)

And now Simons follows with the descriptions of the conversion process quoted in the last section. It has been noted by G. H. Williams especially how the institutions of Anabaptist religious life closely parallel those of the Roman Catholic penitential system.[52] Although the philosophical bases and languages differ, Simons' understanding of faith as a sanctifying process in which subordinate phases are discernible, as it is described in the texts noted above and in others,[53] is in very close parallel to the description of the justification process given in the decree of the Sixth Session of the Council of Trent, Chs. 1-7.

Upon comparison, one must say Simons' views are in fact more nearly in line with the Tridentine decree than they are with the positions of Luther or Calvin. Simons and the fathers at Trent part company, however, over the degree of perfect unity with Christ (= holiness) that the sanctification process effects. Keeney has noted the extremely dynamic character of Simons' teaching on this subject: the process effects a "metaphysical, but [sic] real change," namely, the conferral or creation of a divine nature in the believer.[54] Simons was often charged with "perfectionist" views, but the

---

[52]Williams, *Radical Reformation*, pp. 124, 171, 300, 305, 397.
[53]Cf., in addition to the references cited in the text, CW 130f., 391, 658.
[54]Cf. Keeney, pp. 73, 99, 192.

texts themselves indicate that he was well aware that no Christian was, or perhaps could be, perfect.[55] Yet the ideal was there. Via the discipline of the Spirit, the Christian is to be conformed to Christ; and conformation to Christ means becoming one with Christ's nature.

Unification with Christ's nature is one of Simons' most frequent themes and is both the goal and the source of all he says about the sanctified Christian life. Among the many references to Christ's nature in the texts, the majority occur in the context of Simons' discussion of the Christian as being "changed into" or "united with" Christ's nature. Simons' language in these contexts strikes a more "orthodox" reader as being uncomfortably, almost blatantly clear. Only Peter Ridemann, here as in so many other aspects Simons' true colleague, approximated this degree of linguistic unambiguity.[56] But what puts the extremity of this kind of statement and the ideal it represents into still sharper focus is the fact that the "nature" of Christ with which the Christian becomes one is a nature which, even on its fully human side, has emerged wholly from *God's* being. We are speaking here of course of that famous and infamous doctrine that Simons shared with many other Anabaptists: the "celestial flesh" of Christ.

This matter has been thoroughly examined in the literature and will not be reviewed here, although it would be marginally useful to do so.[57]* For our basic purposes, however, the important point is this. Since the goal of the sanctifying process is union with a nature wholly divinely-sourced, the perceived spiritual, ecclesiastical, and ethical tensions between the church and the world, sin and righteousness, love and justice, are thereby considerably sharpened in Simons' theology. We shall return to this effect at the

---

[55]Cf. CW 53, 55, 144, 233, 397f., 402, 415, 654. Keeney, p. 118, suggests that Simons moderated his early perfectionist views to a "progressivist" view in later writings.

[56]For representative texts from Simons, cf. CW 55f., 58, 92, 139, 268, 299, 409f., 416, 423, 439, 507, 553, 600f., 734ff: from Ridemann, cf. *Account*, pp. 18, 36, 46ff., 53, 62, 77, 85, 135, 162ff., 167, 169, 187, 211.

[57]The matter of the "celestial flesh" of Christ, involving as it does Simons' christology, pneumatology, anthropology, soteriology, and a few other "ologies" as well, is, of course, relevant to the subject of Simons' understanding of the Trinity, which is part of our theme. In particular, such a study might require at least an adjustment of my theses that 1) Simons' effective trinity is an "immanent" one, and 2) ontological or metaphysical considerations are all but inoperative in his thought.

But such a study, or even a complete summary of the research, would require an unacceptably large detour in this text. Secondly, the teachings were very soon rejected by the Mennonites and played no distinct part in the formation of Mennonite ethics or ecclesiology. Thirdly, Simons himself never volunteered his views on the matter. Indeed, he deeply regretted being forced into its dicussion at all. Fourthly, his particular belief on this highly technical matter seems not to affect the general pattern of relationships among his subjects.

These "reasons" for omission are not sufficient, of course. But one other is, I believe. Our basic theme is the relationship among Simons' trinitarian ascriptive pattern, his ecclesiology, and his ethics. And it is this point in our study of Simons where the discipline of sticking very closely to the theme is as necessary as it is hard. Therefore the matter of the "celestial flesh" can be considered only insofar as it highlights our theme. It does so, in that it works to sharpen the intensity of the tensions between love and justice—as will be discussed in the text.

end of the chapter. But now we must see how this gap, widened by Simons' peculiar christology, is to be bridged.

Quite simply, the answer is this: only the power of the Spirit can effect the union. The Spirit achieves this by conforming us to the Word of Christ, to his life and example. And this Word is none other than the plain words of scripture.

Christ revealed his nature—perfect love—most fully by becoming incarnate, suffering, and dying in man's place. It is only because of this great love, which gives itself up in atonement, that the justice of God could be met.[58] But as we have already seen, Simons flatly denies that Christians are connected to the gift of salvation through "sacramental" grace. Neither baptism nor the Lord's Supper is a means by which Christ's salvation is communicated to men. Nor is "Christ the Word," or the "proclamation of the Word," a quasi-sacramental means by which that salvation is communicated. The only agency of salvation (= the sanctification process) is the Holy Spirit of power. And the Holy Spirit works salvation by bringing man into union with Christ's nature. That union is effected when, via the power of the Spirit, we are conformed to the teachings of Christ as they are set down in the scripture.

Although in his rare traditionally trinitarian passages Simons occasionally names the Second Person as "Word," his normal usages quite clearly distinguish Christ's being or nature from his "Word."[59] This is the case with his favorite theologoumenon, "Word and Spirit of Christ," which we have already examined. Perhaps in parallel to his understanding of faith as belief in a content, Simons consistently refers to Christ as the teacher or bringer of the Gospel—"Gospel" defined (as in the section in the *Foundation Book* on "faith") as the "the blessed *announcement* of the favor and grace of God to us, and of forgiveness of sins through Christ Jesus."[60] This Gospel is "infallible" (722), a "decretal" (101), and has at long last again become "clarified" (963). It is the "doctrine of Christ," Simons frequently insists, that is the blueprint of salvation and a chief mark of the church.[61] Franklin Littell has emphasized this distinction between the Second Person and the Word. The living, indwelling Word is not identified with the Second Person; the active agent in the living Word is not the Second Person, but the Holy Spirit.[62]

---

[58]Cf. CW 79, 428, 430, 437f., 515, 771, 792, 797, 799, 804f., 807, 814f., 818. Simons appears to accept a generally Anselmian view of the atonement. This conclusion may have to be modified, however, because of the presence of the "celestial flesh" doctrine, which Simons always develops in close connection with soteriology; and also because of the fact that according to Simons we participate in the gift of salvation only as we become conformed to Christ's life and teaching—a very Abelardian emphasis.

[59]Cf., in addition to the relevant statistical summaries in section A of this Chapter, CW 62, 156, 166, 170, 173f., 185, 193, 200, 206.

[60]CW 115, italics mine. For Christ as teacher, cf. CW 71, 108, 129, 178.

[61]Cf. CW 43, 45, 55f., 86f., 89, 117, 119, 150, 176, 181f., 209, 734ff.

[62]Littell, *Tribute*, pp. 12, 15, 56.

The emphasis on Christ as "teacher" or "bringer" of the Gospel (rather than Christ as Gospel), and the correlative emphasis on Gospel as doctrine and faith as assent, is a characteristic Simons shares with nearly all second-generation reformers, including Melanchthon and Calvin. And it is quite in line with the decree of the Fourth Session of the Council of Trent concerning the canonical scriptures.

Simons, like many other Anabaptists, is often charged with "subjectivism," even by his advocates.[63] While there are some grounds for the charge, it seems strange that it should have been made by reformers whose own doctrines of the Word were more "internal" than Simons'. For when Simons says "conformation to the Word," he means conformation to what the biblical text says, no more, no less, and no other.

Simons' understanding of the Bible as the Word, and of the Christian relationship to that Word, is expressed nowhere better than at the beginning of yet another fruitless plea for toleration:

> And we, before God and His angels, seek nothing on this earth but that we may obey the *clear and printed* Word of the Lord, His Spirit, His example, His command, prohibition, usage, and ordinance (by which everything in Christ's kingdom and church must be regulated if it is to please Him) according to our weakness in all subjection and obedience. (CW 525, emphasis mine).

The scripture, Simons says, everywhere points to Christ and teaches nothing but moral improvement. It is the complete standard for all aspects of life, and Christian faith must be in conformity to both law and Gospel, both inwardly and outwardly.[64] The most important aspect of Simons' approach to the Bible, however, the aspect which most clearly differentiated his church from that of other reforming traditions, is not "biblicism." It is rather how the biblical text was used as a standard or criterion for action. As a general rule, the Lutherans worked on the principle that *where the Bible does not explicitly forbid, there it is permissible* to adapt, invent, or fall back on "tradition" according to circumstantial need. With some qualifications (church order being the chief exception), the Calvinists followed the same principle. But Simons, like many others before and after him, insisted upon an exactly opposite principle: *what the Bible does not explicitly mandate, is forbidden*. This principle is so often and clearly expressed by Simons that it cannot possibly be mistaken.[65] So basic is this difference of

---

[63]Williams, *Radical Reformation*, 821f.; John S. Oyer, "The Reformers Oppose the Anabaptist Theology," in Hershberger, p. 213; Keeney, pp. 120, 192, 194ff.

[64]Cf. CW 191, 216, 219, 224, 268, 328f., 342f., 528, 553, 586f. On the matter of the relation between law and gospel in Simons and in Anabaptist thought generally, cf. Williams, *Radical Reformation*, pp. 468ff., 821ff.; John C. Wenger, "The Biblicism of the Anabaptists," in Hershberger, pp. 173ff; Keeney, pp. 34ff., 192.

[65]Cf. CW 46, 95, 111, 126f., 134, 143, 145, 178f., 238, 242, 264, 300f., 514, 692, 695, 794, 812f., 829.

approach in its implied philosophy, psychology, and ethics, and so vast in its consequences, that it may be seen as the one decision which most profoundly distinguishes the Mennonite from the "orthodox" Protestant understanding of the standards of Christian life.

The increase in spiritual tension between human life and divine life which Simons' doctrine of the "celestial flesh" perhaps only inadvertently fostered is more than paralleled by the increase in ethical and ecclesiastical tension between contemporary social reality and New Testament social reality effected by his restrictive approach to biblical standards. There is only one modification of this sharp contrast of fact and ideal beyond the *de facto* exercise of mercy (". . . according to our weakness . . ."). It is important, but only as a qualification of the notion that Simons was an exclusive biblicist in his theology. As is known by students who have taken the time to read him carefully,[66] Simons does admit that under very tight limits Christian life, faith, and practice can be and are definable, where the Bible is not explicit, on the basis of reason and the usages of the post-New Testament Apostolic church.[67] But such an admission, necessary but minimal, does not significantly lower the tension between the ideals of righteousness and the exigencies of life together in the contemporary world.

Even the existence of the true church itself does not really provide a "medium" to lower the tension between contemporary fact and ancient ideal. The true church, according to Simons, is on the yon side of the gap. The true church is the church which is in (restored) strict conformity to the practices of the Bible and the Apostolic age.[68] That church is and must be outwardly "without spot." In the strongest spiritual sense possible—and in a physical sense too—the church is radically distinct and separate from the world.[69] Its requirements, like those of scripture, take precedence over everything in human life, including the most deeply powerful of merely human values such as marriage and family love.

Only the power, the grace of the Spirit, can close the gap between justice and love, and thereby effect saving union with the divine nature of Christ.

****

In Part One of this study we saw that Luther 1) maintained a vigorously transcendent trinitarian doctrine, 2) along with an equally vigorous "immanent" ascriptive pattern which associated the Father with power, the Son with form or justice, and the Holy Spirit with love. We also saw that for Luther 3) the Son was the originator of the church, hence also the basis from which Luther sought to approach the perceived tensions between 4) power and love. Since both a transcendental and an immanent trinity were maintained, Luther could not resolve the tensions between power and love, but 5) sustained them in a taut dialectical balance.

[66]Cf. Franklin H. Littell, *The Origins of Sectarian Protestantism* (New York: Macmillan Co., 1964), pp. 46, 51, 63ff.; Littell, *Tribute*, p. 24; Keeney, pp. 39f., 42, 178.

[67]CW 41, 81, 99, 129, 159, 268, 292, 422, 573f., 630.

[68]CW 81, 127f., 303, 308f., 407, 415, 424, 475, 554, 582ff.

[69]CW 161f., 304, 308f., 435, 610f., 720, 725, 745, 747f.

Let us now compare, by way of summary, the decisions of Menno Simons on these points.

1) Although he affirms the traditional doctrine of the Trinity as the complete Christian statement about the transcendent God, Simons' theology is not significantly influenced either in structure or content by the doctrine. His writings employ familiar trinitarian usages only when he is attacked on the matter, when the biblical texts suggest it, and when he wishes to evoke the ambience of the Pauline epistolary greetings and benedictions. The relative lack of formally trinitarian language in Simons may be due to his lack of ontological or metaphysical awareness, to his assumption (shared with other reformers) that the Trinity was not at issue, or more probably to the fact that as the persecuted minister of a persecuted church, Simons had far more pressing interests than the allures of nicely-turned but merely professional theological speculation.

2) Simons did maintain, however, a very vigorous and pervasive pattern of immanent trinitarian ascription. It was centered completely on Jesus Christ, and the associations made were of Christ's Spirit with power, Christ's Word with form or justice, and Christ's nature, person, life, or gracious presence, with love. Cognate forms of these terms occur in the text from time to time, e.g., "Holy Spirit," Christ *as* Word, grace *as* power. But their presence indicates that Simons is then speaking not of the internal life of the church of Christ but rather of what we might call the prolegomena to life in the church. Life within the church is described by Simons quite consistently in terms of the trinity of Christ's nature, Word, and Spirit.

3) Within this concrete and wholly confessional perspective, Simons committed himself theologically to the view that it is pre-eminently the power of Christ's Spirit that creates, nourishes, and perfects the church. It is therefore from the perspective of the power of the Spirit that Simons will address the issues of the relationship between 4) justice and love. Only by the power of Christ's Spirit can the Christian become conformed to Christ's teachings, his Word, his justice or righteousness, and so achieve union with Christ's nature of perfect love. But the relationship between justice and love is not expressed in a "vertical" metaphysical tension between creation and redemption, as in Luther or Calvin. The "vertical transcendental" direction is largely missing from, or is at least ineffective in Simons' approach to Christian faith. 5) Hence, there does not exist the need for a taut, dialectically unresolved balance between love and justice expressive of the tensions between transcendent and immanent reality.

As G. H. Williams puts it very clearly, though in a different context:

> Severing, or in their own way identifying, these pairs of opposites [law/gospel, justice/love, state/church, justification/sanctification], the Radicals were on the move away from such doctrinal correlates or supports of the law-grace tensions as the doctrine of predestination, the Anselmian view of the atonement, and the Nicene doctrine of the

Trinity in so far as the last was regarded as a formula for projecting onto the Godhead the sanction for the alleged unity of justice and love.[70]

Not that there is no tension left between justice and love. The tension is rather expressed in what we might call a "horizontal" or historical direction. It is the tension between the human exigencies of love and justice as they impinged upon the daily lives and circumstances of sixteenth-century Mennonites, and the demands of the ancient Gospel for strict conformity to the righteousness of Christ in the interests of saving union with him. Since these latter demands were so specific, so concretely expressed in the text of scripture, and since the former exigencies were so compelling because of the extreme persecution which many Anabaptists experienced, the perceived tensions between love and justice were increased significantly.

To put it quite simply: how was it possible for a persecuted sixteenth-century Mennonite fugitive in the no-man's-land of northern Europe to attempt to embody the ideals of the Sermon on the Mount? Yet that is precisely what was assayed.

Could not the Church and its good offices have been of assistance in supporting Simons' religious ideal? Not really. Although it has not been the focus of our attention, the reader may have noted how closely parallel to Roman Catholic spirituality and teaching are many teachings of Menno Simons. We shall have occasion in the next chapter to ponder more parallels. So recurrent are these parallels that it is tempting to propose the following definition:

> (*Pace* Mennonite friends) Menno Simons' faith and church is an evangelical Roman Catholic faith and church,
> . . .
> (*Pace* Catholic friends) . . . divested of all those institutions, traditions, philosophies, and resources by which one can moderate, evade, ignore, or even reverse the requirements of the Gospel.

The critical barb in this definition can apply as well to the "orthodox" Protestant churches, of course. The ideal stands: the Gospel, undiluted.

The church does of course somewhat assist the religious quest. But it is Christ's church, not man's, and it clearly exists on the *yon* side of the chasm. Like Christ's being, it too is wholly rooted in God. Simons was very determined about its position. That is why, among other reasons, demonstration of a changed life following faith, fear of God, true conversion, and rebaptism (the willingness to undergo which, in the sixteenth century, was a clear sign of willingness to die!) were considered prerequisites

---

[70]Williams, *Radical Reformation*, p. 833.

for entrance into the true church of Christ. The church is not the place in this world where one is assisted in beginning the process of sanctification. It is rather the place where one is assisted in completing it.

How the power of the Spirit works in the church to complete sanctification, how and where that church exists, what are its ethical requirements, and what the ways it both protects and extends itself—these questions are the subjects of the next chapter.

CHAPTER FIVE

Simons: The Sign of Tau

The headwaters of western culture spring from the desert: from the impossibly desert Sinai Peninsula ("wilderness," the biblical word, strikes backpackers as a little mild) and from semi-desert Palestine ("a land flowing with milk and honey" is similarly ironical to farmers). Yet from these unlikely sources flow two life-giving assertions. The first, in time at least, is the Sinai assertion: God has involved, immersed himself actively in the worldly life of his people, thereby giving nature, human existence, and history real significance, in order to accomplish his will. The second is the assertion of the prophets to Jerusalem: God is One, the transcendent creator and master of the universe—and we are therefore his creatures, not he ours.

The first assertion and its implications is an assertion of faith which distinguishes Hebraic from Greek, Indian, and Asian beliefs. The second is a philosophical achievement shared among the world's great cultures. But the joint affirmation that the utterly transcendent God is also specifically immanent in the life of his people, is a dialectical, theological affirmation whose tensions have provided the energy for western evolution.

The Christian faith, with its basic affirmation that Christ is fully God, fully man, and fully one, has embraced and in fact sharpened these tensions by its assertion that the trinitarian God has become the most human of men in order to effect the will of the Creator in his elect. But in these "latter days," the brute reality of history is inescapable: Jesus Christ is himself no longer with us. "Immanuel"—God is with us, but Christ has returned to the bosom of his Father. The implicit problem in this double assertion surfaced early in Christian theology. Christ having returned to the bosom of the Father, what is now the specific, ongoing "point of connection" between God and his world? Where is the life-giving fingertouch of Michelangelo between Adam and the Creator?

The question was answered early and definitively (e.g., in Acts 2 and John 16) and has never been seriously disputed. On our side, the locus of the connection is the church; on his side, the locus of connection is the Holy Spirit. The directional character of this relationship was also declared early and has never been disputed by Christians at all. The arm of Jahweh created Israel, and the fire of the Holy Sprit created the new Israel, the church.

It is a basic hypothesis of this study that the Christian understanding of the church, and hence of ethics, depends upon prior assumptions about God in his trinitarian functions. The point of contact with the world "from God's side" is the Holy Spirit. Therefore the function or functions a theologian asserts or assumes to be pre-eminently associated with the Third Person of the Trinity will provide the basic tone to his understanding of the church and its life in the world.

It is at this point that the traditions begin to diverge. The common tradition (Biblical and patristic) is but a matrix: it assigns all our categorical functions (love/order, power/freedom, form/justice) to each Person. In Acts 2 and elsewhere the Holy Spirit is pre-eminently associated with power; in early second-century theology (John 16) with form or truth; in St. Augustine, with love. Moreover, these functions are in the common tradition understood as mutually inclusive. In Acts 2, the Spirit teaches and unifies; in John 16, the Spirit unifies and effects; in St. Augustine, he effects and teaches. The old dogmatic principle that "the Trinity relates *ad extra* as one" is also a correct principle for historians of Christian thought.

This said, it is also to be said that different emphases were made in what would become the uncommon traditions. Luther emphasized the Word of Christ as the agency creating faith and thereby extending and controlling the church. And possibly in reaction to the excesses of the "Schwermerei," he subordinated the work of the Spirit. Calvin, as we shall see, emphasized the Father's elective love as the agency creating and extending the church, and similarly was very careful about his assertions concerning the work of the Spirit. Menno Simons' position on this issue was the the simplest, most consistent, and most traditional among the Protestant reformers. Once again his view of the priority of th Spirit in the creation, government, and extension of the church appears remarkably parallel to the Roman Catholic teaching, which always recurred to the charism of the Spirit for legitimation of its sacramental, doctrinal, and structural claims. For Simons, it is clear that the Spirit creates and extends the church, and that the Spirit by his power conforms us to Christ's words and example, thereby effecting union with the divine nature.

This emphasis, consistently maintained by Simons, supplies both the perspective from which the characteristic tensions in Mennonite life are seen and the means for their attempted resolution. The occasion for the tension is not, as it is for a more ontologically-rooted theologian, the "vertical" gap between transcendence and immanence. It is rather, for Simons, the brute fact of the historical or "horizontal" gap between sixteenth-century northern European life and the life of Jesus of Nazareth. The Mennonite ideal was to become completely conformed (form, justice) to Christ's words and example, thereby completely one (love, order) with his nature. Simons most vigorously asserted that Christ's Word, life, and Spirit are utterly one divine nature. This is one important point of Simons' teaching about the "celestial flesh" of Christ. But the terrible dichotomy between Jesus' life and sixteenth-century life made it humanly impossible to restore that unity of justice and love.

If one insisted upon absolute conformity to Christ's words and example, the consequence was often a severe strain upon the requirements of love among the brethren. For strict conformity to Christ often entailed sharp separations from otherwise nourishing, natural, God-created worldly relationships. By far the most painful of these required separations was the breakup of family relationships demanded by strict enforcement of the ban. Often the effect was the creation of enmity, bitterness, and mutual recrimination within the Mennonite church. Thus, in the interests of justice, not only was Christian love injured, but thereby also the structures of

Christian justice. Simons' biography as leader of the Mennonite church testifies to the tragedies effected by pushing to the limits endemic to human life.

But if in the interests of love and harmony among the brethren the opposite emphasis was made, the consequences were at least as bad if not worse. Relaxing the requirements of conformity to Christ would have made it easier for the Mennonite church to survive in the world, but then the whole point of the spiritual effort—union with Christ—would have been lost. Worldly associations, maintained, would in the end usher sin back into the church. And there would have been many who, in the Mennonite church as in similar movements before and since, would have left the church because of a perceived loss of purity. The church would be split again when it should have been one. And thus in the interests of love, not only is Christian justice or righteousness diminished, but Christian love and order itself is injured. Once again, Simons' biography is testament to the tragedy.

The basic ethical situation which Simons and the Mennonites had to face, therefore, can be seen as the ongoing need to at least modulate if not resolve the tensions between the demands of love and the requirements of justice. The line between love and justice, however, is in Simons' ethical situation bisected by another line: the demarcation line between the church and the world. Throughout the preceding chapter, we saw that in order to understand Simons' viewpoint on a subject we had to stand within the church and view things according to the Spirit. The same requirement is even more basic when we investigate Simons' ethics, or what he would rather call the regenerate life. This is because, for Simons, there just is no significant ethical situation apart from the church, and only in the church and the Spirit can the tensions between love and justice be addressed. The subject of ethics, like most of Simons' other subjects, presupposes ecclesiology.

Therefore we shall begin with an analysis of Simons' understanding of the church. Then we shall move to an overview of how, firstly, the issues of love and justice arise and are met within the church; and secondly, how the internal solutions affect the way the church views and ethically responds to its worldly environment.

A. *The Free Church*

Luther entitled his most famous treatise "The Freedom of a Christian." Had the pen belonged to Menno Simons, the title would have been "The Freedom of a Christian *Church*." For although Simons described the conversion process in terms of the individual man, he never developed a presentation of sanctified Christian life from such a basis. The primary fact of Christian ethics for Simons is not the individual Christian, but the Christian church. It is not too much to say that for Simons the individual is the creature of the holy community. He "receives himself" from it. Only within its confines does he gain the freedom to make the attempt at a perfected life, and only by the power of the Spirit working in the church is he enabled to accomplish that goal. Outside the church there is no power, no freedom, and no Christian life.

Yet Simons flatly rejected every argument suggesting that there were grounds upon which the church could be understood as an objective entity in its own right, a transpersonal fact whose validity rested on anything other than the free individuals who compose it. Neither state sanction, nor an adminstrative network, nor a sacramental system, nor a closed guild of clergymen, nor the physical fact of a "steeplehouse," to borrow George Fox's word, could provide a basis for the claim to be the "One Holy Catholic Church."

Against each other, as well as against the Roman Catholic Church, the Protestant reformers struggled vigorously for the legitimation of their respective communities. Legitimacy usually meant the recognition that one's church possessed the true doctrine and practice of Christianity. But how was the truth to be demonstrated? In spite of first appearances, the contest was not usually over whose doctrines most agreed with the Bible. For it was discovered early on that the New Testament simply did not answer definitively (when it answered at all) the questions put to it. Rather, with a consuming interest not equalled before or since, the Lutherans, Calvinists, Anglicans, and Roman Catholics of the sixteenth century all contended for the past. The truth of one's doctrine was determined by the degree to which it represented the unbroken tradition of Christian life and thought, the inheritance from the authentic doctors and the righteous churchmen of the past. Continuity—that was the prize at stake.

The Mennonites were virtually without resources for such a contest, and were most vulnerable to the fearsome charge of "novelty." More importantly, however, many Anabaptists rejected in theory the notion that objective historical continuity was a legitimation of the church. In response to a critique by Gellius Faber on just this issue, Menno Simons states clearly both his rejection and his positive alternative.

> [Gellius] admits that the church, deceived and disturbed by the devil through the lusts of the flesh, the pride of the world, conspirators and potentates, has become drowsy, inattentive, ungrateful, and apostate from Christ; has stirred up the wrath of God, and has fallen into all manner of wickedness and sin. Yet he asserts that she has remained the church of Christ, *as if the church could inherit from generation to generation, and as if the church does not consist in faith, Spirit, and power.*[1]

---

[1] CW 754, emphasis mine.

Those last two clauses and their conjunction merit a lengthy essay just by themselves. In a real sense, this section is but an inadequate elaboration of them. The latter clause expresses Simons' understanding of the church, the church whose only basis must be Jesus Christ (I Cor. 3:11). The former expresses Simons' understanding of history, particularly the limitations of history as a grounds of appeal. Simons' understanding of the church is what makes possible his radical dissolution of historical connection. It is his sense of historical bereftness that makes clinging to a church utterly conformed to Christ so necessary.

Let us begin with the historical question. Not only could Anabaptists not avoid being caught up in the general scramble for a legitimating past, but the apparent absence of lineage gave the problem of historical interpretation much greater importance and urgency for the Anabaptists than for other reformed groups. The historical justifications of other groups, self-justifications which were always used as a cudgel against the upstart Anabaptists, had to be broken. If possible the same weapon of historical criticism had to be turned against the critics. In this connection it was not Luther and the sixteenth-century humanists, but the Anabaptists who, to the extent they had access to and could use the material, were the chief beneficiaries of the great increase in knowledge of church history that the crisis of the Great Schism had stimulated.

Secondly, it would have been of tremendous psychological importance for the Anabaptists if this historical study could yield at least a bit of positive support. We spoke earlier of the great "chasm" between sixteenth-century experience and the life of Jesus. The Anabaptist churches were "free" churches in more than one sense. For they were also free, apparently, of the comforts of ancestry. The condition of being orphaned is exceedingly painful for a church as well as for an individual. There seemed no help, no stepping stones, nothing and no one anywhere in the past to provide encouragement or even company to those Anabaptists who had to cross that great gap. If by ransacking the past for weapons a few like-minded brethren could be discovered within that tale of apostasy which was church history, such discoveries would be doubly treasured by the Anabaptists. The cross of Christ is difficult enough to bear without having to bear it alone. Luther had anguished over the thought that he stood alone against the authority of the church and its history. So did the Anabaptist churches, and so did Menno Simons.

But in order to make judgments of "good" and "bad" concerning the church's history, one must have a standard. Menno Simons was quite definite about his standard. It was not "faith, Spirit, and power"; and it was not really the text of the New Testament. It was the "apostolic church." Simons took the New Testament as normative law not only for faith and ethics but also for church order. Yet the "New Testament church" is not coextensive in time with the "church of the New Testament." Simons' standard was the apostolic church, the church whose normative pattern began to develop at Pentecost and was completed in the Nicene Creed.² This apostolic pattern, which Simons insists is identical to Christ's own institution, is thus "fixed" and unalterable, even were the apostles themselves to return and urge us to change it.³ Quite simply, the apostolic church, which is the first church, is also normatively the "last" church, and in the eschatological sense: it cannot be added to. Any addition to its structures is by definition a loss; a change means, by definition, the creation of a different entity which is not the church. From Simons' point of view even such adjectives as "first," "original," or "early" would not really be appropriate designations. They imply the possibility that something else, also properly to be called a "church," might be differently characterized. Now Simons knows all about those "somethings else." But he refuses to call them churches. He usually calls them "great sects."

But what of his own "little sect"? That is called the church, indeed the true church. And it is properly so called because the institutions and experiences of Simons' church are considered identical to those of the apostolic church, which is identical to the New Testament church of Christ. The emphasis here is on the sense of shared eschatological experience. For perfectly understandable reasons, Mennonites had no trouble at all identifying themselves with the persecuted apostolic, i.e., true or "believing" church.⁴*

From this contemporary sense of persecution, Simons like other left-wing reformers developed a distinct sense of the "fall" of the church, of the authentic tradition, of the present ecclesiastical situation, and of the task required of the church in the sixteenth-century crisis. These decisions were of

²CW 630, 667, 967. William E. Keeney, *The Development of Dutch Anabaptist Thought and Practice from 1539 to 1564* (Nieuwkoop: B. de Graaf, 1968), p. 39, is therefore in error when he asserts that Simons accepted only the Apostles' Creed as a legitimate extra-Biblical source of teaching. Cf. Franklin H. Littell, *A Tribute to Menno Simons* (Scottdale, Pa: Herald Press, 1961), p. 24, where in good Anabaptist fashion the author defines "apostolic" as "true to the apostles"!

³CW 81, 127, 216, 219f., 308f.

⁴CW 35, 39, 42, 65, 81, 85f., 141, 202f., 248, 570f. The parallels were indeed quite close. Simons can see parallels in two circumstances particularly. 1) The general persecution of Anabaptists by the state for being subversive disrupters of political and religious order was comparable to the persecutions of the apostolic church under the successors of Nero. 2) More pointedly, Simons saw parallels to the official or "state church" persecutions of the Donatists and related purist movements, symbolized by the issue of baptismal practices. Some of these parallels were intended, of course. At least the Anabaptists, in trying to restore the usages of the ancient church, knew and accepted the persecutions that accompanied that restoration. "Bearing the cross" in this sense was so closely associated with the true church that, as we shall see, suffering was made an important mark of the Anabaptist church. In a few cases the logic was reversed: suffering became the object, not merely an attendant consequence, of becoming a Christian. But even though this perversion of the religious psyche was rare among the Anabaptists, the fact that their communities suffered just like the apostolic communities was a consolation to most Anabaptists.

Other parallels were created, perhaps less intentionally, by the opponents of the Anabaptists. Most important is the imperial recourse to ancient, i.e., Justinian's, law, expressed in the Mandate of Charles V, which required death for such crimes as rebaptism. Menno Simons was well aware of this parallel. Cf. CW 525.

course judgments more of value than of fact. But they reflect a systematic pattern of judgment and so constitute a distinct "salvation history" for many Anabaptist movements.

The apostolic age in general is obviously the "golden age" for Menno Simons. One cannot and need not give a precise date at which the church fell from its original purity. Anabaptists as well as their own later scholars differ over the details of the "fall."[5] Simons appears to believe that the fall was a gradual process beginning perhaps as early as the mid-second century under Pope Hyginus, but surely complete by the time of Augustine. In any case the sign of the falling church is clear: the gradually accumulatiing ecclesiastical legislation concerning the sacrament of baptism.[6*]

In his reading of salvation history, Simons discovered a sense of continuity with the past. The "ancestors" of the true church go back at least as far as Abraham. As might be expected, Simons sees his ancestry in general among the "remnant" of the faithful which has survived, often without leaders, since the beginning. In particular, those who have suffered ecclesiastical and civil persecution because of their baptismal practices are considered direct ancestors of sixteenth-century Mennonites.[7]

While it is commonly termed a "primitivist" theory of value, the Mennonite historical sense of things was not really developed in order to identify a distinct theory of origins. After all, every church claimed the same origin. We must remember that, especially for many Anabaptists, research into the history of the church had as its chief purpose the effective criticism of contemporary ecclesiastical life.[8]

Besides the expected opinions that contemporary rulers do not fear God but violently persecute the truth, and that the "learned ones" are all opposed to each other (hence, all are wrong!),[9] Menno Simons' perspectives on the contemporary scene are enlightening in two respects.

---

[5] Cf. George H. Williams, *The Radical Reformation* (Philadelphia: The Westminster Press, 1962), p. 198; Littell, *Origins*, p. 63f.; Keeney, pp. 175ff.

[6] CW 253, 259, 276ff., 775. In this connection it should be noted that Simons was well aware of the fact that even the "authentic" tradition had seen variations in practice. In different "ages," he allows, there had been minor alterations in the "ordinances" or "usages," especially concerning the symbolic means of entrance into the holy community. These variations were merely adjustments to suit the times, however, and did not touch the matter of true doctrine. Simons' basic differentiating phrase in this connection is the time "before," "under," and "after" the Law, cf. CW 735, 749.

One might suggest that by this admission Simons has at least seriously compromised his case for the unalterability of the teachings of the true church. But Simons made this admission only to account for the Old Testament rootage of the church. From the time of Christ's institution, that is, the time "after the law," there can be no legitimate change in usages. Still, Simons could be pressed on this matter, at least in terms of his philosophy of history. But such an exercise would be of little point: Simons neither had, nor was interested in, an articulated philosophy of historical change.

[7] CW 501f., 504, 582, 584, 683, 735, 749.

[8] This is the view of Littell, *Origins*, p. 51. For general notes on the "primitivist" theories of the Anabaptists, cf. Williams, *Radical Reformation*, p. 848, and Littell, *Origins*, pp. xvi, 44, 57.

Though he had to contend with opponents whom we would identify as Calvinists, Simons does not know them as representatives of an established sect, but in his extremely rare references appears to understand them as a half-organized group of somewhat like-minded individuals.[10] The sects whom he identifies are those already "in place": "papists," Lutherans, Zwinglians, and the "corrupt sects" of the Münsterites, Davidians, and related groups. All of these sects are papist in their own ways since all trust in external ceremonies, works-righteousness, and seek to suppress opposition by political force.[11] Except for references to the Catholic sect, the largest single body of references is to Luther and his associates. Here Simons voices what had already become a general Anabaptist critique: although Luther started out evangelically and accomplished much good for the church, he "drew back," forgot his initial insights, or failed to carry them through to their ultimate conclusions. Desire for fame, weakness of the flesh, and seduction by political powers are the usual reasons cited for his failure.[12]

The second aspect of Simons' evaluation of the contemporary church scene is more significant. In one appeal addressed to "all theologians," Simons listed ten points which he felt were the major areas of contention.[13] But since the ten points cover nearly everything in Christian doctrine, a discussion and analysis of them would not really solve anything—a judgment perhaps shared by "the theologians," if their refusal to accept Simons' invitation be evidence. Yet the ten points in their own way reflect a settled opinion and imply a necessary response which Simons knows is the core of the difficulty: separation from the world of sin.

That "separation" was the immediate source of many Anabaptists' troubles in sixteenth-century Europe was clearly seen by Zwingli, the first magisterial reformer to gain extensive experience with them. In his 1525 treatise *Of Baptism* Zwingli wrote of the Anabaptists:

> But they say: We are the Church, and those who do not belong to our Church are not Christians. The Church was founded by us; before us there was no Church. Answer: Exactly; it is just as I have said from the very first. The root of the trouble is that the Anabaptists will not recognize any Christian except themselves or any Church except their own. And that is always the way with sectarians who separate themselves on their own authority.[14]

[9]Cf. CW 138, 298, 525, 556, 586, 602, 678, 939.

[10]CW 922, 939. "Calvinism," of course, is but a creation of later historians. And especially in Simons' time it would have been highly difficult to see much if any reason to call it a "sect." From Simons' perspective, Calvin was but the crypto-papist "reformer" of Geneva whom a few misguided northerners took for their model. If he had had to give any name to them, he most likely would have classified them as "Zwinglians." [11]CW 279, 725, 735f.

[12]Cf., for example, CW 514, 550, 600, 692, 695, among many other direct and indirect references. [13]CW 538f.

[14]Ulrich Zwingli, *Of Baptism*, in *Zwingli and Bullinger*, trans. C. W. Bromiley, Library of Christian Classics, XXIV (Philadelphia: The Westminster Press, 1953), p. 158.

Simons' understanding of the church is accordingly usually developed by means of a contrast to the "world" or "false churches." And this way of thinking is a habit from his earliest writings on.

Polemics aside, Zwingli has seen that rebaptism is but the first public sign of a people who have already separated themselves from the contemporary religious establishment. He goes on to argue that such innovations (there is that hated word again) as the separatists wish to practice are a danger to the church, and that the responsible course of action is to submit to the church, stay together, and "go slowly" for the sake of the weaker brethren. But what Zwingli did not see clearly then was that the various reforming movements were working from different feelings about the nature of the church.[15] This is no judgment upon his sensitivity, however, for in 1525 no reforming group, Lutheran, Zwinglian, Anabaptist—or Roman Catholic, for that matter—had yet developed a redefinition of the church to meet the needs of the time. And that is the heart of the matter in the Reformation crisis. One might suggest that with few if any "traditions" to slow them down, the Anabaptists were the first to reach clarity on the teaching.

From his earliest writings it is clear that Simons recognizes separation from the world of sin, evidenced by the apostolic practices of baptism and the ban, as a chief mark of the true church.[16] When in his later writings the "marks of the church" are developed more fully and formally, separation as evidenced again by scriptural baptism, but now also by bold confession of faith in the teeth of persecution, remains a chief mark.[17] So long as all who would be Christians do not observe apostolic usages and practice the life of discipline, says Simons in a memorable line, "so long will the world be their church, and their church the world."[18]

> Lest you be alarmed by the word *holy church*, you must learn to know from the Word of God that the holy, Christian church is no assembly of unbelievers, carnal or brazen sinners, . . . [T]he holy Christian church must be a spiritual seed, an assembly of the righteous, and a community of the saints; which church is begotten of God, of the living seed of the divine Word, and not of the teachings, institutions, and fictions of man.[19]

[15]Littell, *Origins*, p. 14.

[16]CW 94f., 101.

[17]CW 739-744; cf. 720, 748, 644ff. Separation as a mark of the church is, of course, also stressed by Dirk Phillips, *Enchiridion*, in George H. Williams, ed., *Spiritual and Anabaptist Writers*, Library of Christian Classics, XXV (Philadelphia: The Westminster Press, 1957), p. 240ff., and by Peter Ridemann, *Account of Our Religion, Doctrine, and Faith*, trans. Kathleen Hasenberg (London, 1950), pp. 92, 140, 164. Cf. Williams, *Radical Reformation*, pp. xxix, 848, Keeney, pp. 147f., 153, 160ff.; and Littell, *Origins*, pp. 83ff.

[18]CW 725.

[19]CW 234. Compare Dirk Phillips, *Enchiridion*, in Williams, *Spiritual and Anabaptist Writers*, p. 234.

As his best student has noted,[20] Simons usually referred to an ecclesiastical instituition as a *Kerk*, and to groups other than true churches as *Secte* ("sects" either "great" such as Lutherans or Roman Catholics, or "corrupt" such as the Münsterites and Davidians). His preferred term for the reality of the true church, however, was *Gemeente*. This term can be variously translated, depending on the perceived nuances in Simons' text, but it always refers in general to that community of the regenerate which alone is the church. Sometimes Simons does speak of the "church" in a singular, collective, or corporate sense.[21] But more often he emphasizes the active binding-together of regenerate people. The church is an "assembly of the righteous and a communion of saints"; a "congregation and church" or a "gathering or congregation"; a "covenant."[22] In line with this active meaning of *Gemeente*, Simons insists that the assembling of the saints be voluntary[23]—a characteristic assumed in all of Simons' doctrines concerning the church, of course, but possibly for that reason very seldom mentioned by him.

Less well known, however, is that in at least one locus Simons, perhaps forced by the assaults of his Calvinist critic Gellius Faber, admits the validity of that great tool of the magisterial reformation, the distinction between the "visible" and the "invisible" church.

> In part I admit this to be right: however, with this understanding: that the visible church, in which the invisible (as he calls it) is contained, must be sound in doctrines, sacraments, and ordinances, and irreproachable in life before the world, so far as man, who is able to judge only that which is visible, can see.[24]

Simons goes on to deny, however, that the "invisible" church can still exist among the corrupted visible churches. He has in fact reversed the normal standard of judgment. Appeal to a supposed presence of the "invisible" church does not excuse the faults of the "visible" church; rather, it is the presence of a perceptibly righteous visible church that allows for the admission of an invisible one. Even if the distinction were a useful one for Simons (which it is not, given his unwillingness to think in a "two-level" theological

---

[20]Cf. Keeney, p. 146f.; also by the same author, "Basic Beliefs of the Dutch Anabaptists," in Walter Klaassen *et al.*, eds., *No Other Foundation* (North Newton, Kansas: Bethel College, 1962), p. 21.

[21]CW 41, 191.

[22]Cf. in order, CW 99, 145, 191, 234, 443, 667, 133, 136. Ridemann also uses the terms in this active sense. Cf. his *Account*, pp. 38, 43. Cf. Keeney, *Development*, p. 160. For less formal, more descriptive names for the church, cf. the list in Table Six in the Appendix.

[23]CW 410, 415.

[24]CW 747; cf. 757, 759. Cf. also Williams, *Radical Reformation*, p. 843; Keeney, *Development*, p. 149f.; John H. Yoder, "The Prophetic Dissent of the Anabaptists," in Guy Hershberger, ed., *The Recovery of the Anabaptist Vision* (Scottdale, Pa.: Herald Press, 1957), p. 99; and Willis M. Stoesz, "The New Creature: Menno Simons' Understanding of the Christian Faith," *MQR* 25 (January 1965): 16.

universe), the press of his ecclesiology is clear: the actual visible congregation of the faithful must be conformed to the will of its Lord or else it simply does not exist as a *Gemeente*. Quite simply, the congregation must be the true "body of Christ"[25] and as such, outwardly perfect.[26] Only in this perfection may there be achieved the goal for which the Mennonites of the sixteenth century girded themselves: the complete restoration of the ancient apostolic usages, the will, and the living presence of Christ and his church.[27]

To pursue a formal definition of the church in Simons' theology, however, would be to miss it completely. As noted before, Simons understands all his subjects in terms of acts, of behaviors: if it doesn't happen, it just isn't there! We must rather seek the church—Christ's life of love, according to Simons—only in the actual daily struggle of the Spirit of power to realize divine righteousness in the midst of an alien world. To our misguided search for ontological definitions Simons replies in a passage as magnificent as that of Luther on the same subject quoted in an earlier chapter.

> No, no, worthy sirs, no! This constitutes the church in Christ: rightly to teach Christ's unadulterated Word in the power of the Spirit; to believe the same with all the heart and to practice it in all obedience; rightly to use the sacraments, such as baptism and holy communion, according to His own commandments and ordinance; to seek God from the heart, to fear Him, love Him, serve Him; to be born of God; to love one's neighbor, to serve him, comfort him, help and assist him; to avoid all false doctrine and the works of darkness; to mortify all carnal lusts that war against God's Word; to deny oneself and the world, to lead a pious, peaceful, chaste, sober, and humble life in righteousness according to the truth. In fine, to be of the same mind as was Christ Jesus! For where these are, there Christ's kingdom and church is.[28]

Therefore, we are best advised to turn our attention to the church not in words but in deeds.

B. *Peace in Strife*

As noted earlier, from Simons' perspective the perceived ethical tensions between the exigencies of love and the requirements of justice do not appear as a simple dialectical tension. That is because for him the ethical question, however it may appear, presumes a settlement of the ecclesiastical question. The line between love and justice is bisected by a more important

---

[25]CW 148, 273, 299, 672, 950. This in spite of what is claimed by Littell, *Tribute*, p. 53.
[26]CW 161, 304, 746.
[27]CW 303, 415, 424, 554.
[28]CW 537f.

one: the distinction between the church and the world. This distinction is operative throughout Simons' thought and must be kept in mind even when it is not explicit in his text in order to understand his position. It is the genuine expression of what theorists have termed the "dualist" or "opposition" pattern of some Christian groups.[29]

Without getting into the question of whether such a dualism is more than a social/ethical stance, it is clear that for Simons the sharp distinction between the righteous church and the corrupted world (including the "sects") is the main structural basis for all ethical judgments. This means that Simons will approach the issues of love and justice and their relationship quite differently when he is speaking from within the realm of the church's life than he will when he is speaking of life in the worldly realm. In fact, as Littell has noted,[30] Anabaptists usually avoided social issues in the latter realm. Simons, as we shall see, usually addressed "public" issues only when and insofar as decisions made or contemplated adversely affected the church.

The reason for the distinction is, as we saw in the preceding chapter, that Simons believed that the Spirit of Christ is operative with his power only within the community of the regenerate. Only in the church, therefore, is there the freedom to achieve the realization of love and justice which the Word of Christ both commands and illustrates. All outside the regenerate church are thus in a realm of powerlessness with respect to God and his own. They are in fact in a realm not of freedom but of bondage to their own sin. In a real, though of course not a physical sense, that world does not exist for Simons. He will have nothing much to say about how, on its own terms, that world should exercise love and administer justice. His closest approach to "worldly" ethics concerns rather how the church should respond in love and justice to the outside realm.

Let us sketch the patterns that will emerge in the concluding sections of this chapter. The ideal realization of the unity of love and justice for Simons is of course seen in the life and teachings of Christ. In the Mennonite community the exigencies of love are met by preserving mutual service, support, and spiritual encouragement among a group of like-minded individuals. In this way an ordered harmony is created and nurtured by the free power of the Spirit. The requirements of justice are met by insistence upon maximal correspondence to the ethical and religious example of Christ and the first Christian communities. In this way a disciplined peace is sustained under the form of the Word. As noted in the introduction, resolving the tensions between love and justice—tensions that if not at least mitigated would destroy the community—must be the focus of greatest spiritual effort

---

[29]H. Richard Niebuhr, *Christ and Culture* (New York: Harper & Row, 1951), pp. 45ff., 76ff.; W. W. Schroeder, *Cognitive Structures and Religious Research: Essays in Sociology and Theology* (East Lansing: Michigan State University Press, 1970), p. 74. Cf. Clarence Bauman, "The Theology of the Two Kingdoms: a Comparison of Luther and the Anabaptists," *MQR* 38 (January 1964): 37-49.

[30]Littell, *Origins*, p. 74.

for the Mennonites. The chief instrument for this purpose is the ban. As Keeney has noted so perceptively, the ban is the characteristic means by which Simons and his church sought to preserve the synthesis of justice and order.[31] The ban is the vital organ of the Mennonite body. Simons' opponents attacked him most vigorously on just this point, and he defended it just as vigorously. Accordingly most of our interest in this section will be directed to a consideration of the ban and related practices.

As far as love and justice in the world are concerned, we need not review the justified, if occasionally rhetorical and polemical, criticisms of Simons. Our concern will be rather to indicate how he views the proper response of the church—its own house in order—to the outside world. In general one may say that according to Simons the church exercises love toward the outside world by its witness, an effort expressed less by active missionary effort than by suffering and martyrdom. It is an effort following systematically from the Mennonite view of the church as the lighthouse of the Spirit and is a most important characteristic of the church's public face. The church exercises justice toward the world in a related way, according to Simons. Christians must individually submit to worldly justice insofar as doing so does not jeopardize religious life. But the key expression of justice in the world is tolerance. Both the individual and the church community must refrain from attempting to impose their own religious persuasions on a general public otherwise inclined. This position, entailing as it does a series of decisions concerning the relationship of church and state, pacifism, and the nature of voluntary associations, to name but a few issues, is a major Anabaptist contribution to modern western social and political theory.

Missionary zeal and religious tolerance are, of course, in great tension. Simons had little occasion and little need to address himself to their resolution. In fact there was theoretically no instrument by which they could be resolved. For that tension exists in the world and is created by the world, not in and by the church. And the world is in disorder. It has no recourse until it becomes regenerate. And then it is no longer the world, but the church. Menno Simons would have appreciated St. Augustine's discussion in the early books of *The City of God*.

* * * * * *

The Scriptures teach that there are two opposing princes and two opposing kingdoms: the one is the prince of peace; the other the prince of strife. Each of these princes had his particular kingdom and as the prince is so is also the kingdom. The Prince of peace is Christ Jesus; His kingdom is the kingdom of peace, which is His church; His

---

[31]Keeney, *Development*, p. 156.

messengers are the messengers of peace; His Word is the word of peace; His body is the body of peace; His children are the seed of peace; and His inheritance and reward are the inheritance and reward of peace. In short, with this King, and in His kingdom and reign, it is nothing but peace. Everything that is seen, heard, and done is peace.

We have heard the word of peace, namely, the consoling Gospel of peace from the mouth of His messengers of peace. We, by His grace, have believed and accepted it in peace and have committed ourselves to the only, eternal, and true Prince of peace, Christ Jesus, in His kingdom of peace and under His reign, and are thus by the gift of His Holy Spirit, by means of faith, incorporated into His body. And henceforth we look with all the children of His peace for the promised inheritance and reward of peace.

Such exceeding grace of God has appeared unto us poor, miserable sinners that we who were formerly no people at all and who knew of no peace are now called to be such a glorious people of God, a church, a kingdom, inheritance, body, and possession of peace. Therefore we desire not to break this peace, but by His great power by which He has called us to this peace and portion, to walk in this grace and peace, unchangeably and unwaveringly unto death.[32]

As is the prince, so is the kingdom. And the only kingdom really worth talking about is the kingdom of Christ and of peace, the church. Notice in the last quoted paragraph Simons' strong conviction that it is only because of the Gospel of Christ that the "people" even exist as such. This is somewhat more than pious rhetoric. G. H. Williams summarized his account of the radical reformation by noting that the Anabaptists were people already deeply alienated from the cultural and religious life of both magisterial Protestantism and Roman Catholicism, and so could separate from all of it on principle.[33] Williams' view can be extended. Those who were to become Anabaptist rank and file, if not its leaders, were those who for generations had been culturally and religiously disenfranchised. Pushed out of, or perhaps never admitted into, the civilized life of Europe, the "poor ones" (as Simons called his flock occasionally) were not *changing* their cultural and social identity: they were *gaining* it. They were not changing their Christian faith from a Catholic to a Protestant version; they were effectively becoming Christian for the first time. Thus it is only in a limited sense that we can speak of the Anabaptist movements as *re*stitutionist movements. Only the historian can see them that way. For the people involved in creating themselves, the movement was *con*stitutionalist. As

[32]CW 554f.

[33]Williams, *Radical Reformation*, p. 848. Cf. Hans. J. Hillerbrand, "Anabaptism and History," *MQR* 45 (April 1971): 110-117; Kenneth R. Davis, "Erasmus as Progenitor of Anabaptist Theology and Piety," *MQR* 47 (July 1973): 163-178.

Simons says, alluding very significantly to the creation of Israel: the Mennonites were "no people" who in the power of the Spirit and under the Word of Christ have become a "glorious people."

This is the perspective from which we must evaluate the seriousness with which Simons stressed Christ's commandments in the New Testament. His emphasis upon Christ as lawgiver and upon faith as a strict observance of his law[34] struck most (already acculturated) critics as excessive legalism, and as socially dangerous besides. For if one took the Sermon on the Mount literally, all traditional social structure would break down! But that is the point: the Mennonites had few traditions they would call their own. Christ's words therefore became the basis for the constitution of a new people. For the same reason one should hesitate to name Simons' approach to ethics a "prescriptive" approach. That term usually suggests general principles of ethics derived from some source other (i.e., "heteronomous" and/or "theonomous") than one's own nature, and applied beyond or even against one's own natural inclinations. Simons' ethics are indeed prescriptive: the words of Christ in the Bible are the absolute standard. But we must remember that they can be exercised only in that people which has already by the power of the Spirit become unified, one flesh with the divine Christ. Therefore in a very real sense Simons' ethical principles are not heteronomous at all. They are indeed theonomous, but they are also natural! It is only in the church community, therefore, a community which Simons believed to be the true bodily presence of Christ (in a stronger sense of the phrase than did any other major reformer except perhaps Peter Ridemann) that the union of love and justice can be realized. And that is why, amidst all the strife in the worldly kingdom, the kingdom of Christ is a kingdom of peace.

Simons was convinced that the harmonious and peaceful environment needed to assist the quest for perfection in Christ could be maintained only if the world's strife and disorder were kept out of the church. And the only way this could be done was to follow exactly the institution of Christ. Thereby what we might visualize as a spiritual perimeter was established for the Mennonite community and for the individual soul. By defining that perimeter, and at least as importantly, by effectuating it, the Mennonites created an instrument for ordered discipline which came closer to achieving the union of love and justice within the community than was achieved in any other Reformation group. That instrument was the ban.

The ban should not be taken as the identifying characteristic of the Mennonite church any more than should adult baptism. Even though at times these related[35] practices seem to become the focus of interest and con-

---

[34]CW 55f., 129, 329, 479, 527, 586f., 985ff.

[35]In his first major treatise on the ban, *A Kind Admonition on Church Discipline* (1541), Simons stresses that it is the voluntary character of the religious community (indicated by adult baptism) that should preclude any theoretical objections to the exercise of spiritual discipline via the ban. Cf. CW 410, 415.

troversy, they are really no more or less than ways by which the visible church seeks to become and remain conformed to Christ. If the ban and the effectuating practice of shunning were often perceived as a major stumbling block and occasion for scandal by opponents of the Mennonites and also by some within the community, that is only because the purely instrumental character of the disciplines was forgotten. The ban neither effects nor demonstrates one's righteousness before God. Menno Simons in a late treatise is very clear about this. Discussing the relationship of the practice of excommunication (the ban) to those in the community who have fallen secretly (i.e., before God alone), and then recovered, he says:

> ... In this matter we are not so to judge; for it is a matter between a man and his God. For since it is evident that we seek our righteousness and salvation, the remission of our sins, satisfaction, reconciliation, and eternal life, *not in or through the ban*, but solely in the righteousness, intercession, merits, death, and blood of Christ, therefore ... we have no binding key of Christ nor any commandment wherewith to punish him yet more, or bind him or shame him before the church.[36]

In the first place, the ban is practiced simply because it is instituted by the Word of Christ in the scripture, and is therefore one of the chief activities of Christ's Spirit in the church.[37] There was, of course, no major disagreement among the reforming groups on this matter. The differences arose rather over questions concerning the agency by which the "binding key" would be exercised, the grounds for its use, and most importantly, the degree of completeness with which its sanctions were to be implemented.

Simons sees no special wisdom, merely by virtue of their position, in ministers and teachers. The position of church leaders is a purely functional and not a formal or sacramental one. They stand under exactly the same evangelical requirements as the rest of the congregaiton.[38] It is the congregation as a whole, including the member whose behavior is at issue, which is the executive agency. For it is the scriptural exercise of the ban, Simons believes, which is a chief mark, not of the individual Christian or the clergy but of the congregation of the faithful.[39]

Simons' three major writings on church discipline (1541, 1550, 1558) span his career and accordingly indicate some changes in his thinking about the grounds and circumstances requiring declaration of the ban. In his earliest writing on the subject (*A Kind Admonition on Church Discipline*), as in the brief discussion in the *Foundation Book*, Simons' focus of application seemed to be upon shunning the corrupt sects.[40] By 1550, however, the

[36]CW 979, emphasis mine.
[37]CW 83ff., 469f., 475, 969ff., 1006.
[38]CW 160ff., 508, 511, 559, 681. Cf. Keeney, *Development*, pp. 46, 50, 52f.; Williams, *Radical Reformation*, p. 392f.
[39]CW 469, 478, 723f., 746, 962. Cf. Williams, *Radical Reformation*, p. 859; Littell, *Origins*, p. 94f.
[40]CW 412.

obvious and simple decisions of the first years were superseded by problems more internal to Mennonite life and so more complex. The "radicals" being no longer an issue, the discipline of the ban began to focus on what we might call "ordinary associations."

One issue: is one to relate any differently to those around us who have not yet been regenerated (= "manifest sinners") than to those who have fallen out from the truth (= "heathen")? "Yes," says Simons throughout an unfortunately labored exegesis of Matthew 18:17. With the unregenerate, one can be polite and civil but must have no unnecessary commerce beyond that. Within the community of the brethren, however, complete shunning of the fallen is required.[41] The logic of this perhaps initially backwards-appearing judgment is very simple and persuasive. We shall return to it below.

Much more problematic, however, were issues forced by unforeseen circumstances strictly within the Mennonite community. In their early enthusiasm, many Anabaptists had underestimated the persistence of sin within the regenerated community.[42] In his last treatise on church discipline, *Instruction on Excommunication* (1558), Simons admitted that in his earlier ministry he had not taken seriously enough the matter of sin within the community.[43] Emphasizing more strongly than before that the ban is "a valid declaration of the eternal death of our soul" (CW 967), Simons goes on to suggest that the biblical "three exhortations" be lessened by one in the case of blatant sinners, heretics, and schismatics, and that it be made more difficult for these people to gain re-entrance into the community.[44]

It was, however, the question of the application of the ban within the family unit that occasioned the greatest test of Mennonite religious conviction and church unity. What made the issue so very difficult was that Simons and others knew that the ban gained its effectiveness only through punishment, i.e., shunning.[45] Besides all the personal difficulties involved in its application within the family, particularly between husband and wife, shunning appeared at least on its face to run counter to the biblical injunction not to separate those whom God had joined together. In spite of what must have been a great spiritual weight upon him, Simons gradually moved to a stricter position on the matter. In his first (1550) response to a question about marital avoidance, Simons equivocated. But by 1558, he insisted that the true apostolic ban makes no exceptions and that the spiritual marriage to Christ takes precedence over human marriage.[46]

[41]CW 460f., 472f. As the editor of Simons' writings indicates in the first reference, Simons, by this decision, is distinguishing himself from the Reformed position, which argued that apostates, no longer in the church, should be treated the same way as those who had not yet entered the church.

[42]Williams, *Radical Reformation*, p. 798; Keeney, *Development*, pp. 118, 122.

[43]CW 964, 975.

[44]CW 976f. Cf. Keeney, *Development*, pp. 156ff., for a discussion of Simons' differentiations with regard to sins.

[45]CW 478, 745, 1007.

[46]CW 478f.; 970ff. It must be noted, however, that Simons' mature views were still not so strict as those of other leaders such as Dirk Phillips. Cf. Keeney, *Development*, pp. 116, 199f., 126, 164f.

Part of Simons' basic argument for the stricter view in this matter is that it is precisely the more intimate personal and social relations which pose greater dangers to the other members of the association, should one member fall into sin. Therefore, even though extreme caution should be taken before rendering judgment, family relations especially should not be less liable to the discipline of Christ than other relations.

This same line of reasoning by extension partially explains why Simons advocated greater strictures against fallen brethren in general than against those not yet regenerated. In a certain sense the sins of the former are greater: they have rejected the body of Christ of which they had been members. Not only has the wayward person retained an intimate and possibly compromising knowledge of the community, should he turn traitor, but also his closest associates in the community are the more liable to his continued influence, should shunning not be required.

Simons defended the ban and shunning as the necessary means by which the church protects itself internally, remains the pure and true church, and maintains a good public report.[47] This largely negative function of the discipline, clearly an exercise in which the concern for justice dominates consideration, was personally distasteful to Simons, especially when it had to be rendered in such areas as family relations.

> I entreat all dear brethren in general that they would always consider with wise and sober minds to what end they have assumed the *gentle* yoke of the living and Almighty God, so that they may act and walk in a becoming manner, in the most holy covenant of grace before Him and all mankind, and live and walk with their life's partner in such piety, love, union, and peace, and with such fidelity and care, that from now on we need never again to hear of *this miserable ban or expulsion,* but of sincere Christian piety, of delight and godly joy.[48]

Yet we would utterly mistake the meaning of the Mennonite discipline were we to rest interpretation upon it as a system of justice. If the discipline has so far appeared negative to us, it is because we have not been presented with what for Simons was a far more important consideration.

First of all the discipline is not really an act of human origin at all. Simons insisted over and over that the ban is an imposition of the Holy Spirit following the institution of Christ (cf. especially CW 470ff. in this connection). He was equally insistent that it is not the congregation which actually excommunicates the erring person, but that the person has already

---

[47]CW 411, 415, 723f., 730, 732f., 962, 969, 1007. Cf. Keeney, "Basic Beliefs," in Klaassen, *No Other Foundation,* p. 22.

[48]CW 973, emphasis mine.

excommunicated himself (CW 423f.). The chief function of the ban, and therefore of the extreme discipline of shunning, is to lead the wayward person to true repentance. Therein, Simons said untiringly, the discipline exhibits itself as a great work of love.[49] By its use the sinner is urged and encouraged in the strongest possible way to rejoin the community of the regenerate, to participate once again with "sincere Christian piety, delight and godly joy" in the Gospel and body of Christ, his true family.

This interpretation of the meaning and purpose of church discipline is shared by all Christian churches, and therefore by itself would not serve to differentiate the Mennonite rationale from that of Lutheranism or Calvinism. It is our thesis in this study that because of differences in understanding the Trinity, the three generic Protestant traditions faced different kinds of issues with respect to the social and ethical tensions among love, power, and justice. Basing itself squarely upon the work of Christ's Spirit of power, the Mennonite community found itself confronted with the task of creating some workable relationship between the needs of love and the requirements of Christ's justice. As suggested earlier, the ban was the way the Mennonites sought to preserve the synthesis of justice and order or love. But how is the relationship of justice and love to be conceived? The most eminent and immediate function of the ban was to preserve the distinction between the church and the world. This distinction, cutting across all other considerations, forced adoption of opposite views of the relationship between love and justice. One view is operative within the church, and the other between the church and the world. It is with the first view that we are concerned at the close of this section.

Simons has insisted that the ban and its implementation was an expression of love. For the Mennonites, this assertion had to be more than a commonplace rationalization, because their community was separated from all worldly means of support. The discipline is an expression of love in at least three senses. Firstly, the community itself must be sustained and protected from injury, not only from the internal threats of sin but also from external adverse public opinion. The ban accomplished this act of love for the righteous brethren. Secondly, the "prodigal son" must be lured and prodded into repentance and hence back into the family, not only for his own sake but also in order that the family might learn and grow. The ban and particularly the practice of shunning accomplished this act of love.

Thirdly and most basically, if the community is not sustained in strict conformity to the word and example of Christ, there is simply no reason for its continued existence. There is then no grace, no joy, no living Gospel, no salvation, no church, nothing for which to leave the world and take up the cross. "We are then," Simons might have said with Paul, "of all men most to be pitied." Christian faith, Simons always insisted, is Christian living. It is act. The Mennonite ban therefore is more than just an instrument of justice for manifesting Christ's gift of himself in love; it is that love made manifest in act. To translate into a language more abstract and less theological: for Menno Simons justice is the expression of love within the community of the church.

[49] CW 411, 413f., 458, 469f., 724, 969.

Let us add but one emphasis to this aspect of Mennonite thought. Simons' ethics are almost entirely a social ethics. The discipline, Christ's righteousness or justice, is exercised wholly by the community, and almost entirely for the community. The exception proves the rule. For when it is a case of a private, i.e., non-social sin, we heard Simons advise earlier, there is neither "binding key" nor commandment. And although the ban is significantly intended for the recovery of the erring individual, we must remember that its first effect is exclusion from the community. In this respect shunning is a particularly effective symbol. For shunning is non-recognition. It teaches the sinner that he in a sense has no individual identity on the outside, and that his only identity before Christ is that given him within and as part of the community of Christ's presence, the church.

This attempt to resolve the tensions between love and justice was, of course, not fully successful. The history of Simons' ministry and that of the Mennonite churches after him bespeak the ongoing difficulties occasioned by differences of opinion over the degree and areas to which the discipline must be applied. Moreover, although for obvious reasons we have little or no direct information from early Mennonite leaders concerning how effective the ban and shunning were in bringing wayward souls back into the church, we may guess that the success rate was less than first anticipated. Simons does give us one hint in this regard. Gellius Faber had charged that of the "several hundreds" whom Simons' group had banned, scarcely a handful could be named who had benefitted thereby, and that the benefit to the unity of the church was even less. Simons does not clearly deny the first charge, responding only with an "even if it were true." Instead he shifts attention to "other" benefits of the practice (CW 730). What of the unity of the church? It is sustained, he says, as a tiny remnant in a world of the unrighteous (CW 732).

That the church continues to be tried by internal disagreement, and that it exists righteously only as a remnant, are grievous facts lamented by Simons. But such conditions, he believed, were not due to the true practice of Christ's Gospel. They were due to the fallenness and intransigence of the world. To the church and its relation to that world we now turn our attention.

C. *A Light in the Wilderness*

No subject has stirred greater research interest among historians in the field than the Anabaptists' views on church-state relations. Yet Menno Simons had little to say on the subject. Because he concentrated upon the realm of the church's life—a realm sharply differentiated from the realm of public social and political life—Simons never attempted either an internal critique of or a constructive model for the latter. Denied all access to influence in constituted political life, many Anabaptists, of course, also had few occasions for such an attempt. Therefore it should not really come as a surprise to find that Simons' views are in large part traditional, and that he is relatively ambiguous and undeveloped even on those issues of greater relevance to Mennonite life.

The notion of a strict separation of church and state such as we moderns have come to uphold is not to be found in Simons, even though his understanding of the church as a wholly volitional community of faith seems to imply that notion. His views on the function of government are fairly similar to Luther's: the prevention and punishment of evil. And even though he places greater emphasis upon governmental non-violence, Simons, like Luther and nearly everyone else at the time, thought it a proper function of government to maintain at least outward conformity to basic religious and Christian beliefs.[50]*

The idea that the commitment to a wholly voluntarist church might imply a truly secular state does not occur to Simons. His position therefore creates some uneasiness. Possibly because he usually spoke in generalities, in familiar biblical language, on the place of government in religious life, Simons apparently did not see the difficulty of reconciling the view stated above with his frequently voiced belief that the "league" of the princes and the "sect-theologians" was unchristian and a danger to the true church. Where does one draw the line? Shall government be limited to the task of maintaining a generally Christian environment in matters of ethics and doctrine—a view which Simons advocated? Or may it enforce more specific practices such as infant baptism and public licensing of ministers and teachers—a view which he most vigorously opposed?

A similar uneasiness of position appears when Simons defends his church against charges of irregularities in such "secular" matters as marriage and economic organization. Although he correctly denied the charges, it is interesting to note that Simons' defenses were not based on the claim that polygamy and communism, for example, were intrinsically and absolutely wrong and hence justifiably illegal. Such practices were instanced in the Bible, after all; they are simply no longer the custom in this dispensation.[51]

The "uneasiness" of Simons' position in both doctrine and social matters is an uneasiness felt by one who is a citizen first and a Christian second.

[50]CW 193, 200, 304, 320, 526, 528f., 551ff. The difference of the Anabaptists from other reforming groups in this matter is that the latter endorsed or accepted civil government involvement in internal church polity, while the former did not. Cf. Williams, *Radical Reformation*, pp. 236, 290; Littell, *Origins*, pp. 65ff. It is of further interest to note that Peter Ridemann, whose church was in some senses further removed from ordinary society than were the Mennonites, had a more purely negative view of civil government. Cf. His *Account*, pp. 102, 104f., 107, 206ff., 218, 220. At the same time, the Hutterites were developing a much fuller alternative lifestyle than were the Mennonites. The new lifestyle included significant changes in personal association, *Account*, pp. 98, 100, 130; in occupations, pp. 111, 126f.; customs, pp. 126, 134; and civil obligations, pp. 113, 115; and most importantly, in the introduction of the practice of group production and consumption of goods, pp. 88, 90, *et alibi*.

There seems an obvious relationship between the degree of negativism with which public life is judged and the degree to which the "withdrawing" religious community creates a full social alternative. The Mennonites, who evidenced no endemic desire to withdraw wholly from the society around them, also did not develop a full social model as alternative.

[51]Cf. CW 558ff. for a good example.

The Mennonites, like the Hutterites, Swiss Brethren, and other maturing Anabaptist groups, did not in fact pose any real threat to the "standing order" of things. Simons is correct in his belief that the turmoil occasioned by his movement was largely, if not wholly, due to the paranoid overreactions of rulers to unfamiliar patterns of Christian commitment. In principle, however, the threat was great. Simons often said that one should obey God in "divine things" and serve the emperor in "human things."[52] But the balance in this otherwise common-enough principle was shifted by Simons' negative standard for civil obedience: one should obey government only in those things which are not contrary to God's Word in the Bible.[53] And the Bible appeared to the Mennonites far more specific and extensive in its constitutive injunctions than it did to other Reformation groups. Moreover, if we see this negative principle in connection with the more basic one, i.e., that what the Bible does not explicitly enjoin is forbidden, then we can see the threat: the ultimate "political" loyalties of Mennonites were to the Kingdom of Christ, his Word and Spirit, and not to any civil authority. They were Christians first and citizens second. And *that* value orientation, unmodified, is subversive in the eyes of the state.

But to Simons it was a basic principle of Christian justice and order. The inherent conflict of these two orientations became sharply visible to Simons with the issue of whether a regenerate Christian could serve in public office. Students have noted ambiguities in the Mennonite position on the question. The ambiguities stem from the fact that although magistrates have as much right and surely as much need to become part of the community of the faithful, they must "use the sword" to exercise their office properly.[54]

Now Menno Simons could as little bear religious diversity as could any other committed Christian of the sixteenth century. Even though he constantly pleaded with authorities to at least tolerate his church, Simons never could accept diverstiy of belief within the Mennonite community. And had the Mennonites ever found themselves in a position of political control of a state or municipality, differences of belief would not have been permitted then either. The issue, however, is not one of relgious tolerance, much less religious freedom. It is rather how conformity of belief is to be accomplished. The state compels by threat and by force of arms if necessary. The church uses "friendly persuasion" and the ban and shunning if necessary.

Throughout his career Simons insisted that Christians never shall, and that magistrates ought not, resort to physical means of compulsion.[55] Simons' position has nothing whatever to do with the fact that his and other Anabaptist groups bore the first heavy onslaughts of religious terrorism.

[52]CW 119f., 203f., 309, 363.

[53]Cf. CW 83, 118f., 285, 518, 549, and 612 for examples of this negative principle.

[54]Williams, *Radical Reformation*, pp. 236, 275; Keeney, *Development*, pp. 129ff. It might be noted here that the Hutterites were not of two minds on this matter at all. One could simply not be a magistrate and a Christian. Cf. Ridemann, *Account*, pp. 102, 104f., 107, 113, 202ff., 214f., 218, 220. Cf. also the discussion in note 50, above.

[55]Cf. CW 94, 117ff., 175, 190ff., 347, 424, 464, 534f., 554ff., 586, 605, 610f., 920, 950f.

Nor should it really be called "pacifism." Simons' position is not a theory of political strategy, an "ism," and it is anything but passive. The question concerns means and motives.

The "sword of the Spirit," Simons always notes in his discussions of non-violence, is much sharper, more powerful, and more effective than the swords of men. Simons knew this from his experience of discipline within the church community. In fact the practice of the ban and shunning within the life of the church is systematically related to the practice of non-violent response in the face of persecution from the world. While for Luther power was the eminent attribute of God the Father, and was hence implied in the creation orders, for Simons power was the eminent attribute of God the Holy Spirit, and hence exercised only within and for the order of salvation, the church. On the difficult question of how the church is to relate to the world, therefore, the issue to Simons was not the just resolution of the claims of love and the use of power, as for Luther, but the effective resolution of the claims of love with the exercise of justice.

The preceding section suggested that Simons' policies expressed the view that justice was the expression of love within the church. The question we have been investigating in this section is the "right relationship," i.e., the question of justice, between the church and the world. In nearly all his discussions of non-violence Simons appeals to Christian love as the only motive for actions which are truly just. Only as that motive is expressed in act can one speak of a Christian ethics, a Christian justice, and a Christian faith. The grounds for the systematic relationship of internal Mennonite discipline and their practice of non-violent response to the outside are therefore clear. As justice is the expression of love within the church, so love is the expression of justice between the church and the world. And love lets life live.

But love as the expression of justice does much more than "let." It seeks, it nourishes, it wishes the best of all things for the beloved, and does everything it has to do in order to share its treasures, even to the extent of giving up its own life. The Mennonites understood their church to be the living presence of Christ, the embodiment of his love. Therefore like Christ they accomplished their mission by witnessing, even unto death.

Just as it is misleading to give the title "pacifism" to Simons' views on non-violent response, so it is misleading to describe his church as a "missionary" church. Some scholars have given great emphasis to the "missionary zeal" of the Anabaptists, tying this impulse closely to adult baptism and assigning it stature as a mark of the church.[56] Without denying the general sense in which this assessment is correct, a careful reading of the literature indicates that vigorously aggressive missionary activity was much more characteristic of the earliest "radical reformers" than of the maturer groups such as the Mennonites and Hutterites. Only rarely, for example,

---

[56]Cf. Williams, *Radical Reformation*, pp. 302ff., 428, 799, 836ff.; Littell, *Origins*, p. 112; Cornelius Krahn, *Dutch Anabaptism: Origin, Spread, Life and Thought 1450-1600* (The Hague: Martinus Nijhoff, 1968), p. 113.

does Simons speak of the mission obligation as we normally understand it: as the active going out by minister and people to convert the non-Christian and to serve his human needs in the name of Christ.[57] And even more rarely does he make explicit reference to the missionary command in Christ's institution of baptism.[58] Almost all his writing on baptism concerns its proper administration and its non-sacramental character. One might even suggest that the Mennonite rejection of infant baptism was a rejection of what to other Christians was an effective instrument for spreading the Gospel. In any case, for the Mennonites baptism was not an instrument of mission. It was a voluntary act signifying that conversion and regeneration of life had already taken place. Similarly with regard to the ban. As Gellius Faber criticized Simons in a passage noted earlier, the Mennonite use of the ban, from Faber's perspective at least, in fact hindered the work of extending the church. Simons did not reply effectively but could only fall back on the belief that the true church was always a tiny remnant in an evil world.[59] It is, however, just this re-emergent assertion of the separation of the church from the world that allows us a more accurate picture of how Simons understood the mission of his church.

For many reasons, some endemic to its view of the church and some due to the difficulties of public exposure in the sixteenth century, the active Mennonite mission was largely confined to the families of those within the community. Simons' most extensive discussion of "mission" in our normal sense of the term is in his late, small treatise *The Nurture of Children* of 1557 (CW 947-952). The burden of his unexceptional discussion is that, while Christian love constrains us to seek the salvation of all the lost, we ought to take a much more active and directly educational role in the spiritual development of those closest to us.

Outside the church and before the world such a direct and active mission is not possible. No "hearings" public or private were allowed by the authorities. And even Simons' appeals for such a hearing soon become appeals for the chance to defend and gain tolerance for his church, not to extend it. But then how, in such an hostile environment, is the proclamation of the Gospel to be made?

The answer was as simple as it was hard. Simons himself had been finally won to a regenerate Christian faith not by argument but by the witness unto death of the first Dutch Anabaptists (CW 668). As we heard Simons confess much earlier in our study: ". . . The Word of Christ remains and is the word of the cross; all who accept it in power and truth must be prepared for the cross. This both Scriptures and experience teach abundantly."

It was in the making of one's confession of faith, not only in words but more importantly in willingness to suffer and die, that Menno Simons and his church practiced the Christian mission. Suffering and martyrdom are

---

[57]CW 508, 559, 653, 736. This sense of mission is discussed by Simons almost exclusively when he is discussing the vocation of preachers.
[58]CW 120, 130, 682.
[59]CW 730ff.

sure signs of the living church. And one enters that church at baptism—a symbol much more often closely associated by Simons with martyrdom than with (our) sense of mission work.[60] No mature Mennonite actively sought martyrdom in order to accomplish his mission. The hostile world was more than happy to provide its own initiative to that end. The Mennonite mission was accomplished, but not via a simple, active programme of converting the heathen. Simons knew that it was the power of the Holy Spirit alone that worked regeneration among men, and not our efforts. And he knew that the Spirit in his freedom worked where and how he wished, regardless of our campaign plans. Scripture and experience testified that the Word of Christ was the way of the cross. And the cross becomes effective by luring men to the divine love manifest in that form. The Mennonite church tried to conform itself to the form of Christ's presence, his love. It thus accomplished its mission to the world by luring men to Christ with its willingness to suffer for its confession.

The church, after all, is supposed to be the light of the world. Had God been pleased to have that light shine in peace and in a world at least willing to look at that light, Simons' joy would have known no bounds. But instead the church had to function as a light in a brutal wilderness of suspicion and hatred, most of it expressed in the name of the Lord. In that situation hundreds of Anabaptists, embodying the love and living the example of their Lord, again proved that a light never shines so brightly as when it is extinguished. And thereby is the justice of Christ fully manifest.

******

The sharp distinction between the righteous church and the evil world was basic to many groups which in spite of other extreme diversities of opinion have been regarded as part of the "Radical Reformation." It is one thing, however, to make this sharp distinction in words and quite another to realize it in fact. The distinction is psychologically and socially easier to sustain in fact if the "withdrawing" group is willing and able to construct a reasonably complete positive alternative to the evil cultural life which they reject. What to an historian were the two most truly unique and noteworthy radical groups of the sixteenth century were able to do this. The Münsterites and the Hutterites, regardless of the great differences in their philosophies and fortunes, accomplished what each regarded as a roundly complete alternative life style.

The distinction is much more difficult to sustain, however, if a group regards "separation" as a largely if not wholly spiritual matter. The pressures of continued persecution and the lures of a relatively open, geographically removed cultural space in vast and underpopulated Russia and the Americas finally would lead later Mennonites to similar decisions. But the original Mennonites, if Simons' writings be any indication, did not wish to leave "this world." They loved it. They wanted to stay with it and in it to the extent the world permitted and (most importantly) to the extent a regenerate Christian life allowed. If one really loves something and knows

[60]CW 75, 109f., 236f., 741. Cf. Vincent Harding, "Menno Simons and the Role of Baptism in the Christian Life," *MQR* 33 (October 1959): 323-334.

that it is destroying itself, he does not abandon it, but rather tries his best to literally keep in touch so that he can have at least a chance to convert it. The first Mennonites did not wish to leave this world for another of their own making. They "hung in there" when and wherever they could so that their witness to the Gospel might find some ears, eyes, and hearts on the other side of the proclaimed Word. To the evil world the Hutterites were "out of sight, out of mind." The early Mennonites continued to function as neighbors wherever in good conscience they could. Therefore their mortality rate by execution was significantly higher than that of the brethren on a secluded estate in eastern Europe.

If desire to be with, in spite of great cost, is an indicator of love, then Menno Simons loved the world. In that respect he shared the passion of both Catholics and Lutherans. But unlike the latter groups, Simons and his church were not allowed. At least not allowed until a deeply committed religious faith became a matter of merely personal (i.e., irrelevant) idiosyncracy in later centuries. We let the "religious freaks" live now. Whether, considering our motives, that situation is a testimony to our increased spirituality or to our more sophisticated sinfulness, is a judgment each will have to make for himself.

Menno Simons apparently knew little if anything about, and so did not locate his own position relative to, the developing movement which would later be called "Hutterite." One of his early great burdens was to publicly dissociate his people from the Münsterites and associated radical extremists. And at last in this respect he was successful. A small victory! But he could not finally persuade his fellow citizens and neighbors that the Mennonites were no threat to public order and the religious establishment. The number of actual martyrdoms diminished. But for those who had only wished to live and work quietly with their families in northwestern Europe's cities, and who only wished to proclaim the Gospel to those who freely chose to look and listen, the suffering continued to be great. The Mennonites, like their Lord, had nowhere to lay their heads, and like the first Christians, could not appear in the light of day. The separation of the church and the world was a joint accomplishment. The evil world in fact forced the Mennonites out, and the Mennonites withdrew from its evil. That separation was a theoretically just one to Simons. The anguish was caused because the "powers and principalities" of the world enforced the separation so unjustly and cruelly.

But instead of abandoning the places of men, the Mennonites tried their best to stay in touch by responding to the situation out of the power of the Holy Spirit they felt working in their midst. Unable to persuade others that physical coercion in religious matters was not Christ-like, they simply refused to be a part of it themselves; and as reward for their pleas for a just toleration, they endured unjust persecution. Wishing only to live and to bring others to life in Christ, they responded to the world's hatred by their willingness to die if need be. In these ways the Mennonites tried to demonstrate to the world that the righteousness or justice of God is perfected in self-giving love. The Mennonites, as Simons wrote time and again, sought to be one with Christ, conformed not only in Word, but more importantly in life, in love, and in Spirit.

And for this desire, the Mennonites believed, they had become Isaiah's suffering servant: men despised and rejected, men of sorrows and acquainted with grief; oppressed and afflicted, yet opening not their mouth. They had become, referring again to the passage quoted near the beginning of the second section, a glorious people after having been no people. Only in their suffering did the Mennonites find some grounds for association with the earlier, more eschatologically-minded Anabaptist groups. What sustained each spiritually was the promise the scripture attached to the suffering of the servant: ". . . he shall see his offspring, he shall prolong his days; the will of the Lord shall prosper in his hand; he shall see the fruit of the travail of his soul and be satisfied." (Is. 53 RSV) Simons risked using a transformed version of the symbol long associated with the radical movements he so hated: the sign of Tau. The regenerate people have

> . . . received the sign TAU in their foreheads by which the servants of God are marked. These are the spiritual bride of Christ, His holy church, his spiritual body, flesh of his flesh, and bone of His bone. These have come to the heavenly Jerusalem, the city of the living God, which came down from heaven. These have come to an innumerable company of angels, to the assembly of the church of the first-born which are written in heaven, and to Jesus the Mediator of the new covenant. They are fellow citizens in the household of God. These have put off the corruptible garment and have put on the incorruptible; have acknowledged the name of God and keep His commandments and the faith in Jesus; the true sheep of Christ, who hear His voice alone, knowing no other; the first fruits of His creatures who have the Spirit and quality of Christ. Therefore they know what the will of the Lord is, yes, the chosen generation, the spiritual and royal priesthood, a holy nation, a peculiar people, who in times past were not a people, but are now the people of God, for God had compassion on them. They are the souls of the slain for the Word of God beneath the altar.
>
> In short, with these people old things have passed away; behold, all things are become new; this is all of God who has reconciled us unto Himself through Jesus Christ. These are they who stand before the throne of God with palms in their hands, clothed in white, saying, Blessing and glory and wisdom and thanksgiving and honor and power and might be unto our God forever and ever. Amen. (CW59f.)

PART THREE

Introduction: The Shaking of the Foundations

The Prologue made a preliminary assessment of the various problems of data selection and interpretive procedure presented to us by Luther, Simons, and Calvin. Compared to Luther's diffuse corpus, the works of Simons and Calvin, each containing a *magnum opus* which they and we could use as a touchstone, considerably simplified the task of data collection. Regarding interpretive matters, Luther's kaleidoscopic riot of language and Simons' endlessly turgid, non-technical commonplaces made evaluation very difficult. Calvin by contrast appeared "luxurious." The *Institutes* offers us a text of spare, very carefully defined and qualified language. Its author was extremely conscious of his placement, word choice, and phrasing. He was well aware of his place in the tradition, and he was very concerned to give his readers a clear, basic teaching instrument whereby the scripture might be meditated upon more profitably. And if Calvin's superb Latin here and there could not completely satisfy a scholar's mind concerning some nuance of the reformer's meaning, a companion French version probably could. Calvin wrote and re-wrote the *Institutes* for a quarter of a century, expanding its contents, adjusting its argument, re-arranging its shape until with the radically revised version of 1559, Calvin pronounced his work satisfactorily completed.

Given all these circumstances, and knowing Calvin's instinct for and training in the classical disciplines conducive to clear thought, organization, and expression, the historical theologian with a topic in systematic theology to pursue naturally feels he will be relatively at ease in Calvin, whether or not he shares the reformer's views. On any particular subject, moreover, Calvin does offer a cogent discussion and development of his position.

But when the student stands back and tries to conceptualize the overall pattern, the relation of the relations, he finds it extremely difficult. There is the *Institutes*, the second bible of the Reformation, not appearing now as the magnificent cathedral of religious thought he assumed it to be, but rather lying there like a monument broken into great pieces by earthquake. Huge chunks of constructive teaching lie amid the rubble of polemics. Foundational doctrines belonging together are here widely separated. Later things are treated sooner and without preparation. One sees where a great fault line had ruptured, evidence of the irresolvable tension in Calvin between the doctrines of God the Creator and God the Redeemer. That line is the only overall pattern there is. It shows us, however, not the unity of Calvin's work, but how and possibly why it broke. For generations scholars have tried to locate the quake's epicenter: God's glory? sovereignty? election? Christian wisdom? piety? Christ? the Holy Spirit? It has not been found yet. Calvin's numerous attempts in the *Institutes* to tell us what he is going to do next usually do not succeed, for he seldom tells us why. The *Institutes* is not one organically conceived and executed book. It is many books, or rather a series of monographs on individual subjects, edited together by a man whose logic appears to many students as unremarkable as the grave in which its author is buried.

A brief consideration of the table of contents of the 1559 *Institutes* may reveal some of the difficulties. The four parts appear to follow in general the order of the Apostles' Creed (I Father, II Son, III Holy Spirit, IV Church), although even on such a simple level of generalization seasoned scholars have come to opposite conclusions.[1] Calvin's famous opening thesis, that knowledge of God depends upon knowledge of man, and vice versa, might lead the reader to expect a consistently maintained dialectical approach comparable to that of Luther. But then the closing line of Chapter 1, that "the order of right teaching requires" beginning with knowledge of God, removes our expectancy without any real explanation for the decision.

It seems of heuristic value to suppose that Calvin ultimately decided to subordinate the dialectical approach (God/man, or perhaps even God the Creator/God the Redeemer) to a more functionally trinitarian approach (creation-soteriology-ecclesiology). But then he perhaps became aware that this historical order of things might suggest a) a sequential change in God's relation to man; b) too close a divine involvement in the world; c) hints of a Sabellian or modalist heresy vis-à-vis the Trinity; and d) consequently a great pressure on the doctrine of divine unity. To counter this, Calvin would have then decided so to apportion his subtopics that the placement and partial development of each, within one of his three major sections, would require continual reference to a supplementary discussion in one or both of the other sections. If such a decision be the case, it worked out reasonably well in some instances, and badly in others. Some illustrations may clarify the point.

This hypothesized integration of the dialectical (God/man) and trinitarian patterns suggested would appear most successful in Calvin's treatment of anthropology. One can see I, 3-5 and 14-15 as concerning man in his natural state (the Creator is the referent); II, 1-5 concerning man as fallen (the Redeemer is the referent); and perhaps II, 2-20 concerning the life of redeemed man (the Sanctifier is the referent).

---

[1] Cf. François Wendel, *Calvin: The Origins and Development of His Religious Thought*, trans. Philip Mairet (New York: Harper & Row, 1963), p. 120f.; John T. McNeill, *The History and Character of Calvinism*, (New York: Oxford University Press, 1954), p. 128; Paul Jacobs, *Prädestination und Verantwortlichkeit bei Calvin*, (Neukirchen: Buchhandlung des Erziehungsvereins, 1937), p. 73. The division of the creed into four articles, as suggested in the text, is based upon Calvin's 1541 French catechism, q. 18. Jacobs' organization (I Trinity II-III soteriology IV ecclesiology) is much more in line with the general theoretical pattern of this study, and is the one I shall follow in organizing the subject matter of these chapters. All references to and quotations from Calvin's *Institutes of the Christian Religion* below are from the Library of Christian Classics edition, and follow the standard notation of Book, Chapter, and Section, e.g., "I,13.2." References to the commentaries are based on the CR volumes, English translations, and will be noted by title, verse number, and page number.

The placement of individual doctrines is in part felicitous. Calvin's discussion of faith and justification under the aegis of the work of the Holy Spirit (III, 2-18) demands intimate consideration of the work of Christ in Bk. II, while his placement of the doctrine of election in Bk. III similarly demands consideration of God the Creator in Bk. I. The consideration of the need for Christ (II, 6) before consideration of the law and its effects (II, 7-8) drives us back to the truth that it is only with Christ (Bk. II) that God's will can be known (Bk. I); while the consideration of law and Gospel in the Bible (II, 9-11) requires us to ponder the interior work of the Holy Spirit (Bk. III). Similarly the introduction of the Trinity in Bk. I drives us to Christ (Bk. II) for understanding, and that of scriptural certification (I, 6-12) to the Holy Spirit in Bk. III.

And yet these decisions also make for great confusion, backtracking, repetitions, false starts, and surprises. Though God and man must be considered together (I,1), the essential discussion of man is put off until Book II. Though the Trinity cannnot be understood apart from the revelation of Christ and the Holy Spirit, the doctrine is "wholly summed up" in Book I. And although Calvin's epistemology assumes the interior witness of the Holy Spirit, the teachings about the validity of the scripture come in Book I and Book II, in the former case prior even to discussion of the revelation in Christ. In many cases, moreover, Calvin either leads us into a subject, only to put it off until later (cf. I, 13.9 and 24, on redemption; II, 1.10 on election), or returns to a subject considered earlier (cf. II, 3.3).

Finally and perhaps most seriously. The tensions between the doctrine of God and the doctrine of Christ first cause Calvin to oscillate concerning the grounds or foundation of such important matters as the doctrine of divine election (cf. III, 21.7 and 23.11).[2] And then in the final, radically revised edition, he widely separated closely related doctrines which had been considered together in earlier editions. The final placement of the doctrines of election and providence[3] is the famous example of the tension broken, while the separation of the doctrines of civil government (IV, 20) and Christian freedom-in-order (II, 19) appears as a secondary aftershock.

We shall consider all these issues more fully later. But one must wonder, at least from the point of view of systematic theology, whether Calvin's final massive revision of the *Institutes* was not rather a mutilation than an improvement of earlier editions.[4] To make such a negative judgment, however, would be to hold Calvin to our canons of systematic writing, when in fact Calvin may not have intended a treatise in systematic theology at all! He called it not a *summa theologiae* but a *summa pietatis*, we must remember.

[2]The tensions between these two subjects, always the classical tension in systematic theology, are discussed in reference to Calvin by, among others, H. Richard Niebuhr, *Christ and Culture* (New York: Harper & Row, 1951), pp. 191ff.; Paul Tillich, *Systematic Theology*, I (Chicago: University of Chicago Press, 1951), p. 228; and Wendel, pp. 229ff.

[3]Cf. Wendel, pp. 178, 264ff.; Jacobs, pp. 57ff.

[4]John T. McNeill, in his introduction to the LCC edition of the *Institutes*, notes this viewpoint, p. xxxvii, but does not share it himself, p. 1f.; but cf. the same author's comments in McNeill, *History and Character of Calvinism*, pp. 201f.

Perhaps it is as a work of piety[5] that we must evaluate the *Institutes*. If so, then the overall disjointed appearance of the work indicates not the failure of systematic thought but rather the successfully maintained and communicated sense that God in his glory and transcendence is infinitely beyond our meager attempts to conceive him. As the twentieth-century Calvin, Karl Barth, put it, "we must speak of God, and we cannot." It is a great temptation for the systematic theologian to require, in effect, God and the things of God to be bound by the requirements of the theologian's logic. But Calvin knew that a god so bound is not God but an idol of man's own making. The *Institutes* represent the convictions of a man who could not and would not allow that to happen. If therefore Calvin's teachings in the *Institutes* seem ultimately not to cohere, perhaps we should take that as a lesson in humility. God's truth is not to be sought in our systems but in the mystery of his Holy Trinity, which surpasses all understanding.

At lower levels of generalization, however, the *Institutes* does offer us a consistently maintained pattern throughout many teachings. In particular it was not so difficult as one might have thought to arrive at a cogent order for presenting the thesis we have been developing in this text. The general themes of Chapters 6 and 7 are, respectively, knowledge of God and knowledge of man. Thereby the terms of Calvin's dialectic are preserved. The interpretive arrangement, however, is trinitarian in form. The first two sections of Chapter 6 concern the Trinity in relative independence of God's relationship to the world, i.e., apart from God's will as made known through Christ and certified in the heart by the Holy Spirit. We shall consider God the Father as love, as seen through his creative and providential order, and examine the functions of the Son and Holy Spirit, and the trinitarian tensions, from this basis. The last section of Chapter 6 and the first of Chapter 7 concern the true knowledge of God (Ch. 6) and man (Ch. 7) as it is made known in Christ, who is the justice or righteousness of God. We shall consider Christ as the definer of the church, therefore, both on its transcendental side as seen in the doctrine of election and on its immanent side as seen in the doctrine of sanctification. The last two sections of Chapter 7 will concern the effectuating work of the Holy Spirit of power by which the individual Christian lives in prayer and perseverance, by which the church grows and realizes in itself God's will for it, and by which it becomes increasingly transformed into a living image of God.

This basic trinitarian pattern, construing an equally basic dialectical pattern, seems to reflect Calvin's format in the *Institutes*. At least it works reasonably well within the confines of our thesis. As noted in the Prologue, Calvin is the most difficult among the men we are studying to distinguish cleanly. This is due to many reasons, among them his own character and his place in Reformation history. But if we cannot finally grasp him, there may be some consolation in knowing that such a circumstance would not be unpleasing to Calvin. "After all," he would say to us his students, "it is not to me or to 'this little handbook' that you must look for Christian wisdom. *Soli deo gloria.*"

[5] A. M. Hunter, *The Teaching of Calvin* (London: James Clarke and Co., Ltd., 1950), p. 296.

CHAPTER SIX

Calvin: Neither Confusion Nor Separation

Like Luther and Simons, Calvin abhorred the charge of "novelty" of teaching, and like Luther he went to some effort to demonstrate his orthodoxy regarding such "received" dogmas as the Trinity. But unlike Luther—though perhaps with less justification—Calvin from virtually the time of the first edition of the *Institutes* in 1536 until his death was attacked directly or indirectly on his trinitarian language. In 1537 came the charge by Pierre Caroli, based upon what in retrospect might be seen as inadequacies in the 1536 edition, that Calvin was Arian. Then there were the continual distractions, from 1531 on, by that gadfly Michael Servetus, culminating with his *Christianismi Restitutio* and his execution by the Geneva authorities in 1553. And finally came the attacks by Valentine Gentile in 1558, which achieved by their timing an historic if unmerited effect because of Calvin's reaction in the final edition.

These experiences are reflected in Calvin's work in at least two ways. First, Calvin's trinitarian language in subsequent editions of the *Institutes* becomes both more carefuly qualified and more traditional. It would thus be particularly fruitless to seek important differentiating features of Calvin's trinitarian thought in his formal considerations of the nature and persons of the Trinity. Secondly, the initial experience with Caroli may have reinforced what was clearly Calvin's instinctive tendency to emphasize the unity of God. This emphasis has effects in Calvin's theology as a whole and also qualifies our approach to the meaning and functions of his trinitarian ascriptive pattern. A brief consideration of Calvin's formal treatment of official trinitarian doctrine in I, 13 will provide an introduction to these matters.

Calvin's trinitarian exercise is placed exquisitely for the orthodox Christian—but scandalously for the Jew and especially the Muslim. For Chapter 13 is bounded fore and aft by a discussion of the corrupted natural tendency to idolatry and polytheism (Ch. 12) and the knowledge of the one true God which, via God's revelation in scripture, nature provided (Ch. 14).[1] Following his introductory discussion (13.1-6), Calvin takes as his major burden the task of defending the full divinity (and therefore the identity with God the Father) of the Second and Third Persons of the Trinity (7-15). Three things might be noted in this discussion.

The doctrine of the full deity of the Holy Spirit (14-15) is relatively underdeveloped compared to that of the Son (7-13). While the main counter-assertion to Servetus' teachings was that the Second Person existed in a fully trinitarian manner prior to creation, we initially miss in Calvin a similar assertion with respect to the Holy Spirit, whose deity (not eternity)

---

[1] Cf. also the opening sentence to 13.2, where Calvin, without subsequent explanation, introduces the Trinity of persons precisely in order to distinguish the true god from idols.

is proved only functionally. Only later, and framing a description of the Holy Spirit as the bond of the Father and the Son (19; cf. 23), do we get a couple of explicit, non-deductive statements about the Spirit's eternality in God (18; 25; cf. 22). This situation again reflects the "afterthought" character of the doctrine of the Holy Spirit, common in the tradition and among the reformers we are studying except for Menno Simons and his brethren.

Secondly, throughout the text Calvin is very conscious that his discussion of the Trinity is epistemologically if not methodologically premature, for the discussion occurs prior to his treatment of God's revelation in the scripture, hence prior to that of knowledge of God the Redeemer. Section 9, for example, begins:

> Further, I do not yet touch upon the person of the Mediator, but postpone it until we reach the treatment of redemption. Despite this, because it ought to be agreed among all that Christ is that Word endued with flesh, the testimonies affirming Christ's deity are suitably included here.[2]

Here we see one evidence of the unresolved tension in Calvin—perhaps it is unresolvable in Christian thought—between the doctrines of creation and redemption. This tension is perhaps made sharper in Calvin by his stress on the unity of the transcendent God. The effects of this stress would then appear most consequentially in Calvin's unmistakable emphasis on the distinction of natures in Christ.

Thirdly, Calvin's arguments for the deity of the Son and Holy Spirit appeal primarily to their exhibited works or powers (9-15)—"power" being "the characteristic mark of the one God" (9). In this respect Calvin is exhibiting the important rule followed in nearly all Reformation theology, i.e., that proper evangelical theology concerns itself with God only *pro nobis*, only as God acts with regard to his world and his people (21).

This characteristic of Calvin, moreover, forces sharp qualifications upon the results of our study. While throughout the text Calvin has tended to emphasize the unity of God, he also clearly indicates something like an order of subordination among the persons of the Trinity (cf. 18 and 25). The fact that this order of subordination is most amply defended by appeal to Christ as mediator (26) suggests that for Calvin these subordinations exist not in God in himself, but only as he acts *pro nobis* and appears to our consciousness.

It is difficult to assess the importance of Calvin's distinction here. Were such a distinction systematically operative more or less throughout Calvin's theology, what then would be his postion relative to the dictum that God relates *ad extra* as one, a dictum that Calvin, in his stress on divine unity, otherwise seems to appreciate? Would we then have at least a partial ex-

---

[2]Cf. further indications of Calvin's awareness of this difficulty elsewhere in sec. 9 and in secs. 22-24.

planation for the apparent brokenness of themes in the *Institutes*? And would we have discovered in Calvin a dialectically opposite approach to theology from that of Luther, who in his own christological emphasis insisted on the unity of relations *ad extra*, and who, perhaps in consequence, at least appeared to speak of God *in se* in a dualistic way?

These and other speculative questions tantalize us as we enter our study. While the thematic limits of this study prevent us from assaying these questions, the circumstances giving rise to the intrigues do qualify our study in the following ways. On the one hand Calvin's distinction gives us confidence with respect to the legitimacy of making real discriminations in his trinitarian ascriptive pattern. On the other hand we must be constantly aware of the dangers of overstating the distinctions, and especially be aware that while according to Calvin such discriminations do exist, they exist only with respect to our understanding. But as mutually exclusive or even supplementary distinctions, they do not exist at all. Were we not to keep this limitation of thought because of an undue zeal for the distinctiveness of the persons, we would fall into just that corruption which Calvin discussed by way of prefacing and concluding his discussion of the Trinity: idolatry.

Calvin concludes Chapter 13: "Finally, I trust that the whole sum of this doctrine has been faithfully explained, if my readers will impose a limit upon their curiosity, and not seek out for themselves more eagerly than is proper troublesome and perplexed disputations."

Calvin's "trust" is, of course, either merely rhetorical, or based upon things comprehended only by himself, or upon things *not* comprehended by him, but rather accepted in faith and piety. In any case the "whole sum" of the teaching is far from tallied. There have been many eagerly curious.

A. *Calvin's Trinitarian Ascriptions*

One of Calvin's most famous similes compared the scripture to spectacles. As spectacles assist the weak-eyed to read a beautiful volume, so the scripture assists our dull minds to read the creation and thereby gain a clearer knowledge of the true God, the Creator—a knowledge distinguishing God's elect from unbelievers. The "spectacles" are really bifocals. For the knowledge of God which the Word provided even the patriarchs, and perforce ourselves, is a twofold knowledge.

> First in order came that kind of knowledge by which one is permitted to grasp *who* that God is who founded and governs the universe. Then that other *inner* knowledge was added, which alone quickens dead souls, whereby God is known not only as the Founder of the universe and the sole Author and Ruler of all that is make, but also *in the person* of the Mediator and Redeemer.[3]

[3] I,6.1, emphasis mine.

One should note that the difference is not that without scriptural aid natural man fails to see any god at all. Calvin's introductory chapters have established the inescapability and corruptibility of that knowledge. It is rather that, "first in order," the scripture reveals who the Creator is, and then (second in order?) "adds" the saving inner knowledge of God in the person of the Redeemer.

Immediately many problems arise with Calvin's assertions and with his continuation in this section. The problem of sequence is first. Calvin's argument for the necessity of scripture for knowledge of God is precisely the fallenness of man and the corruption of his natural knowledge (Chs. 3-5). Yet he postpones consideration of the "inner" knowledge of God because he has not yet treated the matter of the fall. And then he tells us he will make frequent reference to Christ anyway—these references, nevertheless, pointing the the Creator.[4]

Secondly, is the knowledge of who God is merely an "outer" knowledge compared to that of Christ, which is an inner knowledge "alone" quickening the soul? And what does Calvin mean by "first in order"? There cannot be knowledge of God, Calvin asserted in the opening lines of the *Institutes*, without at the same time knowledge of man—and that means knowledge of Christ. And yet he formally began with knowledge of God, giving no more adequate explanation for his decision than that "the order of right teaching" required it.[5]

As we shall see, Calvin occasionally does appeal to at least epistemological "degrees of distance," so to speak, between God and man. God *in se* is most remote, God the sanctifying Spirit most intimate, God the Redeemer spanning the terms. Perhaps the Trinity in this epistemological sense is already in Calvin's mind as he begins his treatment of the knowledge of God. For in the above quotation he does appear to differentiate the twofold knowledge in terms of "person." It is only in the person of the mediator that the inner, soul-quickening knowledge of God is available to us. Yet as Calvin indicates later[6] (fully in accord with Luther's rule), the scripture describes God's attributes not as they exist in Him, but as he is or acts toward us. And that means, presumably, as he is revealed to us in Christ.

We are following Calvin's "order of right teaching." But our introductory assessment, for all its unanswered questions, at least clearly indicates a strong tension in Calvin between the doctrines of God the Creator and God the Redeemer. The former doctrine is more epistemologically remote, but must come first. Calvin compensated by making continual reference to Christ the Mediator, and by asserting that apart from knowledge of Christ even scriptural knowledge of God the Creator is an "outer" and unvivifying knowledge. The doctrine of the Trinity is placed in the first book of the *Institutes*, not in the second or third. And therefore the discussion of the Trinity in our first two sections must be as provisional as is that of Calvin.

[4]Ibid.
[5]I,1.3.
[6]I,10.2.

1. CALVIN'S INFORMAL trinitarian usages are as variable and unsystematic as those of Luther. He is aware of and can use the more-or-less Augustinian trinity of human faculties for his anthropology. But at the same time Calvin explicitly rejects this usage when it is applied to the matter of the supposed image of God in man.[7] Sometimes he will apply a trinitarian analysis in connection with such matters as the chief Christian virtues, the sacraments, the superiority of scriptural knowledge of God, the functions of angels, or the value of prayer.[8] And scattered throughout the text are a variety of otherwise undeveloped trinitarian ascriptions to "God" of "wisdom, power, and goodness." Occasionally one of these terms is omitted or is replaced by another (e.g., "glory" for "power" and "mercy" for "goodness"). Other terms are added, or one is defined by another.[9] Now this variability of usage is not remarkable, excepting perhaps Calvin's habit of differentiating God's "wisdom" from his "judgment" or "righteousness"—a distinction one might take as reflective of the tensions between the doctrines of creation and redemption.

Occasionally, however, Calvin's usages appear to be more formal and functional. We have for example a highly developed trinitarian pattern of analysis in an important early assertion of Calvin's concerning the need for descent into ourselves in order to properly comprehend God's power.[10] The most important example, because of its placement and application, occurs in I,2.1. We have a double trinitarian pattern. Knowledge of the One God is insufficient unless we see him as the one source of all good. This means the good of the world, which God sustains by his power, regulates by his wisdom, and preserves by his goodness. And it means the good of mankind, which God rules by his righteousness and judgment,[11] bears with by his mercy, and watches over by his protection. Only from this sense of God's powers can there issue true piety, and hence true religion.

In Calvin's formal discussion of the doctrine of the Trinity we have a clear and definitive statement of the particular functions he assigns to the various persons. Calvin begins with a note on his linguistic pattern which tends to support our emphasis on the reality of the distinctions of association even when only "God," and not the trinity of persons, is named in his text.[12] Sections 7-15 of Chapter 13 assert the divinity of the Son and Spirit, the argument appealing in good evangelical fashion to the saving work of the Son and Spirit in us. For our purposes the definitive material comes in sections 16-20, where Calvin very carefully defines the distinctions among

[7]I,5.3; 15.3f., 15.6; 15.8; 16.1. Calvin can also use Aristotle's "four causes" schema to suggest the Trinity; cf. III, 14.17.

[8]III,2.41-43; 20.37; 1.1; IV,14.8; 14.22; 15.1; 15.6; I,8.1; 14.11.

[9]Cf. for the following list I,2.1; 4.2; 5.8; 6.3; 14.1; 14.21; 15.1; III,2,26; 8.11; 20.2.

[10]I,5.10. We see the I) a)chief purpose, b)value, and c)reason for pondering God's powers only when by descent into ourselves we contemplate by what means God II) shows us his a)love, b)wisdom, and c)power, and III) exercises in our behalf his a)righteousness, b)goodness, and c)mercy.

[11]Note again the distinction within the "form" ascription mentioned earlier.

[12]I,13.6. Calvin, of course, claims that the trinitarian implication of the term "God" is also biblical.

and the unity of the three persons. Calvin begins and ends this treatment with a stress on the divine unity—a stress continued in the following sections on heresies. Cautiously introducing the biblical testimonies to the real distinctions among the persons (17), Calvin proceeds in section 18 to his position. Amid great fear and trembling he admits that "it is not fitting to suppress the distinction that we observe to be expressed in Scripture. . . ." Calvin's piety and obedience are obviously put to a severe test here! The distinction is this: ". . . To the Father is attributed the beginning of activity, and the fountain and wellspring of all things; to the Son, wisdom, counsel, and the well-ordered disposition of all things; but to the Spirit is assigned the power and efficacy of that activity."[13]

Besides the biblical warrant, Calvin ventures that the distinctions are "not meaningless" from a natural human point of view even though connotations of a temporal distinction must be suppressed. The mind is inclined to observe this "order" of presentation of the persons and their distinct functions (18), although sometimes the fathers appeared to differ over it (19). In section 20 Calvin asserts that this is a "reasoned order" which is rooted not merely in the human mind and asserted by scripture (18) but also in the peculiar qualities of the persons themselves.

Clearly observing his own insistence that the real distinctions among the persons can in no way gainsay the unity of God, Calvin throughout the text frequently assigns all the concepts love, power, and justice, or their cognates, to each person of the Trinity. Yet we may rest confident with the formal distinctions provided in I,13.18. In addition Calvin's discussion of the "order" of these functional or economic distinctions provides us perhaps the closest explanation we are likely to get to the question of Calvin's general ordering of subjects in the *Institutes*.

Before continuing to fill in Calvin's ascriptive pattern in more detail, it might be useful to illustrate how Calvin applies a more or less fully trinitarian description, with both the persons and associated functions named, to major subjects in his theology. We would thereby have more persuasive evidence of the importance of trinitarian thought for Calvin's christology, ecclesiology, and ethics than has been introduced so far.

Occasionally Calvin describes the creation and governing of the spiritual realm, the church, in explicitly trinitarian terms.[14] On the relation of God to Christ, and Christ to us, Calvin can exhibit a trinitarian pattern which even includes the "reasoned order" and the epistemological "degrees of distance" referred to above. In his comment on John 14.10, for example, Calvin says:

> . . . For Christ, so far as regards his hidden divinity, is not better known to us than the Father. But he is said to be the lively image, or Portrait, of God, because in him God has

---

[13] Werner Krusche, *Das Wirken des Heiligen Geistes nach Calvin*, (Göttingen: Vandenhoeck & Ruprecht, 1957), pp. 8ff.

[14] *Commentary on John* 16:14, p. 145; and 20:17, p. 259.

fully revealed himself, so far as God's infinite goodness, wisdom, and power are clearly manifested in him.[15]

This view of the epistemological priority of Christ is further illustrated in his comment on John 6:57:

> For though the Father is the beginning of life, yet the eternal Word himself is strictly life. . . . It must be observed, however, that he [Christ] points out here three degrees of life. In the first rank is the living Father, who is the source, but remote and hidden. Next follows the Son, who is exhibited to us as an open fountain, and by whom life flows to us. The third is the life which we draw from him [the Holy Spirit?]. We now perceive what is stated to amount to this, that God the Father, in whom life dwells, is at a great distance from us, and that Christ, placed between us, is the second cause of life, in order that what would otherwise be concealed in God may proceed from him to us.[16]

It is in the *Institutes*, however, that the trinitarian patterns in Calvin are utilized most fully and explicitly. Let me quote but two examples, important because they concern matters central to our thesis: the church, and Christian life in faith.

Calvin begins his presentation of the creedal definition of the church as "the communion of saints" by noting that our security in the church rests upon a) God's election, b) the steadfastness of Christ, and c) the promise of God's powerful participation in the church. He then notes that, nevertheless, the church so understood is not visible, but must be grasped by faith.

> For here we are not bidden to distinguish between reprobate and elect—that is for God alone, not for us, to do—but to establish with certainty in our hearts that all those who, by the kindness of God the Father, through the working of the Holy Spirit, have entered into fellowship with Christ, are set apart as God's property and personal possession; and that when we are of their number we share that great grace.[17]

---

[15] *Com. on John* 14:10, p. 87; cf. also *Institutes* IV,8.5.
[16] *Com. on John* 6:57, p. 269; cf. *Com. on Romans* 8:9, p. 290f.
[17] IV,1.3.

And what is the faith which sees the church this way? Calvin begins his definition in III,2.6 by describing faith as a "knowledge of God's will toward us, perceived from his Word. But the foundation of this is a preconceived conviction of God's truth." Yet Calvin is not satisfied with this. He opines that if "God's will" be understood rather in terms of "God's benevolence or his mercy," a closer definition of faith emerges. He is then able to close the section with a fully rounded trinitarian definition.

> Now we shall possess a right definition of faith if we call it a firm and certain knowledge of God's benevolence toward us, founded upon the truth of the freely given promise in Christ, both revealed to our minds and sealed upon our hearts through the Holy Spirit.

2. AMONG THE REASONS for the selection of the above quotations is the fact that Calvin in his formal definition of trinitarian distinctions at I,13.18 did not explicitly associate love with the Father, but instead ascribed to him the "beginning of activity." The above quotations, however, illustrate Calvin's attribution of love to the Father at key points in his theology. This subsection will elaborate on this association.

Throughout the *Institutes* Calvin goes to great lengths to stress that it is God's love, mercy, benevolence, or goodness that basically defines his relationship to the world.[18] While both Luther and Calvin assert that it is only in Christ that God's love to us is clearly seen, Luther's stress on God as power resulted in a more balanced presentation of God's wrath in relation to God's love than is seen in Calvin. Calvin asserts that God's wrath really falls only on the reprobate, and that the scripture commands believers to meditate upon it only in order to become aware of their sinfulness and the value of Christ's work. When Christians experience suffering at the hand of God, they are to take this not as the wrath of a judge but rather as the strong chastisement of a loving father.[19] The primary result of the difference of ascriptive pattern can be seen in the descriptions by the two men of Christ's atonement. While Luther, especially in the famous passages in the Galatians commentary, stresses God's powerful wrath unleashing itself impersonally against Christ on the cross, Calvin's introductory treatment of the atonement in II,16.2ff. is devoid of that application. Instead Calvin's stress on God's personal love for us in the atonement is more intense than almost anywhere else in the *Institutes*.

---

[18]While there are differences of nuance among these terms, they are not important for our purposes. Cf. note 61 to II,8.14 of the LCC edition.

[19]Cf. II,16.2; III,4.31ff. For other references to God's wrath, cf. II,1.8; 8.4; 10.19; III,11.2; IV,12.17; 20.4; 20.25ff., and *Sermons on Deuteronomy* 5:8-10, p. 269.

Only after this emphasis has been made can Calvin describe the sufferings of Christ (16.5-7). And only once in these sections does Calvin come close to saying explicitly that it is God who is attacking Christ on the cross.[20]

Calvin begins the *Institutes* by asserting that the only reason for the creation and preservation of the world is God's goodness. The very order of the creation is a testimony to God's love.[21] It is in fact by considering God's preservation of the world that his love is most clearly seen. Calvin's order of presentation expresses this beautifully. For the chapters on the creation of the world (14) and the creation of man (15) are followed immediately by the chapter on providence (16). Without considering God's providence we cannot properly grasp what creation means. Were we to consider the order of the world to reflect merely a supposed natural and connotatively impartial operation of things, no room would be left for considering God's favor to man.[22] We must instead meditate upon God's ceaseless, immediate, all-inclusive, wholly active providential care, i.e., his goodness. Then we can see that the world and its workings are not impartial. We see that God in his love creates and maintains the world for the sake of man, and especially for the sake of his elect.[23] The blessings from God's providential care for his church of course flow over into the world at large, which therefore can enjoy justice, equity, and civil order from God's particular concern with his own.[24] The knowledge that the world is personally ordered for the elect is a great source of comfort. This knowledge is especially effective in times of adversity, for properly evaluating God's wrath, as we have seen. But this knowledge also lays upon Christians a great responsibility for the world, as Calvin indicates in I,17.3-5. The theme of the responsibilities of Christian love for the world in response to God's loving gift of the world to Christians will be a theme of our ethical considerations in the next chapter. But we might say here in anticipation that since according to Calvin the ultimate goal of life is to be loved by God, then we, constantly meditating upon God's created gifts of love to us, ought to be moved to love him, and in him one another and the world, in return.[25]

God's creative love is understood only if God's providential love is appreciated. And God's providential love is fully appreciated only if God's elective love is experienced, according to Calvin.[26]*

[20] II,16.6: "The Father destroyed the force of sin when the curse of sin was transferred [note the passive voice] to Christ's flesh."

[21] I,5.6; 14.2. In fact, all of Chapter 14.

[22] I,16.1; 16.5.

[23] I,14,2; 14.22; 16.6; 17.1; 17.6; *Com. on Romans* 11:2, p. 411f.

[24] I,17.2; III,14.2; IV,20.4; 20.8; 20.15.

[25] I,14.22; II,1.4; 2.18; III,7.6; cf. q. 218 of the 1541 French Catechism.

[26] I do not wish at this point to enter into the discussion of the general systematic relationships between the doctrines of providence and election in Calvin. The suggestion here is that, regarding knowledge of God and his works, the doctrine of election functions epistemologically to disclose the interior meaning of the doctrine of providence. As the continuation in the text will indicate, however, election by itself is not a sufficient ground for this knowledge.

In other contexts, the relationship of these doctrines will appear reversed. Thus, for example, when the responsibilities which knowledge of election places upon the Christian become

Both the centrality of Christ to God's over-all plan for mankind and the interior effects of Christ's work in those whom he has elected are themes developed by Calvin in terms of God's love. God's election of Israel—a relationship which Calvin, here very comfortable with biblical usage, always describes in terms of a marriage covenant—is motivated solely by God's love.[27] Our election, like that of Israel, is election in Christ and is rooted in the love God knew for his own before the creation.[28] It is only because of God's love, moreover, that his promises are extended to us. And it is God's love alone which is the reason our works are acceptable in his sight. The faith which grasps this knowledge is itself the pledge of God's love.[29]

To put it most simply and unconditionally, as Calvin usually does in his catechisms: although we ought to know God as almighty and perfectly good, such knowledge by itself is insufficient. We must rather be certain that God loves us and desires to be our Father and Savior.[30] A truly spiritual insight into the things of God (so Calvin begins his introduction to the knowledge of Christ in Bk. II of the *Institutes*) consists of a) knowing God, b) knowing his fatherly favor for us, and c) knowing how to frame our life according to his law. It is the second aspect which is so beyond the possibilities of the natural mind; only the interior work of the Holy Spirit makes this possible.[31]

A true knowledge of God's providential care is gained only via knowledge of God's election. But God's elective love, Calvin insists throughout the *Institutes*, is perceived correctly only in the work of Christ. And knowledge of Christ is a dead, exterior, hence false knowledge, Calvin insists no less frequently, except it be certified and made effective in our hearts by the sanctifying work of the Holy Spirit. Thus in order for us to gain a real sense of what Calvin asserts to be the priority of the Father's love in his dealings with men, we must turn to Calvin's discussion of the work of the Son and the Holy Spirit.

B. *A Reasoned Order*

In these two opening sections we are attempting to assess Calvin's trinitarian ascriptive pattern in relative independence of his views of God's relationship to the world. But that procedure is nearly impossible to maintain when we turn to the functions Calvin assigns to the Second Person, and is only slightly less difficult to respect to the functions of the Third Person. The reason for the near-impossibility is clear: Calvin's stress on the full

---

the focus of our attention, the doctrine of providence will be seen to function as a clarification of the doctrine of election. For a general discussion of these doctrines in their complex relationship to each other and to the doctrines of God and of Christ, cf. the works of Wendel and Jacobs, noted earlier.

[27] III,21.5; cf. II,8.18.

[28] II,16.4; 17.2; III,2.12; 21.1; 22.9; cf. *Com. on Romans* 9:4, p. 340; on 9.16, p. 357; *Com. on Eph.* 1:4, p. 99.

[29] II,8.4; III,2.32; 17.3; 22.10.

[30] Cf. the 1541 French Catechism, qq. 9-11.

[31] II,2.18.

divinity, hence equality and unity in God, of the Second and Third Persons. It is via the Second and Third Persons that God's relationship to the world is wholly expressed and certified. And the Second Person of the Trinity (and this is Calvin's particular emphasis) is identical to the person of Christ the mediator. Menno Simons, in whose theology the transcendental referent in christology had little if any functional importance, did not experience the tensions between trinitarian and christological discourse that Calvin did. And Luther, who shared Calvin's transcendentalism but who concentrated upon the divine-human unity in Christ incarnate,[32] did not experience the theological writer's difficulties over this systematic matter to the degree the Geneva reformer did. Moreover Calvin's writing in the *Institutes* is noticeably affected by the positions of Servetus and other contemporary anti-trinitarians who, in Calvin's view, stressed the distinction between the Word of God and the incarnate Son of God (implying thereby the subordination of the latter).[33]

A second difficulty emerges with regard to Calvin's treatment of the functional interrelationship of the Son and the Holy Spirit. While his text exhibits little awareness of comparable transcendent-immanent tensions with regard to the person of the Holy Spirit (yet another indication of the "afterthought" character of the doctrine of the Spirit), Calvin consistently discusses the work of Christ only in relation to that of the Holy Spirit, and vice versa.[34] The distinctions of functions are relatively precise. Yet it is the mutual inclusiveness of function that is Calvin's emphasis against Rome, the Anabaptists, the mere philosophers of religion, and the anti-trinitarians. Once again, although Calvin gives us few explicit affirmations here, the reason for his emphasis must be presumed to be the unity of the Godhead.

These circumstances dictate the approach, the arrangement of materials, and the qualification of conclusion imposed upon our study in this section. The distinct functions of the "Second Person" (distinct from "Christ the mediator") can be noted without serious distortion so long as we remain aware that for Calvin such distinctions are, in the strongest possible sense of the phrase, "merely analytical." We must also consider jointly the work of the Second and Third Persons, and with the same qualification as before. We may then ponder the tensions in Calvin's trinitarian thought, knowing that his emphasis is on the divine unity, and may offer the thesis that the basis of this unity is the love of God the Father.

1. THROUGHOUT HIS writings Calvin asserts—usually as an introduction to a subject—that a true, adequate, and effective knowledge of divine things is possible only via God's self-revelation in Christ and self-authentication via the Holy Spirit. Christ is the mediator between God and man. But while his affirmation concerning the union of God and man effected by Christ's incarnation cannot be faulted by comparison to current

[32]Krusche, p. 143.
[33]Cf. especially Calvin's discussion in II,14.3-5. The same effect is of course noticeable in his formal discussion of the Trinity in Bk. I.
[34]Krusche, pp. 127ff; 219.

standards of orthodoxy, Calvin appears to take special care to limit the extent of union to areas he considers proper. For our present purposes the most significant example of Calvin's concern occurs in his response to the Lutheran Osiander at II,11.5. The general issue is the degree to which the terms "righteous," or "just," can be considered "essential" qualifications of the Christian, beyond the forensic, declarative, or otherwise "external" qualitative relationship between God and man asserted by the younger Luther and, with qualification, by Calvin. Picking up on one of Osiander's arguments, Calvin admits that while it is correct to say that the whole Trinity and its virtues are in us because of our union with Christ, that is true only indirectly. Father and Spirit are wholly present in the Son. But they and their virtues are present in us only through and in the distinct form of the Son and his work for us. "Separate" considerations of the Father and Spirit and their effects in us, Calvin maintains, are "deceptive."[35]

The distinct functions of the Son and Spirit must be seen as special instances of their general functions with regard to the knowledge of God. Calvin puts it somewhat negatively:

> To sum up: since our hearts cannot, in God's mercy, either seize upon life ardently enough or accept it with the gratefulness we owe, unless our minds are first struck and overwhelmed by fear of God's wrath and by dread of eternal death, we are taught by Scripture to perceive that apart from Christ, God is, so to speak, hostile to us, and his hand is armed for our destruction; to embrace his benevolence and fatherly love in Christ alone. (II,16.2)

As indicated earlier, Calvin sees the epistemological function of Christ to be that of bringing God "closer" to us. It is only as God is thus brought closer that we can see him as Father, as love. The function of Christ, therefore, is to qualify our knowledge of God as a knowledge of God's fatherly love. Only through Christ can God be seen in this way, i.e., seen truly.[36] The epistemological function of the Holy Spirit is also to be seen in this way. If Christ brings God closer to us so that we can know him more correctly, it is the Holy Spirit who joins God in Christ to us most intimately by certifying that knowledge in our hearts. The whole of scripture points us to Christ, first of all. The function of the Spirit, therefore, is to open our eyes to the correct interpretation of scripture (cf. Calvin's discussion in I,7.4 and 9.2f.). Given the specific revelation of Christ and especially of his atoning work for us, the function of the Spirit is to effectively instill that work and its results in our hearts, i.e., in our life of faith (cf. Calvin's discussion in III,1 and 2.33-39).

---

[35]Cf. *Com. on John* 2:19, p. 98; to 6:51, p. 262; to 6:57, p. 269; to 14:10, p. 87; *Com. on Romans* 8:9, p. 290f.; *Com. on I Corinthians* 1:13, p. 70.

[36]II,6.1; 14.5; 16.2ff.; 17.3; III,2.32; 20.36 *et passim*; cf. the 1541 Catechism, qq. 10-14; 22; 260; 262; *Com. on John* 3:16, p. 123f.; on 15:9, p. 112.

This concentration upon Christ and the Spirit relative to true knowledge of God is nowhere more required than with respect to the doctrine of election. As we shall see later, God's election is the most profound indication of his love. But election is always election in Christ. Only in Christ the Word can we even begin to approach a correct understanding of this doctrine.[37] And only in the Spirit of Christ can we gain the internal assurance of faith which is so much the object of God's act in electing us in Christ.[38]

When this joint epistemological function is not explicitly Calvin's subject, the special functions of the Son and Spirit begin to appear more distinctly and begin to approximate Calvin's formal trinitarian ascriptive pattern.

Exhibiting language characteristic of Simons, of nearly all second-generation magisterial reformers, and of Tridentine Catholicism as well, Calvin tends to distinguish "Christ" and "Gospel." While for Luther Christ is the Gospel, Calvin more frequently speaks of "Gospel" as something brought by Christ, or as something "pointing to" Christ. Thus the Gospel is Christ's "heavenly philosophy," the perfect sum of doctrine, perfect wisdom, with which Christ is "clothed." It is that proclamation of the grace manifested in Christ, a clear manifestation of the mystery of Christ. We can have to do with Christ only if we have perceived the right understanding of him from the word of the Gospel.[39]

The relationship between Christ and God's Word is one of mutual inclusiveness within the general formal, justice, or "wisdom" function which Calvin has assigned to the Second Person. God's Word leads to or points to Christ, and Christ is the teacher of this doctrine. The distinction between Christ and God's Word maintained by Calvin (perhaps this distinction is related to his stress on the distinction of natures in Christ) either reflects or produces additional differences from Luther's approach to the nature of revelation. The most important of these differences is Calvin's greater stress on the unity of revelation. Law is evaluated more positively than in Luther, who stressed the contrast between law and Christ (= Gospel).[40] Calvin, not making the identification of Christ and Gospel, can subsume law and Gospel under the general aegis of God's expressed covenant with man—a covenant of which Christ is both the ultimate embodiment and the perfect mediator. Not only is God's revelation one revelation in Christ, but also reflexively, man and his world are brought into unity with themselves and with God by means of Christ. Here is the justice or form function of the Second Person: it gives "shape" to the Father's love; it produces order.

[37]III,21.2; 22.1; 24.3ff.

[38]III,1.3f.; 2.11f.; 21.3; cf. 1541 Catechism, q. 89; *Com. on John* 6:40, p. 254f.; *Com. on Eph.* 1:13, p. 208.

[39]I,11.7; 15.2; 13.7; III,2.6; II,9.2; III,6.4.

[40]The chief indications in the *Institutes* of this more positive, integrated valuation of law are Calvin's stress on the "third use" of the law, and most importantly, his decision to include the topic of law in Book II as an introduction to his treatment of Christ the Redeemer. Cf. II,6-11.

> The meaning [Eph.1.10, "that he might gather together in one"] appears to me to be, that out of Christ all things are disordered, and that through him they have been restored to order. And truly, out of Christ, what can we perceive in the world but mere ruins? We are alienated from God by sin, and how can we but present a broken and shattered aspect? The proper condition of creatures is to keep close to God. Such a gathering together as might bring us back to regular order, the apostle tells us, has been made in Christ. Formed into one body, we are united to God, and closely connected with each other. Without Christ, on the other hand, the whole world is a shapeless chaos and frightful confusion. We are brought into actual unity by Christ alone. . . . By gathering both [men and angels] into his own body, Christ hath united them to God the Father, and established actual harmony between heaven and earth.[41]

The above description is a description of the living church, founded upon Christ, and not of a merely possible or abstract ideal. That this unity has been and is being accomplished is due to the special work of the Holy Spirit. If the "ordered disposition of all things" be the activity of the Son, the "power and efficacy" of that activity is the business of the Holy Spirit (I,13.18).

The variety of specific functions that Calvin assigns to the Holy Spirit can be grouped around a single theme: the effective unification of God and man. That unification is accomplished by the Spirit from both sides. The Spirit effectuates God's way to man, and man's way to God.

In a sense all features of this process are encompassed in the Spirit's agency with regard to the Holy Scripture. The Spirit is eternally present strengthening and preserving the natural world, of course. But the Spirit's chief function occurs in reference to God's more explicit way to man: his word in the scripture. The Holy Spirit is the inspirer (in this sense the author) of the scripture, and only under his guidance can it be interpreted correctly. But correct interpretation means that the scripture must be seen to point to God's most explicit and complete way to man. The Holy Spirit everywhere in scripture commends Christ to us. And Christ is fully and intimately joined to us only as the Spirit authenticates the scriptural word and Christ's work in our hearts.

This union itself is fully effected only as the Holy Spirit, reflexively operative in our souls, minds, and hearts, joins us to Christ. Calvin's *locus classicus* for this theme is the opening sections of Book III.[42] The Spirit is the means by which Christ unites us to himself. Christ joins us to himself by inspiring in us his own life-giving Spirit with its grace and power.[43] Creating

---

[41]*Com. on Eph.* 1:10, p. 205; cf. *Com. on Ezek.* 13:9, p. 281.

[42]Cf. for the following discussion François Wendel, *Calvin: The Origins and Development of His Religious Thought*, trans. Philip Mairet (New York: Harper & Row, 1963), pp. 236ff.

[43]Cf. III,1.1; 1.3; 2.34 *et passim*.

in us faith (the Spirit's "principal work," III,1.4), the Spirit communicates the power and grace of Christ to us through the Word and sacraments⁴⁴ so that the recreation, reformation, and sanctification of our life (i.e., of our living faith) may become complete. Only through this activity of the Spirit are we then enabled to approach heavenly things.

> Therefore, as we cannot come to Christ unless we be drawn by the Spirit of God, so when we are drawn we are lifted up in mind and heart above our understanding. For the soul, illumined by him, takes on a new keenness, as it were, to contemplate the heavenly mysteries, whose splendor had previously blinded it. And man's understanding, thus beamed by the light of the Holy Spirit, then at last truly begins to taste those things which belong to the kingdom of God, having formerly been quite foolish and dull in tasting them (III,2.34).

2.
> He [Christ] calls the Spirit another Comforter, on account of the difference between the blessings which we obtain from both. The peculiar office of Christ was, to appease the wrath of God by atoning for the sins of the world, to redeem men from death, to procure righteousness and life; and the peculiar office of the Spirit is, to make us partakers not only of Christ himself, but of all his blessings. And yet there would be no impropriety in inferring from this passage a distinction of Persons; for there must be some peculiarity in which the Spirit differs from the Son so as to be another than the Son (*Com. on John* 14.16, p. 92f.).

Not only are the distinct trinitarian functions which Calvin formally posited at 1,13.18ff. operative throughout his theology, as we have seen, but so too is the "reasoned order" of subordination. In the previous subsection the joint image "God's way to man—man's way to God" was utilized to organize the brief discussion of the functions of the Holy Spirit. The general organization and sequence of materials suggested by this image was exemplified in the church fathers, and Calvin could not have been unaware of its classic illustrations in the systematic writings of Augustine, Hugh of St. Victor, and Thomas Aquinas. But were we to suppose Calvin made his own organizational decisions for the *Institutes* with these precedents consciously in mind, we would have to conclude that he rejected the arrangement on the grounds of sequence and the theology suggested by the sequence.⁴⁵*

⁴⁴IV,14.8f; 8.17; 16.25; 17.12, 24, 31, 33.

⁴⁵St. Augustine's *De civitate dei*, with its double dialectical pattern (the two cities, and then the initial and final visions of the heavenly city) provides the first classic example. Hugh of St. Victor's *De Sacramentis*, structured in terms of creation and redemption, and further-

Calvin's order of subordination in I,13.18 (Father-Son-Holy Spirit) reflects the first side of the image. But for Calvin, as we have seen, the order of subordination is limited to an epistemological subordination. Perfectly illustrating a key distinguishing feature of Protestant evangelical thought in this area—and thereby also drawing the Roman Catholic charge of "subjectivism"—Calvin knew that only living, personal experience with scripture could show us the mediator Christ, and thereby provide us true knowledge of God. The epistemological sequence here must be Holy Spirit-Son-Father (a sequence suggesting the second side of the image).

To continue our supposition: Calvin either would or could not choose one sequence or separate the two, even though to have done so would have afforded his later students a much "neater" text to investigate. What we have instead is a theology in which both orders of subordination are exhibited on most important topics.

Calvin's "God-to-man" order is exhibited more fully in the first half of the *Institutes*. Knowledge of the Creator comes before the "inner" knowledge of the Redeemer. It is the way of the Father, himself infinite, says Calvin in a positive reference to Irenaeus, to become finite in the Son as an accommodation to our limited minds. God in fact has never manifested himself in any other way than through the Son.[46] Even within the context of God's saving acts, Calvin subordinates the Son to the Father. God's elective decisions are focused wholly through Christ. Yet Christ's merits are not only "subordinate" to the Father's mercy, but also non-existent apart from God's good pleasure. It is God alone who justifies—but we transfer this function to Christ because that is the Father's will. The love of God the Father is always stated by Calvin to be the first, or efficient, and the final cause of our salvation. It is God's election which produces faith in Christ, not vice versa.[47]

The subordination extends between Son and Spirit as well. The Spirit's teaching is wholly confined to the doctrine brought by Christ, of course. God was fully, bodily present in Christ, but since Christ has ascended, God is present in the world only through Christ's Spirit, by which Christ exercises his rule over us.[48] Yet it is just at this point that Calvin begins to exhibit

---

more oriented to the life of the church, as the title indicates, must have initially appealed to Calvin as it did to St. Thomas. Thomas' own *Summa Theologica*, the major sections of which can be divided into 1)God 2)Man 3)God's way to man, and 4)Man's way to God, also may have seemed suggestive to Calvin. The last example may be particularly instructive vis-à-vis Calvin's decisions. Calvin could never have given the pride of place to the subject "Man's way to God" as did Thomas. There could be no suggestion of God-man reciprocity, neat as such an organization of materials would be. There is only one direction in religion: God to man. Thus Calvin begins with God, moves in Book II to "God's way to man," and then to first the internal (Bk. III) and then the external (Bk. IV) means by which God's way to man is effected.

[46]I,6.1; II,6,4; 14.5; III,8.4; cf. *Com. on John* 1:1, p. 30.

[47]III,22.1; II,17.1; III,11.7; 14.17,21; IV,15.6; cf. *Com. on Romans*. 3:22, pp. 138ff.; III,22.10; 24.1.

[48]III,11.5; cf. *Com. on John* 2:19, p. 98; IV,17.26; cf. *Com. on John* 14:6, p. 92; to 14:18, p. 94; to 20:17, p. 259.

his epistemological man-to-God sequence. For the Holy Spirit is the bond: the bond between Father and Son, between the Son and us, and between us and the Father.[49]

Thus Calvin can say that we gain access to Christ's work, to true knowledge of him only when our minds "become intent upon the Spirit," whose principal work is faith. Christ cannot be known otherwise than by this inward work of the Spirit, and Christ's work is ineffective without the Spirit's illumination.[50] It is via the Spirit that we meet Christ. And, continuing the man-Godward direction of thought, we see Christ as the sole foundation of the church and as the author of election.[51] Finally, when we encounter Christ in this way, we are led back to the Father. Faith embraces Christ only as he is offered to us by the Father.[52]

We have noted only a few instances of Calvin's "reasoned order" of trinitarian subordination. Usually he expresses both the man-ward and the God-ward directions of thought in the same passage or discussion. That is because Christ is the mediator in both directions and because the Spirit is the efficacy of that mediation in both directions. Although for Calvin the God-manward direction of thought is paramount (the very titles of Books II and III provide the only evidence we really need for that assertion), yet his thematic organization of the *Institutes* exhibits a constant shifting from one direction to another. If we consider God (Bk. I) and the church (Bk. IV) as its termini, the commerce of thought is especially well revealed in the arrangement of materials in Books II and III. In Book II, chapters 1-5 in a general way concern the impossibility of man's attempts to reach God on his own. Chapters 6-14 deal with God's way to man via the law and especially via Christ. Chapters 15-17 affirm that because of Christ's work we are now enabled to draw closer to God. In Book III, chapters 1-10 concern the same subject, focusing upon the Spirit's gift of faith as the means of the return. Chapters 11-19 again reverse the direction, concentrating upon God's own justification of us, freely-initiated and completed apart from our efforts.

Chapters 20-21 are particularly revealing of Calvin's habit of thought. Chapter 20 is a classic, beautiful essay on prayer as the way by which, through the agency of the Holy Spirit and of Christ, we may confidently approach the Father for all our anticipated needs. And this chapter functions as the introduction to the subject of God's eternal predestination, for which the work of Christ and the efficacy of the Spirit are agents (Ch. 21).

* * * * * *

For Calvin, the special function of the Second Person is that of providing form: providing the structure in the world and in God's preservation of it, righteousness of relationship between God and man, and as we shall

---
[49]Krusche, p. 7.
[50]III,1.3; 2.8; I,7.2.
[51]II,6.2; cf. *Com. on John* 5:20, p. 199; to 13:18, p. 64f.; *Com. on I Cor.* 3:11, p. 135f.
[52]*Com. on John* 10:36, p. 420; to 15:9, p. 112.

emphasize later, justice among men. Calvin sees the special function of the Holy Spirit in terms of power: the efficacy of God's rule over the world, the achievement of a sanctified Christian life, and as we shall emphasize later, the proper exercise of Christian freedom-in-order. But we must again recall that for Calvin the emphasis was always upon the mutuality rather than the distinctiveness of these functions.

One cannot, however, prove the mutuality simply by asserting it, or as illustrated in this subsection, by alternating contrasting directions of thought in the same context. The unity of form and power must be rooted somewhere. The unity between the distinct work of the Son and Spirit asserted in Calvin's theology must be sought "further back," in a causal though not temporal sense. We are led once again to Calvin's "reasoned order," to his "first" and "final" causes.

It is the Father, Calvin says, whom we see as the source of all things. And the chief defining characteristic Calvin assigns to the Father is love. It is the love of the Father to which we must recur if we would gain the foundation for the asserted unity of operations of the Son and Spirit. God's love, according to the hypothesis guiding our study, manifests itself among us as the desire for ordered harmony—for the unity of form and power. From our perspectives, Calvin very clearly appears to exhibit the effects of the fact that his consideration of the distinct functions of the Son and Spirit is rooted in God's love. Christ, whom as we have seen Calvin discusses in a variety of special contexts as the "form" of God in his dealings with the world, is formally and substantively presented as mediator. The Holy Spirit, whom Calvin in a variety of contexts discusses as the "power" of God, is primarily the epistemological "lock" or the certifier of God's relationship to the world. Mediation and certification—that is how God's love, his drive for reunion with man, effectively transfigures and unifies Calvin's presentations of the distinct works of the Son and Spirit.

The argument in the above paragraph, however, is unsatisfyingly abstract. The hungry question arises: where, specifically, is the point at which God-to-man and man-to-God may be seen in their interrelationship? For Calvin there is a specific point of contact. In its divine aspect, that point is Christ; in its worldly aspect, it is the church. There is also a mutual dynamism effecting the togetherness of Christ and the church, according to Calvin. God in his love elects the church in Christ; the church of Christ strives to become sanctified unto God.

In the next two sections we shall consider the themes Christ, election, the church, and sanctification.

C. *Justice in Love*

The God who is both the *arche* and the *telos* of all righteousness is very far removed from us, Calvin believes. Were we able to contemplate the divine majesty in itself, or foolish enough to wish to attempt that, we would end up at best with what Luther called a "theology of glory." Such a theology mistakes God's truth, ignores his revealed, actual relations to us, and consequently leaves us in our sins, bereft of hope and confidence. Throughout this study, one of the initial questions we put to the reformers has been, "What do you see to be the 'general relationship' of God and the world?" Such a question, because it seeks the "general" (one might have said "absolute" or "metaphysical") rather than the "specific" or "revealed," betrays the urge to a theology of glory and its attendant dangers.

Calvin was just as aware of these dangers as was Luther, although Calvin's sensitivities appear to differ somewhat from those of his German colleague. Calvin seems most aware of the dangers such speculative thought posed for the doctrine of God, especially regarding God's unity. It may have been true in Calvin's time (a time when the inadequacies of classical Greek thought on the matter were becoming known, but prior to the work of Copernicus and Newton) that the "general relationship of God and the world" was a wide-open subject of inquiry. But Calvin did not think faith well-served by such scholastic offerings on the matter as the distinction between God's "absolute" and "ordained" will. Such a distinction, he says, impiously and profanely separates God's justice from his power. Instead Calvin would commend to us what the scripture and Christian wisdom say about this matter: "providence—the determinative principle of all things, from which flows nothing but right, although the reasons have been hidden from us" (I,17.2). Only this way, presumably, may God's power and justice be kept together in our theology.

Why can this presumption be made? Because, Calvin insists, all of God's dealings with men, including his care for the world's order, are adequately made known to us in Christ. Christ is "Immanuel"—God with us—the mediator and certifier of his will. Christ's teachings, and most of all his sacraficial death for us, reveal God's justice. Christ's Spirit, operative in the church to accomplish our sanctification, reveal God's power. The realities of God's power and justice asre integrated in Christ. This integration in our thought is possible because Christ shows us the roots of that power and justice: God's love.

1. BECAUSE CALVIN HAS, to his own mind, adequately defended the full divinity of Christ in his consideration of the Trinity in Book I, he tells us that his focus in the christological section of Book II will be upon the full humanity of Christ (II,13.1). We might have expected him to stress the completeness of God's involvement with man's "flesh" in this connection, as does Luther. But it is not so. Without (to his mind) diminishing in any way the Christian doctrine concerning the intimacy of God's union with man in Christ, Calvin takes as the first of his two major foci of interest in II,13-17 the necessary qualifications upon that union. Calvin's own theological temperament is a partial explanation for this stress. What he perceived to be the excesses in the other direction of the Lutheran Osiander and of some Anabaptists is also clearly another reason.

Calvin's explicit consideration of Christ's incarnation and saving work comes as the conclusion to a lengthy consideration of God's law. This order of association has been commented upon by many students. Without prejudicing other considerations, a definite hint into Calvin's thinking can be seen if we focus on his qualifications of the God-man union in Christ.

Calvin's essay on the mediator can be divided roughly into two sections: 12.1-14.8 on Christ's person and 16.1-17.6 on Christ's work, with Chapter 15 as a bridge joining the "relation-to-God" and "relation-to-man" sections.

The very first lines of his essay reflect Calvin's interest. We can uncover no reason, no necessity either upon or within God's being, for the incarnation. The incarnation stemmed from a "heavenly decree" even though it is clear that we would necessarily be lost, even were we free from stain, without it (12.1). Calvin's subsequent description of the necessity (if we are to be saved) of the incarnation cannot be taken to suggest any exigencies or impositions influencing God's decisions. Divinity and humanity are joined together by God's "eternal" or "secret" decree, his "unchangeable ordinance," his "predestination." We are not to inquire further (12.5). Christ is always head of his church, independently of the fact of incarnation. No "historical contingency" can qualify God's decision (12.7).

Inordinate stress upon Christ's unity with us could also lead to similar impious attempts to limit God's freedom. Chapters 13 and 14 are addressed in part to these dangers. Calvin insists against the "Manichees" that the saving bond of men with Christ is not flesh by itself, but a spiritual bond initiated by the Holy Spirit and accomplished through faith (13.2). God's "immeasurable essence" cannot be confined to the limits of flesh (13.4). We must remember that Christ is not to be understood simply as the union of divine and human natures. He is mediator. That function cannot properly apply jointly to both body and soul, flesh and spirit, human nature and divine (14.1f.). It properly belongs to Christ's person (and that divine) as mediator. The title "Lord" belongs exclusively to the person of Christ "only in so far as it represents a degree midway between God and us" (14.3). And Christ is called Lord and Son of God, *"even* according to, but *not by reason of,* his humanity" (14.4, emphases mine; cf. 14.6).

It seems clear that Calvin has stressed the distinction of divine and human aspects with regard to the mediatorial role of Christ in this discussion. Why does he insist that our saving bond with Christ is spiritual, not physical,[53]* and that properly speaking Christ saves us by reason of his

[51] II,6.2; cf. *Com. on John* 5:20, p. 199; to 13:18, p. 64f.; *Com. on I Cor.* 3:11, p. 135f.

[52] *Com. on John* 10:36, p. 420; to 15:9, p. 112.

[53] Calvin's emphasis here may be in part reflective of what has been called his "antiphysical" bias. Such a term may be an overstatement, and in any case it is deceptive or misleading to modern readers. Yet when some of Calvin's modern advocates, for example McNeill and Wendel, go to the lengths they do to "exonerate" Calvin of the charge, one gets the impression that they are protesting too much. Throughout the *Institutes* there are far too many allusions to the "prison house" of the body and related phrases to ignore. Calvin's statements that, for example, one cannot avoid pleasure in God's created gifts, and that one ought not despise what God in his wisdom has given man to enjoy, do not really balance the overall impression. In comparison to Luther in particular, Calvin the man and theologian seems much cooler, much more reserved, less appreciative of and less affected by physical life in all its variety of sensations.

Regarding this comparison, however, it must be said that it is Luther, not Calvin, who is

divinity, not his humanity? Besides his instinctive preference for maintaining God's distinctiveness from man, Calvin clearly indicates that the purpose is to maintain the eternity, the unchangeableness, of God's decision to save. And that means God must be seen to be free of any contingency of decision, whether the contingency arise from the creation, from sin, or even from union with human nature in the person of Christ. The appeal to the eternity of God's acts is a regular theme throughout this section, and in fact continues in the "bridging" Chapter 15 (cf. 15.3). But why does Calvin make this appeal? Partly, of course, to satisfy the requirements of the traditional doctrine of God's aseity, and of his unchangeability as the "unmoved mover." There is, however, a more important reason. The subsection noted above concerning the eternity of Christ's rule of the church is followed immediately by a meditation on the wretchedness of our life apart from such a rule (15.4). The point: if we make our salvation—its causes, realization, or consequences— to rest on anything other than, or in addition to, God's own radically free decision, our hope and confidence are lost. They are lost because we would then have lost the essence of God's relationship to us. We would have begun to consider his act in Christ to be in some way a contract, an act whose effectiveness or availability to us was conditioned in some small way by its object. Such a view might seem to respect the divine justice, might seem to respect God's law (a subject, recall, that Calvin includes in his general discussion of Christ the mediator). But such a view would not only miss the object of God's giving of the law, miss the real point of the incarnation, but would radically overlook the basic fact about God, the heart of God's self-initiated relationship to man as revealed in both the law and the Gospel: God's love. Love offered only upon conditions may be man's way, but it is not God's way. God's love is an unconditional, free, powerful, and creative love.

Calvin's second major section (Chapters 16f.) very vividly picks up this emphasis on God's love. Throughout Calvin's description of Christ's suffering, his constant stress is that, appearances notwithstanding, the atonement struggle is evidence not of God's wrath, but of his love. Indeed Calvin's references to God's love in these early sections of Chapter 16 (cf. secs. 2-5 particularly) are more frequent than anywhere else in the *Institutes*. Calvin's emphasis can be put into sharper focus if one compares his treatment of Christ's sufferings on the cross with that of Luther in the 1534 Galatians commentary. Luther's descriptions are almost wholly in terms of a struggle between divine and demonic *powers*.

It is in Chapter 17, the final chapter of Book II, that Calvin most clearly gives evidence of the sharp limitations he feels compelled to put on all discussions of Christ and his work. As much as Calvin wishes to affirm the "merit" acquired by Christ's obedience, he very carefully insists that ultimately it is God's predestination, ordinance, and good pleasure alone that is the reason for our salvation (17.1). Calvin is aware of the difficulty: he says that "in some ineffable way, God loved us and yet was angry

the exception to the general attitude of his professional peers. It was he, and not either Calvin or Menno Simons, who was accused of coarseness of language and life by his peers, including those of his own church.

toward us at the same time, until he became reconciled to us in Christ" (17.2). What is the relationship between God's love and his righteousness or justice? Which has causal precedence? Calvin, admitting this to be a mystery, offers what he too must surely have known was not a solution but a description.

> How did God *begin to embrace with his favor* those whom he had *loved before the creation* of the world? Only in that he *revealed his love* when he was reconciled to us by Christ's blood. God is the fountainhead of all righteousness. Hence man, so long as he remains a sinner, must consider him an enemy and a judge. *Therefore, the beginning of love is righteousness*, as Paul describes it: "For our sake he made him to be sin who had done no sin, so that in him we *might become* the righteousness of God (17.2, emphases mine).

This passage becomes more puzzling the more it is studied. It makes no logical sense at all. Calvin at first appears to give precedence to divine love, in spite of the troubling distinctions emphasized in the first two sentences. One might have expected him to assert that "the beginning of righteousness is love." But his "therefore," itself unexpected, leads to the reverse conclusion! A conclusion buttressed, moreover, by II Corinthians 5:21, which seems at least irrelevant and at most appears to support his original line of approach! In the continuation Calvin again returns to the priority of God's love.

Perhaps in spite of himself Calvin is, at the end of his essay in christology, being drawn through focus on Christ's merited righteousness back into the Father's free love. And that means, as Calvin insisted at the beginning of his essay, that it is God's elective love which must be taken as the ultimate source for our salvation through Christ, and as the ultimate basis of the church of which Christ is the head.

2. THE THEOLOGICAL tensions between the doctrines of God the Creator and God the Redeemer—tensions which in the present context appear in Calvin in the form of the relationship between love and justice—continue to be felt as Calvin raises his thoughts to the highest mystery of God's relationship to man: his eternal election. These perceived tensions have often been expressed by students this way: are Christ and his work to be seen as the instrument or the realization of God's election, or is divine election the instrument or certification of Christ and his work?[54] Calvin himself seems to work both ways, indeed both ways at once. We seem to be back to the matter of his "reasoned order" of subordination. One

---

[54]Paul Jacobs, *Prädestination und Verantwortlichkeit bei Calvin* (Neukirchen: Buchhandlung des Erziehungsvereins, 1937), p. 54.

of the problems Calvin faced in his christological essay was the relationship between God's free grace and Christ's earned merits. The christological focus perhaps rendered Calvin's response somewhat provisional. But when he focuses on the matter of divine election, Calvin's response to the issue is firmer. For the subject of election is seen by Calvin, as by his opponents, as explicitly a matter of the relationship between divine love and divine justice. And Calvin's answer is clear. God's election is the just or righteous expression of his love. Christ is the instrumental form by which God's elective love is revealed and accomplished.

The doctrine of double election is not a premise for subsequent thought or experience. It is rather a retrospective conclusion of faith concerning its experience and its sources.[55] The teaching originates in experience, in the experience of God's Word and its varied effects. "In actual fact," Calvin begins his topic, "the covenant of life is not preached equally among all men, and among those to whom it is preached, it does not gain the same acceptance either constantly or in equal degree."[56] No one of us can dispute this most obvious fact! The question is, why is it the "actual fact" of life? As in his presentation of the doctrine of divine providence, Calvin rejected all answers appealing to fate, fortune, or human free decision. God alone is ceaselessly active and omnipresent. It is he alone who by his free acts determines not only all things but also every particular thing that happens. *Soli deo gloria.* Therefore if some men hear the Word and others not, if among those who do some are moved and others not, that too is God's decision; his elective decision; his predestination.

The doctrine of election is not, however, an attempt to express a general, neutral metaphysical law about the way the universe works. It is rather a confession of Christian faith about God's *trustworthiness*. The teaching arises from the experience of the preached word to the church; and in order to avoid the grievous effects upon the human mind and heart that consideration of the teaching apart from God's revelation would entail, we must constantly root our thoughts in God's Word, that is, in Christ and the experience of his church.[57] Already we see two characteristics of Calvin's teaching emerge: the doctrine is rooted in the activity of the church, and it is governed by the revelation brought by Christ. All evangelical teachings must share these characteristics, of course. But for Calvin it is particularly important that the doctrine of double election exhibit them. For only in this way can we learn that God's elective decisions are intended for the church, and that as seen in Christ, these decisions are the ultimate expression of God's love. Election is how God is Immanuel, God with us. Eternally with us. We may therefore rest secure in this. Predestination is a *comforting* doctrine.[58]

[55] Wendel, p. 265.
[56] III,21.1; cf. 21.6; 22.1; cf. A. M. Hunter, *The Teaching of Calvin* (London: James Clarke and Co., Ltd., 1950), p. 101f.
[57] III,21.2,7; 22.7; 24.1,3,5; 22.1.
[58] Hunter, p. 132f.

Just as the doctrine of providence meant for Calvin our assurance that God in his love has and will continue to care for our physical lives against the contingencies of a dark and uncertain future (cf. I,17.10), so the doctrine of election meant that our spiritual lives were likewise secured against the future.[59]* Calvin always began his positive teaching about election with a vigorous emphasis upon the divine love as the primary motive for God's election (cf. III,21.5 for the key illustration of Calvin's sense on this matter).[60] Calvin's emphasis vis-à-vis the doctrine of election is of course systematically and intrinsically related to his similar emphasis when describing the work of Christ. It is the eternity, the unchangeableness of God's decisions which is the basis of our security. No contingencies, no conditions, neither creation, nor sin, nor God's taking on of flesh, nor the variabilities of our faith, nor the temporal conditions of the church's life in the world, can affect God's eternal decision to elect us as his own.

Calvin's order of presentation itself suggests this emphasis. He leads us from Christ's work (Bk. II), to faith and justification before God (Bk. III, 2ff.), to election (Bk. III,21 ff.). We are following Calvin's reasoned order of epistemological subordination, from our own experience of Christ as heard in the preached Word, to the gracious decision of God to accept the results in us of Christ's work, to the ultimate grounds in the divine life for his gracious decision. In this connection it can be seen that the doctrine of election is for Calvin the ultimate guarantee of the doctrine of justification by faith alone (cf. III,24.9). Were we to allow that God's decision to covenant

[59]We must recall here that from the late sixteenth century onward until perhaps World War I, the future looked increasingly promising to thinking people in Europe. This was due in part to the Renaissance, revived now after a century's hiatus for what was considered the "final solution" to the old benighted religious problem. It was due in part to the rapid growth of scientific knowledge, and to the increasing control that man began to exercise over the natural world and then over his own society. In this context, when the future looked open to growth, adventure, and freedom, a doctrine that suggested that our individual and collective futures were irrevocably determined in the past struck the soul as terribly unjust, enslaving, impossible to bear, and just plain wrong. It had to be no more than an atavistic hangover from the dark ages of religious conflict.

But consider the quite different world-view of the late middle ages, taking the Reformation era not as the beginning of modern times, but as the culmination of medieval times, as did the reformers. Then, it was the past that looked glorious, free, reassuring, the present dubious at best, and the future deeply foreboding. One might note in this contrast the distinct characteristics of the two phases of the Renaissance, as symbolized in the "watchword" associated with each. *"Sapere aude!"* ("Think boldly!") was the forward-looking command of the seventeenth century; *"Ad fontes!"* ("Back to the sources!"), the wise counsel of the fifteenth. The watchword of the Protestant Reformation, itself a reactionary movement from the point of view of both Catholicism and the later Renaissance—*"sola scriptura"*—can be seen as the religious analog to the earlier Renaissance counsel. The events of the sixteenth century appeared to nearly all reformers to bode the impending end of the world, with the lengthy terrors thought to precede it. In this context, the doctrine suggesting that, no matter what may happen, our lives have been eternally secured by God's antecedent decision, appeared very comforting indeed.

[60]Cf. also II,16.4; 17.3; III,22.9; *Com. on Rom.* 1:7, p. 49; on 4:14, p. 171; on 9:4, p. 340; on 9:16, p. 357; *Com. on Eph.* 1:4, p. 199. Cf. Jacobs, p. 130.

with us is based on anything except or in addition to his own internally determined, freely exercised love, the evangelical doctrine of justification by faith alone (faith itself being an unmerited gift of God's grace) would fall. And with it our peace. God does not love as man loves. God loves absolutely and without condition. This is seen not only in Christ's incarnation and death but also in the benefits that are ours because of Christ. Our justification, our salvation, is complete and unconditional because it, like Christ's incarnation and atonement, is wholly rooted in God's unconditional, eternal elective decision. Spiritual peace is the highest gift of God's love. Calvin quotes or refers to Romans 8:38f. only a few times in the *Institutes*, but these references occur in the sections on faith, justification, and election.

Our emphasis upon election as the eminent sign of God's love is both possible and necessary because the doctrine exists wholly within the experience of the church of Christ. Calvin would have preferred to limit himself, as did Luther, to consideration of God's expressed will to and for the elect. Indeed, his opening two chapters (III,21f.) on the teaching are almost wholly confined to God's election of the church, Calvin's subordinate task being to refute all notions suggesting that this election was based on anything outside the absolutely free decision of God. But throughout this discussion a question about the divine justice emerges with increasing frequency and sharpness. It arises because Calvin has taken the facts of human temporal experience—that some are moved by the preached word and others not—and rooted them in God's eternal decisions. That means double election. And God's election of the majority of men to damnation appears as unjust as his election of some to salvation. This is the "dreadful decree" (23.7). Once the matter of the reprobate is broached in the final section of Chapter 22, Calvin cannot and will not avoid the admittedly non-existential discussion in Chapter 23.[61] Why not? Because the necessary affirmation of both sides of the teaching (23.1) has raised questions, from circles outside the elect church, about God's justice in relation to his love. It appears that God is either cruel or unjust. Since the matter of the exercise of divine justice concerns the reprobate while that of divine love and mercy concerns the elect (21.7), Calvin might properly have ignored the issue, restricting himself to an affirmation of faith's experience. But he could not permit the charge to stand, even though, as he himself is perfectly well aware, he cannot refute it on its own terms and assumptions.

Calvin's first response to the matter—the assertion in 21.6 that "the very inequality of [God's] grace proves that it is free"—is a logical and verbal sleight of hand. His one reasonably direct response, that by reason of universal sinfulness we all are justly condemned (23.3), is of value only within the context of the church's faith, and even there is only of limited value. For the problems of God's decisions to attribute to and realize in all mankind the guilt and effects of Adam's sin (23.8), and to prevent some of those whom he calls to salvation from hearing it (21.6f.; 22.10; 23.1f., 8, 11), find no theological solution. Even apart from these intra-faith considerations, the general acknowledgement that all men by reason of actual

[61]Jacobs, p. 57.

sins, at least, are justly condemned, does not vacate the charge of divine injustice.[62] For the exercise of justice must be impartial (thus the implicit objection to Calvin's discussions of God's call—objections made explicit at 23.10f.).

To all of this Calvin has finally but one "answer," which is no answer at all: "Silence!" he would say. "Who are you, O man, to impose your standards of justice upon God? God has willed what he has willed. His will is just, though we cannot say why. Ours it is but humbly to accept God's decisions and to praise the righteousness of his judgment." (Cf. 21.2; 22.1,8,10f., 23.2,4,5,8; 24.14.17)

Although Calvin offers no answers to these objections, the objections themselves contain an implicit demand whose consequences, if allowed, would strike a blow to Calvin's faith and theology right where it lives. For the demands of justice, at least as justice is humanly conceived, would either eliminate the real meaning of God's love or preclude its exercise for us. And that is why Calvin, although he cannot finally respond adequately to the objections, must at least take them on in order to throw them off and out of the church's consciousness.

In his introduction to the topic of election Calvin stressed God's free love and mercy as the heart of the teaching.[63] In his running battle with objectors to the teaching, however, Calvin found himself, as did Luther in so many of his discussions, forced to shift his responses into the categories and subjects of his oppoonents. Thus the main theme of Calvin's essay, God's elective love, soon is transformed into a dispute concerning God's justice. It appears that just below the surface of the discussion of divine justice (in Chapters 22f.) is what Calvin's faith took to be an increasingly pointed, two-phased attack upon the divine love as he knows it.

The first phase: if, as Calvin seems to say, we are predestined to hell by God without even having had a real chance to deserve it, if God in the interests of effecting his own prior decisions either ignores or even prevents our sincere attempts to achieve the good—well, then, that god is not a god of love but of its opposite, a god of unremitting, irrational, unexceptional, and inhuman cruelty (cf. 23.4).

That Calvin did not evidence a particular concern with this attack should not surprise us. After all, it is based on the assumption that mankind really did not merit such treatment by God. But Calvin has already (Bk. I), to his own satisfaction at least, demonstrated that all men are individually without excuse for their own free decision to abandon true knowledge of God. Calvin assumes that, even without logically convincing proof,[64] his objectors really know in their heart of hearts that they themselves deserve God's condemnation. An *ad hominem* argument, admittedly. But nevertheless it is an argument which Calvin feels compromises the assumptions of the opponents enough to render their conclusions non-persuasive.

The second phase of the attack, however, is more serious. Granting that all men are justly deserving of God's condemnation, there would be no problem if God were to exercise a general mercy—a love which transcends

[62]Hunter, p. 119.   [63]Ibid., p. 132f.   [64]Ibid., p. 120f.

justice—on us all. But it must be general to be just. And, to quote Calvin, "the beginning of [God's] love is righteousness" or justice (II,27.3). As he said, when we think of God's glory—his chief characteristic—we should think of his justice (23.8). Therefore, presuming that we all are equally guilty, we must believe that God will condemn us all equally. He cannot be said to exercise mercy on an undeserving some of us while withholding it from a no less (un)deserving most of us. For him to do that would leave God failed of his own proclaimed standards of justice and righteousness.

Perhaps it has now become clear why this phase of the attack is far more threatening to Calvin's faith than the first. The first, after all, was based on the difference between merely human opinions concerning the sense of justice, and those of God. But now the attack plays upon a constructed conflict in the divine nature itself: a conflict between God's love and his justice. God's unity of operation is put in doubt. In order to avoid this difficulty, we are bidden to subordinate divine love to our own requirements for divine justice.

The attack, and the beginning of Calvin's vigorous response to it, breaks out at 23.11. Again without attempting to respond adequately to the philosophical problem, Calvin vigorously rejects the notion that the requirements of justice to be universally applied can preclude the exercise of love. Yet he is bidden to come down on one side or the other of the alternative subordination proposed between divine love and divine justice. And he must do so without violating his own principles concerning the absolute equality and mutuality of divine operations1

No adequate response is possible, and Calvin knows it. Calvin's recourse is to the authority of Augustine in the remainder of the chapter (irrelevant Augustinian citations at that). This indicates that Calvin is aware that his attempt to respond to external criticism on its own terms has reached the end of its limited usefulness. The only alternative is to reconstruct the issue in terms of the church's experience. And that experience is primarily the experience of divine love. Divine justice must be understood in this context. That is Calvin's decision. It is worked out in Chapter 24, his conclusion to the essay on double election.

Calvin began his essay on election with appeal to experience. Throughout most of the first two chapters he concentrated on God's elective love and developed his thoughts wholly within the context of God's call of the church through Christ. The objections raised in Chapter 23 forced the discussion back into the divine nature itself. Calvin finally did not either satisfy the objections or explain his own commitment to God's love (appeals to God's authority and to the virtues of "learned ignorance" being recurring themes throughout the essay). But at the end of Chapter 23 questions about God's purpose *ad nos* (12-14) gave Calvin a chance to return to his preferred theme. Chapter 24 thus reflects his God-to-us order of thought, Calvin beginning with God's call of the church through Christ (1-2), proceeding to a description of faith and perseverance as the effects of that call (3-10), and then concluding with an assertion of divine justice regarding the reprobate (12-17). And throughout these latter sections, experience is a major basis of his appeal, as it was at the beginning of the essay.

Calvin asserts throughout his writings that Christ is the pledge and mirror of God's love. "We may contemplate in him, as in a mirror, God's paternal love towards us all; because he is not loved apart, or for his own private advantage, but that he may unite us with Him to the Father."[65] Christ is loved by the Father as head of the church; in him dwells the whole love of God, which therefore flows from him to us. It is in this sense that Calvin can say that Christ is the author of election and the sole foundation of the church.[66] God's election, as seen and realized in Christ, is therefore the eminent expression of his love. And that election is the foundation of the church.

Calvin's beginning discussion of the church in Book IV brings together many of the themes we have been considering throughout this chapter.

> But because a small and contemptible number are hidden in a huge multitude, . . . we must leave to God alone the knowledge of his church, whose foundation is his secret election. . . . The basis on which we believe the church is that we are fully convinced we are members of it. In this way our salvation rests upon sure and firm supports, so that, even if the whole fabric of the world were overthrown, the church could neither totter nor fall. First, it stands by God's election, and cannot waver or fail anymore than his eternal providence can. Secondly, it has in a way been joined to the steadfastness of Christ. . . . And our faith is no worse because it recognizes a church beyond our ken. For here we are not bidden to distinguish between reprobate and elect—that is for God alone, not for us, to do—but to establish with certainty in our hearts that all those who, by the kindness of God the Father, through the working of the Holy Spirit, have entered into fellowship with Christ, are set apart as God's property and personal possession; and that when we are of their number we share that great grace.[67]

* * * * * *

The basic relationship of God to the world is love. That love is manifested through and in Christ as elective love. It is realized in those whom God in his love has chosen, the church. But the question now arises again: what of divine justice? How can the particular decisions of God's eternal love be said at the same time to express the equally eternal requirement of God's righteousness or justice?

[65] *Com. on John* 15:9, p. 112; *Com. on Is.* 33:24, p. 578; cf. *Institutes* II,14.5; 16.2; III,22.10.

[66] *Com. on John* 5:20, p. 199; on 13:18, p. 64f.; cf. *Institutes* III,21.7; 24.5; II,6.2; *Com. on I Cor.* 1:2, p. 51.

[67] IV,1.2f., in part, conflated.

Calvin's answer to the objectors, that the reprobate justly deserve their end, is as we have seen inadequate on their own terms. Much more expressive of Calvin's piety and faith is his assertion that God's predestination of the reprobate shows forth the divine glory.[68] This assertion, of course, is even more scandalous than the first one to the objectors. In fact nothing more can be said that would advance the discussion with those outside the church. If we are to understand how God's love can be expressed righteously or justly—if we are to understand Calvin's statement, previously quoted, that "the beginning of love is righteousness"—we must seek our answers only within the context of the church's experience. When we do that, Calvin's answer emerges at once: God's elective love in Christ is completed only as it transforms us, who are unrighteous, into the living image of divine righteousness.

> Men indeed ought to be taught that God's loving-kindness is set forth to all who seek it, without exception. But since it is those on whom heavenly grace has breathed who at length begin to seek after it, they should not claim for themselves the slightest part of his praise. It is obviously the privilege of the elect that, regenerated through the Spirit of God, they are moved and governed by his leading.[69]

Divine love creates righteousness and justice in those whom God elects. The question about divine justice in love is a question about the powerful working of the Holy Spirit to sanctify those who are justified in Christ. True knowledge of God can be sought only in that which is revealed in the church of Christ's elect. True knowledge of man must also be sought only in that which is effected by Christ's Spirit in the church.

True knowledge of man, moved by the Spirit to a regenerate, just life in the world and before God, is the subject of the next chapter.

---

[68] III,21.1. 22.11; 23.6,8; 24.14.
[69] II,3.10.

CATECHISMVS
Ecclesiæ Geneuésis,
HOC EST, FORMVLA
erudiendi pueros in doctrina Christi.

IO. CALVINO AVTHORE.

GENEVAE.
M. D. L.

CHAPTER SEVEN

Calvin: Justice and Freedom

> Suppose we but once begin to raise our thoughts to God, and to ponder his nature, and how completely perfect are his righteousness, wisdom, and power—the straightedge to which we must be shaped. Then, what masquerading earlier as righteousness was pleasing in us will soon grow filthy in its consummate wickedness. What wonderfully impressed us under the name of wisdom will stink in its very foolishness. What wore the face of power will prove itself the most miserable weakness. that is, what in us seems perfection itself corresponds ill to the purity of God. (I,1.2)

The *Institutes* is not a scholarly treatise on the psychology or phenomenology of religion, of which the purpose is to show how man creates and perceives God in his own image. It is rather from cover to cover wholly a confession of the church's piety, faith, and experience of itself in the light of God's image. With the opening lines of his text, Calvin expressed awareness of the alternate perspective centers from which one might assay knowledge of God and knowledge of man. Though the formal presentation of the doctrine of the church does not come until the end, it should be clear even from the prefatory address and from the very title of the work that the perspective of the confessing church dominates from the beginning. Thus Calvin, without any felt need for explanation, follows the "order of right teaching" and commits himself to the alternative of viewing man in the light of knowledge of God.

Our opening quotation therefore does not reflect Calvin's assessment of the natural human condition apart from or prior to knowledge of salvation in the church. It reflects the continuing self-understanding of the church in the light of the salvation already accomplished for it by Christ and in the light of the righteousness yet to be perfected in it by Christ's Spirit. The expressed polarity between God's perfection and human imperfection thus can in no way be construed to apply to the supposed polarity of the church and the world, such as would be possible in the theology of Menno Simons. Rather it applies wholly to the church's sense of itself as both being and becoming. We are God's elect; this is revealed, achieved, and certified by Christ and the Spirit. But we are elected to be holy; and this remains to be completed by Christ and the Spirit. The task is undertaken in that gymnasium of faith, the church. The body of Christ in its imperfections is the church visible; the perfect body of Christ is the church invisible. Menno

Simons thought that distinction nothing but a convenient tool by which men sought to evade the requirements of the Gospel. For Calvin, however, it reflects the essence, the structure, and the dynamism of Christian life.

A. *The Invisible Church: Toward the Image of God*

The opening two lines of Book IV of the *Institutes* state the dialectic of being and becoming which is the experience of the church. By faith Christ becomes ours, and we are partakers of salvation. Yet we need outward helps to beget, increase, and advance faith to its goal.

With the introduction of the subject of "the external means or aids by which God invites us into the society of Christ and holds us therein," Calvin immediately realized that he had broached the controversial subject of the distinction between the visible and the invisible church. As in so many other instances in the *Institutes*, Calvin's new essay had not been very well anticipated. For Calvin's line of discussion in Book IV not only presumes the distinction, but further also presumes a determinate relationship between the *distincta*. Both presumptions, of course, were—and are—highly controversial.

Reading IV,1-8, one gets the feeling that Calvin was surprised and unprepared for the issues that occurred to his own self-conscious and systematic mind when he started to write. He finally settled down to his chosen subject in IV,1.9. But his opening sections are an organized chaos.

The very title of Book IV contains Calvin's subordinate assumption concerning the relationship of the assumed two entities, the visible and the invisible churches. The visible church, which is the subject of Book IV, is understood as an external means or aid by which we are led into and remain in the society of Christ. Now, even if the basic distinction could be presumed, Calvin's specified relationship would be contested by many Anabaptists. Menno Simons, as we have seen, will grudgingly allow the distinction of an "invisible church," but only on the prior condition of an actually righteous visible church (*vide supra*, p. 110). He understands "invisible church" to refer to a presumed "spiritual inside" of an already actual, visible, physically righteous church. Simons' position is one application of a more basic one which Calvin scores in relation to its application to sacramental theory. "But they [the Anabaptists] repeatedly go wrong through their deluded notion that the thing ought always to precede the sign in order of time."[1]* Calvin's view of the relationship is opposite. The "exter-

---

[1]IV,16.21 on baptism. Obviously the basic difference illustrated here is an epistemological one. But it also involves a metaphysical one. As suggested a number of times earlier in our study, Simons was simply not willing or able to accept the notion that there is an ideal, transcendental, "invisible" reality which exists metaphysically prior to, and more "really," than the actual physical reality which we experience and set our values by. Correspondingly, Simons could never admit that one ought to judge the quality of an actually existent thing in the light of a supposed "higher reality" of which the thing was but an anticipation. It becomes a matter of epistemology: can—does—a thing appear before its ideal or essential reality exists, or must a thing actually be before we can visualize its perfected, ideal future state?

nal" or visible church is justified as, and only as, a means by which the invisible church, existing prior to physical life (existing in God's eternal decisions), gains and sustains the actual temporal elect.

Calvin would like to get to the subject of the visible church. But because he did not prepare for it by giving the basic distinction a sufficiently explicit systematic setting, he is first compelled to do a quick pick-up of his missed stitches. His opening clause refers back to Book III. In fact, the whole of the positive teachings in Book III ("The Way in Which We Receive the Grace of Christ; What Benefits Come to Us from It, and What Effects Follow")—faith, regeneration/repentance, self-denial, justification, Christian freedom, prayer, election—comprises a discussion of the experience of the invisible church, even though that term was never used, much less discussed, in Book III. Section 2 defines the invisible church as an object of faith. Section 3 continues this line, but Calvin, wanting to introduce the "outward" church, begins by making a very weak connection between the creedal phrase "communion of saints" and the idea that church people should share their private possessions. In section 4 Calvin asserts a questionable identification between the visible church and "the mother of belief." In sections 5 and 6 he gets into a rather specific discussion of the validity of the visible church's educational ministry—but ends with an appreciation of its limits. Then in sections 7 and 8 he returns to a discussion of the invisible church, only to conclude with a shakey definition (understandably so!) of the visible church, or at least of those who presumably belong to it.

> And, since assurance of faith was not necessary, he [God] substituted for it a certain charitable judgment whereby we recognize as members of the church those who, by confession of faith, by example of life, and by partaking of the sacraments, profess the same God and Christ with us (IV,1.8).

What we must do is to view the church from the inside out, as did Calvin in fact if not clearly in print. Thus we must begin the presentation with a review of Calvin's description of the life of the invisible church in Book III of the *Institutes*. Only after doing that may we turn to a discussion of how that life is expressed, exercised, nourished, and perfected via the agencies of the external or visible church.

Calvin and Simons came down on opposite sides of these questions. In a certain way, the issues can be symbolized in two New Testament quotations appealed to frequently by the reformers: "A good tree bears good fruit," and "By their fruits you shall know them."

1. AT THE END of the preceding chapter we were faced with the urgent question: how do the decisions of God's elective love provide for the establishment of his justice or righteousness in us? The urgency of this question also impressed Calvin. Surrounded by antinomians and libertines on one side, Anabaptists and Catholic merit-mongers on the other, Calvin felt a particular need to stress his conviction that holiness of life is the object of God's deed in Christ. That is the major reason why Calvin, after introducing the meaning of faith at the beginning of Book III, continues not as we might expect with the matter of justification, but with regeneration and repentance.² Considering the misapplication of and the attacks against the evangelical doctrine of justification from both the right and the left, Calvin's placement can be appreciated.

Calvin begins with a double emphasis: it is the Spirit who is the bond or connection between the believer and Christ; and that bond is achieved through faith, which is the Spirit's principal work.³ Thereby the theological dangers of too immediate an identification of the believer and Christ can be avoided. To Calvin, the dangers of ignoring the mediating function of the Holy Spirit were represented in the position of Osiander, discussed earlier (*vide supra*, p. 145). The danger of downplaying the role of faith in this bonding is represented both in the Anabpatist's latent universalism of salvation (cf. II,13.2) and in their denial of legitimacy to a less-than-perfectly righteous church (cf. IV,1.).

Calvin gives a well-rounded trinitarian definition of faith at the end of III,2.7. Faith is "a firm and certain knowledge of God's benevolence toward us, founded upon the truth of the freely given promise in Christ, both revealed to our minds and sealed upon our hearts through the Holy Spirit." After some clarifications and refutations (secs. 8-13), he devotes the bulk of the remainder of the chapter to his own clear emphasis. The chief benefit of faith as the gift of God's grace is that via faith we gain certainty of knowledge (secs. 14-37). The internalization of God's promises, their certification in the heart, and the resultant constancy of the heart in the face of fear, is the chief thing in faith. And this certification is the work of the Holy Spirit, who operates within even as the Word works without.⁴

Calvin begins his treatment of the effects of faith by asserting that the sum of the Gospel is repentance and forgiveness of sins, and that these are attained through faith (III,3.1). The second element, forgiveness of sins, is identified with free reconciliation. Calvin decided to put off consideration of this matter until later, where in the definition of justification the earlier terms "forgiveness of sins"/"free reconciliation" are replaced by "remisssion of sins"/"imputation of Christ's righteousness" (III,11.2). His entire focus in Chapters 3-10 is upon the first element, repentance. As suggested earlier, this sequence was decided upon largely in order to offset the charge that

---

²III,3.1.
³III,1.1,4; cf. III,2.30.
⁴III,2.16, 33-37; cf. II,5.5.

evangelical doctrines over-emphasized divine love at the expense of divine righteousness. Calvin had to deal with this matter earlier, concerning Christ's satisfaction (II,17) and will have to do so again later, concerning God's election (III,23).

Calvin's main point in the early sections is that there is no simple cause-effect relationship between faith and repentance. Clearly repentance does not produce faith. But it is also wrong to conclude from Calvin's assertion that faith has a kind of priority, or that repentance is produced from it "as fruit from a tree" (III,3.12). Rather, as indicated in the first subsection of Chapter Three, faith receives or attains repentance (and forgiveness of sins) from the Gospel. Calvin wishes to resist the notion that repentance is in some way a "work of faith," even though to our experience it does seem to "follow" faith or is "born of" faith. Faith itself is something received from the Gospel. As Calvin indicated in the 1541 French catechism, the Gospel in us *is* faith and repentance.[5] Though we creatures must distinguish them, faith and repentance must be held together most intimately (III,3.5). Or perhaps more clearly, they are mutually implicative features of the same phenomenon: the certification in our hearts by the Holy Spirit of the salvation achieved for us by God in Christ. In the passage from 16.1 on justification by faith which will be quoted below, Calvin expressed this mutuality of effect by affirming that justification and sanctification happen "at the same time." One cannot help but hear in this passage echoes of Luther's *simul iustus et peccator*.

In fact the parallel is nearly exact. For to confess that we, justified, are at the same time sinners, is to repent. But what is the relationship between repentance and sanctification? On the presumption that for Calvin sanctification and regeneration refer basically to the same process, we can rephrase the question. What is the relationship between regeneration and repentance? Calvin's answer is clear: repentance is regeneration (III,3.9).

Calvin's main burden in the later chapters of his essay (III,4-10) is to work this identification (with a growing emphasis on regeneration) in both a negative and a positive way. First Roman views on the nature of repentance are answered (Chs. 4-5), and then Calvin launches into a positive description of what faith as regeneration entails for the Christian life. (Chs. 6-10).

It is at the beginning of Chapter Six that we get the answer to our question concerning the relationship of divine love to divine righteousness. "The object of regeneration, as we have said [cf. III,3.9], is to manifest in the life of believers a harmony and agreement between God's righteousness and their obedience, and thus to confirm the adoption that they have received as sons." God's righteousness is his holiness. God in his love has accepted us. His loving acceptance, however, is not a passive act. Rather, that act sets in motion, and is, the process whereby we are conformed to a likeness of God's holiness or righteousness. And that act is not finished until the harmony is achieved.

[5]Cf. the 1541 Catechism, q. 127.

Calvin continues with a statement of where may be found the pattern by which our obedience is structured so as to achieve this harmony and agreement. We shall return to this matter in the next section.

It is now possible to understand what may have been in Calvin's mind when at II,17.2 he asserted that "the beginning of love is righteousness"—a passage that gave us trouble in the last chapter. The fruits of repentance (= regeneration) are "the duties of piety toward God, of charity toward men, and in the whole of life, holiness and purity" (III,3.16). It can all be summed up as love: love to God and love to the neighbor. As emphasized in the last chapter, God's love is the source of our righteousness. In that sense one must say that "the beginning of righteousness is love." But now, of our imputed righteousness and as a co-ordinate aspect of our faith and repentance, is born an inward love for God and for man, and from this inward love flow outward works of love. That is the *simul* relationship between justification and sanctification—distinct causally and in meaning to our experience, but indissolubly linked gifts of God. And that is the sense in which Calvin could say at II,17.2 that "righteousness is the beginning of love." Or as he put it at III,14.6, "justification is the beginning of love."[6]

Calvin's emphasis on faith as a certain knowledge would be insufficient did not the evangelical doctrine of justification back it up. And the doctrine of justification would be insufficient support were it not founded on the doctrine of election. That is the order of Calvin's presentation in Book III. Here we see again evidence of one side of his "order of subordination." He begins with the Christian experience (faith, regeneration), moves to the declared relationship between the Christian and God (justification), and ends with God's own absolute decisions (election).

Calvin's essay on justification is a model of balance, his position one to which only the antinomians in the Lutheran camp and the perfectionists in the Anabaptist camp might take exception. Defined as God's acceptance of us, justification consists of two elements: remission of sins and the imputation of Christ's righteousness (III,11.2). The second element, imputation, is then developed first against Osiander (secs. 5-12) and then against Rome (secs. 13-20), Calvin stressing throughout that Christian righteousness and sanctification, though inseparable, are nevertheless distinct and not to be confused.[7] Then Calvin introduces the first element, remission of sins (secs. 21-23), his own preferred interest indicated by the fact that the next two chapters are devoted to topics cognate with the subject of human sinfulness. Echoing the theme with which the *Institutes* began and which was quoted at the beginning of this chapter, Calvin emphasizes the need for God's forgiving justification of us—a need driven home to us when we compare our own righteousness with God's (Ch.12). Then returning to the theme with which he began the essay on faith, Calvin describes how, properly humbled by

[6] II,1.3; 2.8f; III,2.41; 14.9; 19.13. Cf. Paul Jacobs, *Prädestination und Verantwortlichkeit bei Calvin* (Neukirchen: Buchhandlung des Erziehungsvereins, 1937), p. 107; François Wendel, *Calvin: The Origins and Development of His Religious Thought*, trans. Philip Mairet (New York: Harper & Row, 1963), p. 256f.

[7] III,11.6; cf. 11.11; IV,9-11.

viewing ourselves according to God's "straightedge," we may have complete peace of conscience from the sure knowledge of God's justification (Ch. 13).

Only once he has established the sure foundation of the doctrine of justification does Calvin feel free to turn to a consideration of the place of works in the life of faith. His discussion in Chapters 14-18 is on the one hand basically defensive and polemical against Roman Catholic views, and on the other hand largely devoted to "external works" in relation to faith. The doctrine of justification established, the question now is how one is to understand the relationship between faith and the internally regenerate life which makes external good works possible. Calvin states the relationship very clearly in the midst of his defense against the Catholic objections to his positions.

> Why, then, are we justified by faith? Because by faith we grasp Christ's righteousness, by which alone we are reconciled to God. Yet you could not grasp this without *at the same time* grasping sanctification also. . . . Therefore Christ justifies no one whom he does not *at the same time* sanctify. These benefits are joined together by an everlasting and indissoluble bond, so that those whom he illumines by his wisdom, he redeems; those whom he redeems, he justifies; those whom he justifies, he sanctifies (16.1, emphasis mine).

Calvin followed his opening assertion about the object of regeneration by saying he was not interested in composing an essay on the particular virtues we are to manifest in the world. The Christian life which is his subject in the essay to follow is still the inward life of regeneration.[8]* It is the regenerate life of the invisible church, a life of which the internal structure is defined by the example of Christ and is internally effected by the power of the Holy Spirit.

2. THOUGH THE EXTERNAL church be many and various, the internal church is wholly one. This unity or harmony is not merely a harmony

---

[8]It should be clear that Calvin's positive teachings in Book III are all teachings concerning the internal life of the church. The phrase in the title of Book III, ". . . and What Effects Follow," should not be taken to suggest anything else. The effects are internal. Faith, repentance, regeneration, self-denial, justification, freedom, election—all these are clearly matters of the heart, of the disposition, of motive. They cannot be defined by outward observances. Outward observances are at best merely an expression of the inward fact. Calvin does not begin to consider the life of the outer man and the visible church until Book IV, "The External Means or Aids . . ."

among those earthly souls who make up the true church on earth. It extends to include the saints already in glory, the angels, and also, in principle at least, God's created world. For it is Christ who as the sole foundation of the church creates this unity.[9] One of Christ's two distinct powers, according to Calvin, is that manifest in the structures of the world and the order of nature. The other is that power by which fallen nature is renewed and restored. And for Calvin this power of regeneration is virtually identifed with the work of the Holy Spirit.[10] The whole purpose of Christ's incarnation, death, and resurrection is that our humanity and his divinity might grow together "by mutual connection."[11] The mutual connection of Christ and us, that by which it becomes possible to define the church as the "society of Christ" (title, Book IV), is that relationship effected by the secret power of the Holy Spirit.[12]

Even though Calvin includes the living church, the saints in glory, the angels, and the (restored) earth itself in his understanding of the unifying function of Christ's Spirit, he does not wish to suggest that there is an identity among these entities. To do that would leave the way open for at least two erroneous consequences, consequences which could be illustrated in certain positions of some Anabaptists. Identification of the true church on earth with the saints in glory or the angel could suggest that the church on earth was a perfected body. But Calvin insists that the church is defined by its life of faith, which therefore constantly involves repentance.[13] "The whole life of Christians," says Calvin, "ought to be a sort of practice of godliness, for we have been called to sanctification."[14] This passage is a strong echo of Luther's first thesis that the whole life of the Christian people should be one of repentance.

Too close an identification of the body of Christ with restored earthly nature could issue in a kind of universalism of salvation, a theory many early Anabaptists developed largely on the basis of a mistranslation of Mark 16.15 as ". . . the gospel of all creatures."[15] Calvin may be making oblique reference to the consequences of this error when he insists against the Anabaptists that not Christ's flesh, but faith and the inward work of the Spirit is the distinguishing feature of our spiritual union with Christ.[16] Without such a differentiating feature, the doctrine of God's special election would be devoid of real meaning.

[9]II,6.2; *Com. on I Cor.* 3:11, p. 135f.; cf. *Com. on Rom.* 3:12, p. 126; *Com. on Eph.* 1:10, p. 205.
[10]*Com. on John* 1.6, p. 34.
[11]II,12.1; III,2.24.
[12]III,11.5; cf. III,1.1,3.
[13]III,3.2.
[14]III,19.2.
[15]Cf. the discussion of this topic in George H. Williams, *The Radical Reformation* (Philadelphia: The Westminster Press, 1962), particularly pp. 836ff.
[16]II,13.2; III,1.1. Calvin's rejection of the Lutheran idea of the ubiquity of Christ's resurrected body may also be based at least partly on the same idea.

Both errors—perfectionism and universalism—can be avoided only if the body of Christ be understood in light of the work of the Spirit. As we have seen, the object of regeneration is not the identity, but the harmony or agreement between God's righteousness and our obedience (III,6.1). This is the ongoing function of the Holy Spirit. Since that regenerating activity of the Holy Spirit is identified by Calvin with repentance, all thought of perfection is excluded. The same activity of the Spirit excludes all thoughts of universalism as well. For repentance is born of faith. And repentance and faith are the effects of the inward working Spirit—the Spirit who by this activity distinguishes God's elect from the rest of creation.

Calvin insists that even though the Spirit's power fills creation, the Spirit of sanctification dwells only in believers. Only the elect receive the full grace of the Spirit.[17] Therefore only in the church, the community of the elect, is there forgiveness of sins. Forgiveness of sins in fact "is for us the first entry into the church and the Kingdom of God. Without it, there is for us no covenant or bond with God."[18] The difference between the elect and the non-elect is that forgiveness of sins and all that it implies is sealed by the Spirit only in the hearts of the elect.[19] Similarly and consequently, only in the elect is there truly a will toward the good.[20]

As we have seen, Calvin insisted that the only access we have to Christ and the Father is through the Holy Spirit. Throughout the *Institutes* Calvin associates the Holy Spirit with a teaching function, i.e., with the function of commending to us Christ's Gospel and true religion as these are found in the Holy Scripture.[21] But this association should not be taken to suggest that the chief function of the Spirit is other than the power/freedom function specified in our thesis. For Calvin always emphasizes in his discussion of the Spirit's functions relative to the Word that the Spirit is not the originator of any new or supplemental revelation beyond the teachings of Christ.[22] More to the point: to Calvin there is no such thing as a true knowledge of God or man except insofar as that knowledge is inscribed in the heart and expressed in a regenerate life. That is why the work of the Spirit is so necessary. Without it the doctrine of Christ, and Christ himself, are useless, barren things.[23] For Calvin, the agency of the Holy Spirit relative to certifying the Word in our hearts and lives comes under the general rubric of sanctification.

Calvin has stated that the difference between the elect and non-elect is that the former enjoy a special grace of the Spirit. One cannot understand this grace as a kind of indwelling virtue, as either a quantifiable difference in, or a qualification of, the human soul, such as this grace was understood

[17] II,2.6,16.
[18] IV,1.20; cf. III,20.9,45; 1541 Catechism, q. 104.
[19] III,2.11.
[20] II,2.26f.; 3.8.
[21] Cf. I,5.13; 7.3f.; 91ff.; *Com. on John* 14:25, p. 101; on 16:8, p. 138.
[22] Cf. Werner Krusche, *Das Wirken des Heiligen Geistes bei Calvin* (Göttingen: Vandenhoeck & Ruprecht, 1957), p. 215; Ronald S. Wallace, *Calvin's Doctrine of the Word and Sacrament* (Edinburgh: Oliver & Boyd, 1953), p. 130.
[23] I,8.5; III,1.3; 2.33ff. Calvin of course completely shares Luther's rejection of what the latter termed a "merely historical faith" which even the devils share.

by Rome and by many Anabaptists. Rather, Calvin concentrates attention on grace as a form of God's will (indeed, as God's law), by which man becomes conformed to Christ, who is the righteousness of God.

> Hence it appears that God's grace, as this word is understood in discussing regeneration, is the rule of the Spirit to regulate man's will. The Spirit cannot regulate without correcting, without reforming, without renewing. For this reason we say that the beginning of our regeneration is to wipe out what is ours. Likewise, he cannot carry out these functions without moving, acting, impelling, bearing, keeping. Hence we are right in saying that all the actions that arise from grace are wholly his.[24]

Calvin's definition of grace seems to make two emphases directed against what he considered errors in Roman Catholic and Anabaptist teaching on the subject of regeneration. Against Rome, Calvin's emphasis, like Luther's, was that sanctification is a process the sole agent of which is God. There is nothing indwelling man which can be appealed to as either a contributing or even a non-resisting factor.

The general context in which this definition occurs, however, indicates that Calvin's chief emphasis is against the perfectionist tendencies he usually associates with Anabaptist thought. We may put the issue this way: what is the end or ideal pattern to which the work of the Spirit in us is directed? Says Calvin at I,15.4, ". . . the end of regeneration is that Christ should reform us to God's image." There are two major places in the *Institutes* where the object of the Spirit's regenerating work is the major theme. The *imago dei* is discussed by Calvin specifically at I,15.3-5 and more generally at II,2-12. The earlier discussion of man's original spiritual nature presumes the later discussion of man's nature as restored by Christ—another illustration of the systematic problems caused by the tension between the doctrines of creation and redemption. In both these sections the major opponent is neither the Anabaptists, nor even Servetus, but the Lutheran, Osiander. What Osiander shares with the general Anabaptist view, however, is a consequent tendency toward perfectionism in the matter of sanctification.[25]*

[24]II,5.15. Cf. I,9.1; III,7.1; *Com. on John* 3:6, p. 114; on 14:18, p. 94; on 20:17, p. 259.

[25]Much of the material in these sections is either new in the 1559 edition or significantly reworked from earlier editions. One might argue that Calvin's concentration against the views of Osiander is due to the fact that by 1559 the controversies stirred by the latter's views had come to Calvin's attention. One such as Calvin, however, always had a range of possible opponents to which to address himself. And so we have to ask ourselves, why is this opponent chosen here rather than another? Why Osiander, when on the issue of sanctification, the Anabaptist views would appear a much more obvious counterfoil?

Part of the answer might be that the professional status of Osiander, and the apparent proximity of his "Lutheran" theology to Calvin's, made him a much more serious threat to Calvin than the Anabaptists. Another possibility might be the general unavailability to Calvin of Anabaptist sources. For further thoughts on this question, cf. the continuation in the text.

Even though the original *imago dei* is evidenced in the natural world and among the angels (I,15.3), Calvin insists that properly speaking the "image of God" is a designation of the human spirit or soul, the function of which designation is to distinguish man's restored (and original) spiritual nature from the nature of other creatures and from angels (II,12.6). Calvin's line of analysis on this matter is systematically related to his parallel line of analysis regarding the definition of the true church: he is concerned to avoid occasion for any notions of perfectionism or universalism.

We must remember that Calvin's descriptions and definitions, apart from those in Book IV, are of the inward, invisible, true church. It is an important matter for Calvin that the restored and original ideal *imago dei* be understood to include the whole man, i.e., his "flesh" or otherwise visible, public, or scientifically ascertainable characteristics. We shall consider these characteristics below in the sections concerning the visible church. But basically the *imago dei* is a term for man's invisible, restored, originating spiritual nature, the "inner good of the soul" (I,15.4). For Calvin the *imago dei* is seen "in the light of the mind, in the uprightness of the heart, and in the soundness of all the parts"—"the perfect excellence of human nature which shone in Adam before his defection . . ." (I,15.4). It is these spiritual gifts, which Calvin later enumerates as faith, love for God and neighbor, and the zeal for holiness and righteousness (II,2.12), that are restored to fallen man via the power of the Spirit.

It has been suggested that Calvin's immediate interest in the issue of the *imago dei* is to combat tendencies toward perfectionist and universalist ideas regarding the doctrine of sanctification. Yet one of the basic assumptions in this study is that, to the Reformation theologian if not to the modern sociologist or psychologist or religion, one's understanding of the trinitarian interrelationships determines one's evaluation of worldly human relationships, and not the reverse. If we are willing to accept this assumption, Calvin's decision to address Osiander, the professional Lutheran theologian, on the matter of sanctification, rather than what to Calvin were untutored Anabaptist lay spokesmen, will make more sense.

According to Calvin, Osiander's position in favor of the view that Christians are actually, substantially righteous (=sanctified or holy) is consequent upon certain prior errors concerning the nature of the relationships among the persons of the Trinity. Calvin accepts one of Osiander's basic premises that Christ is the perfect "image of God" to whom we Christians are and ought to be conformed (I,15.4). But to Calvin, Osiander appears to "mingle heaven and earth" by extending the *imago dei* to include the body. Christ's actual body is then said to be a manifestation of a supposed trinitarian image which, according to Osiander, has eternally and necessarily existed as God's ideal for our human being.

Calvin sees in this position a number of insidious implications, the chief of which is a confusion of functions of the Son and Holy Spirit. Osiander's position would make the incarnation necessary even if Adam had not sinned, and would suggest that Christ's function was that of an ideal human prototype which actually becomes ours with the birth of faith.

As much as this view superficially maintains a sense of the unconditionality of the divine life (and to that extent would be acceptable to Calvin), it effectively removes any real meaning from the function of Christ as redeemer. Calvin insists, as we have seen, that Christ's incarnation was not necessary except for the fall. But this conditionality does not apply to the *imago dei* or to Christ's lordship of the church (II,12.7). If one needs a basis upon which to anchor trust that God is unconditioned in his relationship to us, that basis is not a supposed eternal, ideal type existing in God's mind, but is rather the eternal decisions of God's elective will.

Osiander's position, exchanging as it does the knowledge of Christ as redeemer from sin for that of Christ as the ideal for human perfection, thereby also confuses the functions of Christ and the Spirit, and mistakes the role of the latter. Whereas Osiander has confused trinitarian relationships, Calvin insists that the Son and the Holy Spirit must be cleanly distinguished in being and function (I,15.3). The Holy Spirit, after all, is spirit, not flesh. As we have seen, Calvin insisted that the only access we have to the Father and the Son is through the Spirit. The Spirit's work of sanctification in us is wholly a spiritual work: to reform, renew, and purify our "spiritual nature" so that the image of God might shine in it.

By restricting so sharply the power of the Spirit to an inward, spiritual function, Calvin has, to his mind at least, prevented all the perfectionist implications of Osiander's (and Anabaptist) views. Most importantly for our following discussion: we are prevented from mistaking Calvin's strong affirmation of the "third and principal " use of the law (II,7.12) as a re-introduction, in the doctrine of regeneration, of the works-righteousness eliminated in the doctrine of justification. The third use of the law is an entirely spiritual use. It ". . . finds its place among believers in whose hearts the Spirit of God already lives and reigns." The Spirit's function here is necessary precisely because Christians are not perfect either inwardly or outwardly.

Inwardly: the law "is the best instrument for them to learn more thoroughly each day the nature of the Lord's will to which they aspire, and to confirm them in the understanding of it."

Outwardly: ". . .because we need not only teaching but also exhortation, the servant of God will also avail himself of this benefit of the law: by frequent meditation upon it to be aroused to obedience, be strengthened in it, and be drawn back from the slippery path of transgression. In this way the saints must press on: for however eagerly they may in accordance with the Spirit strive toward God's righteousness, the listless flesh always so burdens them that they do not proceed with due readiness" (II,7.12).

B. *The Visible Church: An Ordered Life*

At Question 55 of his 1541 French catechism, Calvin states that the Christian doctrine of the atonement concerns itself only with Christ's birth and death, and not with his life, "because nothing is said here about what belongs properly to the substance of our redemption."

Luther generally understood Christ's Sermon on the Mount not as a positive instruction on the kind of life one must live in order to enter and remain in the church, but as an attack upon our underestimation of God's righteousness, the object of which attack is to make us, already in the church, realize how impossible it is for us to observe God's law.

Had Menno Simons read these views, he would have been shocked beyond belief. Imagine! Men offering themselves as evangelical theologians and pastors, who claim that Christ's life and teachings are not the substance of what it means to be righteous!

As formulated in the opening chapter and illustrated particularly in Part Two, one of the basic differences between Simons on the one hand and Luther and Calvin on the other was that the two latter shared what we might today call a transcendentalist approach to salvation history which Simons did not accept. Luther and Calvin believed that sin and salvation were realities transcending our present actual existence. Sin is a state of being and not primarily an act. Salvation was accomplished once for all, perfectly, on the cross long ago by God himself, and is granted to us now as a free, unmerited gift. Simons was critical of both views. The first was to him simply an illusion. And both by implication seemed to him to encourage a certain laxity in Christian discipline which would prove fatal to the attainment of salvation.

The same transcendentalism was also reflected in a distinction more specific to the positions noted above, and more germane to the themes of the following sections: the distinction between the visible and the invisible church. While all the parties (including Simons) would identify the invisible church as the true church, the issue was whether the actual behavior of those who claim to constitute the visible church ought to be taken as indication of the degree of identity of that visible church with the true church. More simply: is visibly righteous behavior one of the marks of the holy community?

Here Calvin and Simons, though still quite distinct because of their differences in ontological foundation, are much closer together than Simons and Luther. The reason for this relatively greater accord is that Calvin and Simons share in their trinitarian ascriptive patterns the assignment to the Holy Spirit of the functions of sanctifying power. Yet because of his transcendentalism, Calvin also significantly differs from Simons on the matter of the formal importance of discipline in the definition of the true church.

Our concern here is to define Calvin's mediate position on this matter, especially in relationship to the position of Simons, but also with regard to that of Luther. Often it is seen in print or heard in lecture on Calvin that 1)in contrast to Luther, Calvin insisted that a Christian must work "through" his vocation, rather than "in" it; and that 2)like Simons, Calvin made discipline a mark of the church. But if these advocates of Calvin would make but a cursory study of the *Institutes*, they would learn that both positions are wrong. Calvin insisted that one work in the vocation in which tradition and circumstances have placed him; and for him, discipline is not a formal mark of the church.

In this and the final section of our consideration of Calvin's theology, the discussion concerns Calvin's understanding of how the Holy Spirit, via the external aid which is the visible ecclesiastical order, effects in us the inward discipline and sustains us in that vocation. Or in the words of the title of Book IV, how we are invited into and held within the divine community which is Christ's church.

1. THE SIMPLE FACT that Calvin's basic discussion of the Christian life comes in Book III rather than in Book IV on the "external aids" should lead us to suspect that his views on discipline relative to the definition of the church will be different from Simons'.

Calvin's order of thought in III,3-24 is at first glance unexpected, but upon further meditation it can be seen to provide the placement, content, and relationship of our themes of discipline and vocation. Having specified repentance and forgiveness of sins as the effects of faith, Calvin further defines repentance as newness of life and then as regeneration. He defines forgiveness of sins as free reconciliation (III,3.1-9). He decides to concentrate first[26]* on repentance/regeneration. The "fruits of repentance" involve "the duties of piety toward God, of charity toward men, and in the whole of life, holiness and purity" (III,3.16). Otherwise put, the "object of regeneration is conformity to God's righteousness." This is what constitutes the life of the Christian man (title, Ch. 6). Calvin devotes five chapters to its elucidation. He tells us right at the beginning that he is not going to compose an essay on the virtues, but rather will point to a universal rule of life (sec. 1) of which Chirst is the pattern (sec. 3). Of what rule is Christ the pattern for us? Now comes the unexpected answer: self-denial. That is the sum of the Christian life of which Christ is the pattern. Calvin devotes three chapters to the subject of self-denial.

It must be clear to anyone who thinks about it that the discipline of self-denial is a wholly internal, spiritual discipline. The whole matter, in any application, involves one's inner attitudes or dispositions regarding goods, whether those goods be external or internal. External abstinence does not necessarily imply self-denial. External indulgence (moderate, of course!) does not necessarily imply the absence of internal discipline. Who knows what it is that tempts a man? How is one to assess externally our discipline concerning purely inward matters (the most important arena for the exercise of self-denial)? Only the inward self knows whether, for example, it indulges a vanity concerning one's intelligence or physical appearance, or a vanity concerning the personal suffering one has endured.

Calvin's discussion in these chapters concerns the inward disposition to goods, including those of the self. It concerns the inner, indeed invisible life, the life in which the Holy Spirit himself is directly operative. Calvin's ap-

---

[26]Calvin insists, however, that repentance and forgiveness of sins are intrinsically related (19ff.). And he follows with what he feels is a presently necessary defensive excursus against Roman views on repentance.

proach here is closely parallel to Luther's use of the "Spirit-Flesh" language to describe not entities, but attitudes of the "hidden" Christian. It is only in this sense that it would be proper to say that for Calvin discipline (=self-denial) is a mark of the church. Of the invisible church!

The subordinate point—or perhaps better, the conclusion of his discussion—is again like Luther's conclusion on the same matter. Christian life is not bound to any particular external behavioral code beyond the general rules by which all civilized men must live. This point is driven home by Calvin in Chapter 10, the end of his essay. Regarding all outward goods, we are free to relate to them as seems best to us (or rather, as seems best to the discerning Spirit within us). Our general guide is simply the revealed end to which God intends these goods. Calvin specified this end at the beginning of his essay: the glory of God and the service of the brethren.

It is now possible for us to assess more correctly Calvin's positions on discipline, obedience, law, and the marks of the church, within the general theme of this section: the relationship of freedom and justice as that relationship is effected by the work of the Holy Spirit.

It would be wrong to see the self-denial Calvin commends as a virtue which, as the saying goes, is its own reward. Nor does the discipline of self-denial have as its primary object the internal, aesthetic "distancing" of the Christian soul from the good things of this world. As elsewhere, Calvin the evangelical reformed theologian sees man's will only in the context of God's will. Therefore we must not consider self-denial as a mere virtue adorning the soul whom the Holy Spirit has reconstructed with his grace. It is rather, as Calvin titled his chapter, the sum of the Christian life. Christian life is the discipline of self-denial—a discipline whose object is service of God. That is to say, it is our vocation. As Calvin put it grandly in a beautifully trinitarian passage:

> We are not our own: let not our reason, nor our will, therefore, sway our plans and deeds. We are not our own: let us therefore not set it as our goal to seek what is expedient for us according to the flesh. We are not our own: in so far as we can, let us therefore forget ourselves and all that is ours.
>
> Conversely, we are God's: let us therefore live for him and die for him. We are God's: let his wisdom and will therefore rule all our actions. We are God's: let all the parts of our life accordingly strive toward him as our only lawful goal. . . .
>
> Let this therefore be the first step, that a man depart from himself in order that he may apply the whole force of his ability in the service of the Lord. I call "service" not only what lies in obedience to God's Word but what turns the mind of man, empty of its own carnal sense, wholly to the bidding of God's Spirit.[27]

---

[27] III,7.1; on vocation, cf. Jacobs, pp. 110f., 122.

The life of self-denial in service of God is a life of obedience. Only out of a life of obedience, Calvin says, are perfect faith and right knowledge of God born.[28] There is no way we can love God, know him truly as Lord, Savior, and Father, unless that love be inseparably joined with faith and obedience.[29] And it is only on the basis of love to God, Calvin says, that we may properly serve God and man.[30]

The service of God, born of love out of faith and obedience, is not, however, something man can accomplish by consulting his own best philosophy. Nor does it consist in a generalized if passionate "benevolent feeling" toward everyone. As Calvin continues in the passage quoted above, ". . .The Christian philosophy bids reason give way to, submit to and subject itself to, the Holy Spirit so that man himself may no longer live but hear Christ living and reigning within him." Hear Christ! That means that the proper service of God requires constant meditation upon the pattern Christ has established in his Word. The condition of our adoption by God is that our lives express Christ, the bond of adoption. The work of the spirit therefore is to conform us in service to the specific patterns of obligation established by God's Word, that is, by God's law.[31]

We need not produce an essay on Calvin's sense of law in the Christian life—a subject that has stirred the pens of friends and opponents alike since his own time. Rather, it should simply be pointed out that we mistake Calvin's intent if we interpret the so-called "third use" of the law as but one distinct kind of law, and "law" in general as but one aspect of God's revelation. To do either would lead to the same kind of misinterpretation that would occur if we took self-denial as but one of the virtues of a Christian man: we would be led into an evangelical form of works-righteousness.[32*]

Rather, law in its positive Christian use must be understood in the same way as self-denial: as the sum of the Christian life. Just as self-denial names the whole reality of Christian living in service of God, so law is the whole reality of God's will for that service. It is "the pattern of perfect righteousness"; it is not only the Ten Commandments, but "the form of religion handed down by God through Moses"; "the best instrument for [believers] to learn more thoroughly each day the nature of the Lord's will to which they aspire, and to confirm them in the understanding of it."[33]

[28]I,6.2; cf. III,2.6.
[29]1541 Catechism, q. 218; cf. *Institutes* II,2.18; III,3.14.
[30]I,5.3.; III,7.5ff.
[31]III,6.3; cf. 3.16.
[32]This "splitting up" of both human characteristics and God's revelation was characteristic of high and late medieval theology, due perhaps to the relatively unguarded use of the syllogistic method of analysis. We also see it recurring in evangelical form, both under Lutheranism and Calvinism, with the development of the *loci* method of composing doctrinal instruments. The magisterial reformers all saw the various Anabaptist groups as "worksmongers," of course. And there is some basis for this judgment. My own explanation for the presence of "works-righteousness" tendencies in the theology of Simons is not his method of writing or thinking, but the effective absence of ontological foundation. It is, however, best to remember Christ's words about the log in one's own eye, before we rush to remove the mote from someone else's vision. [33]II,2.24; 7.1,12; cf. Wendel, p. 203ff.

For Calvin, the Christian discipline is the Christian vocation. That life of vocation, which Calvin summed up as the discipline of self-denial, is a life of service guided by the revealed will of God, which Calvin summed up as law. Only if we take self-denial and law as strictly correlative terms, terms moreover naming the whole interrelation of man and God, can we avoid the dangers of works-righteousness and the sense of spiritual bondage which such a misinterpretation forces upon us.

No less than did Luther, Calvin insisted that Christians will freely observe the law and that the law, properly understood, created freedom of response in us. That such freedom is possible is because God's will toward us, just like our responsive service to him, is an expression of love. The root of that love, the fact that makes God's law of positive value to our lives, and our life of self-denial one of service to God, is the righteousness accomplished for us by Christ. Here we have another sense of that phrase of Calvin's recurred to so frequently: "the beginning of love is righteousness" (II,17.2). Calvin's lengthy essay on our justification by Christ's righteousness (III,11-18) is bounded fore and aft by chapters on Christian freedom. The life of self-denial, of freedom from bondage to things of this world (Ch. 10), would not, however, be of itself fit service to God unless it issued from the certain conviction that Christ has freed us from bondage to the law's demands (Chs. 11-18). Only then can our response to God's will be a loving, joyous, and free response (Ch. 19).

Calvin construes that freedom which "is especially an appendage of justification and is of no little avail in understanding its power" (III,19.1) as 1)freedom of conscience before God; 2)freedom for doing the law; and (echoing the theme of Chapter 10) 3) freedom from the "indifferent" things and practices of this life. His growing emphasis throughout Chapter 19 is that our life of self-denial, of free service to God's will as revealed in the law, must be a life of self-denial, of freedom-in-order. The pattern established by Christ for our lives presumes an internal freedom, of course, a freedom which only the Holy Spirit achieves within each of us by his power. Yet that internal freedom, like self-denial, is also not a virtue in itself. It is there for the purpose of service. And that means service of the brethren.[34] The internal freedom Christ accomplished for us is meant to facilitate the achievement of an ordered life, the life for which Christ sets the pattern. Calvin concludes his chapter on the freedom which attends justification with an emphasis upon order within the church (secs. 10-13) and between the church and the world (secs. 14-16). Christ is the pattern of perfect justice or righteousness. Only the power of the Holy Spirit creates in us the freedom to achieve that pattern. That pattern is an ordered harmony which the Father in his love intends for his own. We now turn our attention to the subjects of freedom and justice as the instruments by which order is achieved in the church and between the church and the world.

2.IN THE COURSE of his introduction of faith as repentance/regeneration, Calvin scored the Anabaptists for a perfectionism which, by abolishing the distinctions among vices and virtues, leads to

[34]Jacobs, p. 91.

disorder. The sanctifying work of the Holy Spirit, Calvin says, leads not to license but to order.[35] In his essay on justification, Calvin argued that unless one recognizes the difference between the righteous and the unrighteous, no order will remain in the world.[36] Later, at the end of his chapter on Christian freedom, Calvin introduced the subject of the "twofold government" in man in order to preclude the possibility of disorder's arising from a misunderstanding of Christian freedom.[37] When in Book IV Calvin turns to the matter of church discipline, he asserts throughout that the general purpose of discipline is that the church be sustained in proper order.[38]

Calvin's stress on faith as a process of sanctification has brought him to a position which could appear very close to the views of both Anabaptists and Roman Catholics on the nature of Christian life. Calvin himself sees all the difference in the world. Book III, on sanctification, is developed largely with Anabaptist perfectionist views as a counterfoil; Book IV, on the visible church, with the Roman Catholic ecclesiastical system as the main counterfoil. The subjects of sanctification and life in the church are inextricably interwoven in Calvin's theology. There is no real church except the communion of saints; and it is only in the church community and by means of it that holiness is created, exercised, and brought to fulness. But he sees the Anabaptist and Roman Catholic positions as opposite errors, errors which, however, produce the same result: disorder in both church and world. By obliterating all distinctions as a consequence of an unwarranted stress on freedom from the values of the world, the Anabaptists not only scandalize consciences, but also create yet another unnecessary and competitive political power.

Calvin's position, to his own mind at least, is a middle position which by a careful balance of freedom and justice avoids the extremes and so allows God's intended order to be established.

The key to the balance is the proper distinction of the "twofold government." The spiritual jurisdiction or government pertains to the inner life, the soul, or conscience; the temporal government to the present life, outward behavior, and life in society.[39] Although Calvin does not think the matter "very obscure or involved," he does find it necessary in this chapter on Christian freedom to stress the sharp distinctions of jurisdiction. We need not develop a lengthy presentation on the subject of the "two realms" in Calvin's theology. This matter (like the question of the place of law in the Christian life, with which the matter of the two realms is closely related) has been fully examined in the literature. Two points, however, need to be stressed relative to the themes of this and the following section. 1)The distinction introduced does not suggest an opposition between church government and civil government. It is rather a distinction of the

---

[35]III,3.14; cf. Ronald S. Wallace, *Calvin's Doctrine of the Christian Life* (Edinburgh: Oliver & Boyd, 1959), pp. 103ff.
[36]III,14.2.
[37]III,19.14f.
[38]IV,12.1ff.
[39]III,19.15.

legitimacies of jurisdiction. And it is not a distinction suggesting an opposition between the rights of free conscience and the obligations of social justice. It is rather a distinction of jurisdictional function, the object of which is to maintain order by means of a proper balance of freedom and justice. 2) The phrasing of Calvin's definition suggests what to him was perhaps a more basic distinction. The "temporal" jurisdiction concerns present existence. What of the "spiritual" jurisdiction? Does it concern the future? More correctly, do we have here a sense of the distinction of being and becoming? Is that why Calvin immediately proceeds from his introduction of the "two realms" in the chapter on Christian freedom in this world to a long, beautiful chapter on prayer and perseverance?

Calvin assumes that it is natural and necessary for all human societies of whatever sort to be organized and governed according to law. The church, far from being an exception, must reflect order as much as possible.[40] Of the various forms of social organization he sees possible—monarchy, aristocracy, and democracy—Calvin prefers a combination of the latter two, largely because he feels that such a system is less liable to misuse than either monarchy or each form by itself.[41] Whatever the form, civil government has a definite function, at least while we live in this world. But now comes the shock to the modern western mind. The purposes of civil government are:

1. to cherish and protect the outward worship of God,
2. to defend sound doctrine of piety and the position of the church,
3. to adjust our life to the society of men,
4. to form our social behavior to civil righteousness,
5. to reconcile us with one another, and
6. to promote general peace and tranquility.[42]

In the continuation Calvin indicates that he is aware of the reactions his definition could cause. But he insists that maintenance of religious propriety is a legitimate function of civil government. Indeed he seems to suggest that it is the major function. Only if religious propriety is maintained can the other functions of government be discharged well. For "no government can be happily established unless piety is the first concern; . . . those laws are preposterous which neglect God's right and provide only for men."[43]

Although we might raise principled objections to Calvin's inclusion of the maintenance of public piety among the proper functions of civil government, neither Luther nor Simons would have objected in principle. Luther, with his darker estimate of the human social condition, might have demur-

[40]IV,10.27; 12.1; cf. Krusche, pp. 110ff.
[41]IV,20.8. Yet he allows that differing conditions may alter this valuation; cf. IV,20.15.
[42]IV,20.2.
[43]IV,20.3,9. For Calvin's views on the nature of civil justice, the legitimacy of war, and the relation of civil to natural law, cf. III,7.3; IV,20.4,100ff., *et passim*. On the true king as God's minister, cf. the preface, p. 12; IV,11.4; 20.4f.

red at Calvin's implication that government could "reconcile" people and "promote" peace and tranquility (5 and 6), preferring instead to define this function more negatively by putting 3 and 4 in somewhat more vigorous language. Menno Simons would have no trouble at all with 4, 5, and 6. He was as concerned as was Calvin—and with more reason—that civil righteousness, reconciliation, and peace be established by a truly just, even if non-Christian, magistrate. But Simons would hestitiate at Calvin's first two points. If a government would exercise its functions justly, i.e., without prejudice against any group whose behavior and beliefs fell within the general limits of what we could agree is the Christian religion, Simons would fully defend it. But that is the hook in Calvin's definitions. The questions are: whose opinion of true worship and piety? the position of which church? and what society of men?

Calvin's spare definitions of the nature of the "temporal" jurisdiction immediately involve us, via Simons' questions, in the matter of the nature of the "spiritual" jurisdiciton. What is that entity which the civil government is mandated by God to protect above all else? What is the church?

That question—one of the two basic doctrinal questions the answers to which have never been agreed upon by any majority of Christians[44]*—is answered differently by Calvin and Luther, by Rome, and Simons. Luther and Calvin would define the church in terms of doctrine and sacrament. Rome would subordinate these marks to that of the unbroken tradition and the succession of bishops. Simons, rejecting Roman accretions, would substitute as the chief mark of the church the discipline of Christ.

Our concern here is to distinguish Calvin's position from that of Luther and Simons. In the remainder of this subsection, the distinction of Calvin's and Simons' positions will be uppermost in our thought; that between Calvin and Luther in the following section.

Many of the apparent complexities involved in assessing Calvin's definitions of the "marks" of the church relative to those of Simons could be dispelled if we but recalled one distinction and made the one required application of it. The distinction is that between the visible and the invisible church. As we have seen, Simons, though finally accepting the distinction, reversed the valuation of it that Luther and Calvin shared. Simons insisted that the "invisible [true] church" existed only if and to the extent that a visibly righteous church existed. And by "visibly righteous" he meant behavior: Christian discipline.

The issue then is not whether discipline constitutes one of the marks of the church, but of which church discipline is a mark. That is the required application of the distinction. Calvin's difference from Simons is clear and simple, and it is not obscured by a suspicion they are working from different presumptions. When in the *Institutes* he found it appropriate to

---

[44]"The other doctrinal question concerns the atonement: how do Christ's incarnation, death, and resurrection affect or otherwise communicate their presumed benefits to us? The two questions are quite clearly related. Depending on how Christ can be said to have accomplished salvation for us, the church will be defined as the medium by which that salvation is communicated.

define the marks of the church, Calvin, like Luther, worked within the general subject of the visible church. We must recall that Book IV of the *Institutes* is entitled "The External Means. . . ." "Marks of the invisible church" is a contradiction in thought if not in terms. There may be some befogging difference of assumption between Calvin and Simons over whether or not the visible church functions as merely an "external means" by which the invisible church is extended. But the issue here is very clear: what are the marks of the visible church? And the difference between Simons and Calvin is equally clear.

As has been remarked upon by many students, Calvin, largely influenced by Bucer, almost committed himself to adding discipline as a third mark of the visible church.[45] In the *Institutes* the near-decision surfaces most clearly at IV,1.8. Calvin, having introduced the distinction of the visible and invisible church, at first says that "since assurance of faith was not necessary, [God] substituted for it a certain charitable judgment whereby we recognize as members of the church those who, by confession of faith, *by example of life*, and by partaking of the sacraments, profess the same God and Christ with us" (emphasis mine). We have commented on the provisional character of this definition earlier in the chapter. But Calvin continues immediately.

> He has, moreover, set off by plainer marks the knowledge of his very body to us, knowing how necessary it is to our salvation. . . .From this the face of the church comes forth and becomes visible to our eyes. Wherever we see the Word of God purely preached and heard, and the sacraments administered according to Christ's institution, there, it is not to be doubted, a church of God exists.

This is Calvin's formal position. It is sustained throughout the *Institutes*,[46] even though the matter of discipline continues to assert a strong influence, as in the definition above ("preached *and heard*"), throughout the text.

Calvin's difficulty with regard to dicipline as a formal mark of the church is much like Luther's difficulty concerning whether confession of sins should be considered a formal sacrament. In neither case was there a sure external sign to confirm the internal reality. But perhaps more importantly: to make confession of sins a formal sacrament and discipline a formal mark of the church (the two matters are closely interrelated) might lead to just the binding of the interior conscience that both reformers saw wrong with the positions of Rome and the Anabaptists. And so, as much as each valued and stressed the importance of confession and discipline, Luther and Calvin each had to make the same hard theological decision in order to maintain

---

[45]Cf. W. P. Stephens., *The Holy Spirit in the Theology of Martin Bucer* (Cambridge: Cambridge University Press, 1970), p. 262; Wendel, pp. 142ff.

[46]Preface, p. 24; IV,1.1,5,7 *et passim*.

the distinction of the visible and invisible churches, and to maintain Christian freedom of conscience in the midst of the demands of justice or righteousness.

Freedom in justice: this now becomes Calvin's emphasis as he sketches the actual discipline of the church. There are some general rules of operation which the visible church of Christ must observe, of course, but it must be free to frame its own order, free to adjust its actions to the circumstances of its life, within the bounds of faith and conscience.[47]

In his chapters on Christian freedom, from which many of the above references are drawn, Calvin's stress was on the distinction of the twofold jurisdiction. Since discipline or self-denial is a matter of the spiritual, inner man, it is just not possible to measure accurately its presence by external standards any more than the external sacrament of confession could measure true repentance. As we shall see, whenever Calvin had occasion to discuss the two realms, his language and mood indicate that his real attention is not with the exterior, "present" order, but with the interior life of faith and piety which looks to God and the future for its consummation. The chapter on the final resurrection, after all, comes at the end of book III on the interior Christian life, and not at the end of Book IV on the external means.

That focus of attention at least partially explains why Calvin is rather conservative on the various issues connected with merely civil justice. The Holy Spirit comes not to establish a new and different kingdom on earth; we must obey constituted government and work within our given secular callings.[48] To put it most sharply: Calvin feels there is no particular need to change even admittedly bad civil arrangements such as slavery because it is perfectly possible for spiritual freedom to exist along with civil bondage.[49] Why this relative unconcern? Just because the interior life of faith and discipline is free from bondage to merely present external order. As Calvin put it, introducing his definition of the functions of civil government quoted earlier:

> But as we have just now pointed out that this kind of government is distinct from that spiritual and inward Kingdom of Christ, so we must know that they are not at variance. For spiritual government, indeed, is already initiating in us upon earth certain beginnings of the Heavenly Kingdom, and in this mortal and fleeting life affords a certain forecast of an immortal and incorruptible blessedness.[50]

---

[47]III,10.1,2,4; IV,1.5; 6.9; 8.1. Cf. *Com. on I Cor* 2:2, p. 352; *Com. on Rom.* 9:3, p. 335; *Institutes*, III,19.13.

[48]*Com. on John* 16:14, p. 145. Cf. IV,20.22-29; III,10.6; 19.9, and Wallace, *Christian Life*, pp. 166, 181. For Calvin's sense of both history and the progressive character of God's revelation in history, cf. Preface. pp. 11, 15ff.; I,11.13; II,2.6; 7.2; 10.20; 11.13; 16.2; III,18.9; IV,4.3; *Com. on I Cor.* 11:2, p. 352.

[49]IV,20.1.

[50]IV,20.2.

Calvin's center of gravity is not in the external present but in God's futurity. And the true church, the church whose marks of Word, sacrament, and discipline are known only to God, is a church whose being is defined in terms of prayer, perseverance, and the becoming of perfect righteousness.

C. *The Church: Being and Becoming*

At III,3.1 Calvin specified repentance and forgiveness of sins as the chief effects of faith. He felt that the "order of right teaching" required him to concentrate first on repentance, defined as regeneration or newness of life. And he closed the section on the new life with a moving portrait of the Christian ethos of self-denial.

Calvin picks up the theme of forgiveness of sins, defined as free reconciliation, at III,11. His major burden in the early sections is to define justification against misunderstanding by Osiander and by Rome. Calvin's stress against both sides is that righteousness (=forgiveness of sins, 11.21ff.) and sanctification, though inseparable, must not be confused.[51] His emphasis is necessary just because he began his discussion of the effects of faith with regeneration rather than justification. Such a procedure might have led one to think that "justification" was but a term for God's recognition of a newness of life, regeneration, or sanctification achieved. The only issue then between Osiander and the Anabaptists on one side and Rome on the other would be when that goal was achieved. The former would claim that sanctification (=justification) was achieved upon entrance into a truly Christian life of repentance and faith; the latter, that full justification (=sanctification) was achieved at best only at the end of a life of good works.

Calvin saw the problem here not simply as one of a false identification of justification and sanctification. The more basic difficulty was the perceived relationship of justification and sanctification to a mistaken notion of (so to speak) "Christian time." The Catholics seemed to think of Christian time—or perhaps better, Christian life—purely in terms of a linear becoming of justification. To Calvin, this not only led to wrong conceptions of the place of works in the life of Christians, but more importantly robbed people of Christ's work and the peace of conscience afforded by that work. Osiander and the Anabaptists, on the other hand, seemed to think of Christian life wholly in terms of a quantitative being of sanctification. To Calvin, this not only led to a depreciation of God's law and the disciplines which God wills for our life, but more importantly threatened to efface the distinction between righteous God and sinful men.

Calvin sought a more balanced emphasis on being and becoming, one that he felt accorded with scripture and hence avoided the problems sketched above. Since the *Institutes* was a text for the evangelical church, Calvin felt particularly compelled to address himself to the issues posed from within the Protestant camp. Hence his main stress throughout III,11-25,

---

[51]III,11.6; 14.9-11; cf. 11.11.

which concerns the being of salvation already achieved (justification and election are the major themes of this section), is upon the becoming of righteousness in Christian life.

To describe Christian life as a "becoming" means that such a life must constantly be seen to involve recognition of one's continued sinfulness, one's distance from the righteousness which God alone by his Spirit can achieve in us. And such a life involves the equally constant recognition that God, by forgiving our sins and freely reconciling us to himself, by his Spirit daily achieves some progress toward that righteousness. The invisible church may be; the visible becomes. The life of Christians in that visible community of the church is accordingly a life of prayer, perseverance, and striving for the perfection of the Kingdom of God.

1. IN THE INTRODUCTION to section B we noted the common but erroneous view that Calvin, unlike Luther, insisted that Christians must work through, not in, their vocations. The error is not so much in the distinction itself, but in that to which it is usually applied. Without in any way diminishing his strong sense of the obligations that Christians as men and citizens had for improving the conditions of life, one must still assert that Calvin does not see one's Christian vocation as a means by or through which the temporal social order might be transformed into a closer approximation to the Kingdom of God. We must recall that for Calvin one's vocation is the spiritual discipline of self-denial, and that this discipline is the ethos of the interior, invisible church and not of the exterior, visible one.

The contrast with Luther is meaningful, however, if it is applied to its proper subject: the perfect righteousness of the Kingdom of God, a purely spiritual righteousness upon which the eye of our souls must be fixed constantly. In the early Luther the sense of Christian life as a continual struggle through the circumstances of this world toward the righteousness of God is very strong (cf. in particular the Luther of the Romans lectures). But Luther's well known shift from the earlier "theology of the cross" to the "theology of the Word" in the early 1520's may be indicative of a diminution of the eschatological sense of things. His subsequent growing interest in the "orders of creation" then also suggests a greater feeling of "at-homeness" in the world than is characteristic of Calvin.

For Calvin never relinquished the eschatological "theology of the cross."[52] Indeed he emphasized it more and more. His entire description of Christian life is a description of "bearing the cross" (cf. III,8)—another way of saying "self-denial." Once again we must emphasize that "cross-bearing" or self-denial is not a mere virtue characterizing the being of Christian man. It rather describes the dynamics of Christian becoming. The object of that becoming is the perfect righteousness or justice of God. The chief instrument through which that righteousness becomes realized in us is self-denial. The power by which that instrument is used effectively is that of the Holy Spirit: the power of prayer.

[52] Cf. Jacobs, p. 112f.; Wallace, *Christian Life*, p. 251.

Throughout his essay on justification, Calvin applied the evangelical doctrine in two interrelated ways. The doctrine insured that true knowledge of God and of his honor would be maintained, with the consequence that true knowledge of man and his sinfulness would also be maintained (III,12f.). And it insured that sanctification would be properly understood as the progressive, lifelong struggle for the righteousness of God (III,14-18).

The sense of sanctification as a lifelong struggle toward God's righteousness is evident throughout the *Institutes*. Even our highest understanding of perfection, we heard Calvin say at the beginning of this chapter, ill accords with the reality of God. Yet it is precisely holiness of life which is the goal of our election in Christ.[53] One cannot short-circuit the process of sanctification by a false sense of perfection, as Calvin thinks the Anabaptists do.[54] Yet even though justification and the new creature are distinct things, God justifies no one whom he does not also immediately begin to sanctify.[55] That is why sanctification can be understood as a progressive struggle.[56] Because of the work of the Holy Spirit in us, our life can be fairly described as a sort of "practice of godliness" whereby the image of God is gradually restored in us.[57]

Sanctification is, however, also a progressive struggle because of the sin remaining within us. And that is why the Christian life is one of self-denial, of cross-bearing, and especially of prayer.

As noted earlier, Calvin quite pointedly framed his discussion of justification with chapters on Christian freedom (III,10, 19). But the frame for the doctrine of justification, which is "the main hinge on which religion turns" (III,11.1), is broader than the issue of freedom. For Calvin, equally pointedly, prefaced Chapter 10 with a discussion of self-denial and cross-bearing (Chs. 7-9) and followed Chapter 19 with a lengthy, beautiful essay on prayer (Ch. 20).

Now the subjects of self-denial, cross-bearing, perseverance, meditation on the future life, and prayer are not of particular interest to most modern readers. We feel more at home in the world, less pilgrims in an alien land. We feel more like honored guests at life's banquet, and less like lonely vigil-keepers on the watchtower. Hence the above subjects, reflective as they are of a sense of things medieval and far removed from us, are often passed over quickly in a study of the reformers of the sixteenth century. And to assign them pride of place, as we do here at the conclusion of our study of Calvin, can seem intentionally contrary at best or sadly quixotic at worst.

But we must subordinate our interests to the evaluations, piety, and judgment of the men we are studying. We are now considering what the reformers described, from their own distinct perspectives, as the reality of Christian life. And on this matter the reformers, in spite of their principled

[53]III,23.12.
[54]III,3.14 *et passim*.
[55]III,11.6; 16.1.
[56]III,7.5; 2.4; 14.9; *Com. on John* 3:3, p. 108; *Com. on Rom.* 1:17, p. 65.
[57]III,19.2; II,7.5; III,3.8; 20.45; IV,1.21.

differences, agreed: Christian life is a life of prayer. For Luther, prayer was the inestimably precious personal lifeline sustaining him amidst the continual onslaughts of the world, the flesh, and the Devil. For Simons, prayer was second nature, literally the form in which he thought and wrote, and also the chief instrument by which the holy community maintained its unity of consciousness and extended its mission in the world. But no one estimated prayer more highly than Calvin. With the deceptively spare language so characteristic of him, Calvin evaluates prayer simply as "the chief exercise of faith" (title, III,20).

Calvin said that the whole life of a Christian man ought to be a sort of practice of godliness. Since that life is a life of faith, it is just as appropriate to say that the life of a Christian man ought to be a life of prayer, the chief exercise of faith. Yet we must not take "practice" and "exercise" to refer primarily to an outward behavior by which faith is measured. Rather, Calvin defines prayer wholly in terms of an internal discipline.

Though the Lord's Prayer sets an objective standard to which all prayer ought to conform, prayer for Calvin is defined as "an intimate conversation" of the heart with God, an "emotion of the heart within, which is poured out an laid open before God, the searcher of hearts."[58] We are bidden to prayer both by God's command and by the promises he offers to those who seek him. Just as the Gospel gives birth to faith, so faith trains our hearts to call upon God in prayer.[59] Calvin has said that repentance and forgiveness of sins are the chief effects of faith. That is why the most important characteristic of prayer, as the exercise of faith, must be repentance and the plea for forgiveness of sins.[60] The sense of God's just vengeance must be combined with the firm assurance of God's favor, Calvin said, referring[61] explicitly to his earlier discussion of the bond between repentance and faith.

Although prayer originates as an interior discipline of faith, it is by no means exercised for purely private ends. Prayer is not only the chief exercise of faith, but is also the chief part of worship.[62] Provided the hearts which utter it in worship are pure, prayer in speech and in song is a way by which the whole church is edified, according to Calvin.[63] All prayer, whether uttered privately or publicly, must originate from a sense of one's communion with the church and must be directed toward the benefit of the church. This rule is brought home to us very clearly in the Lord's Prayer: the recurrent use of the pronouns "our" and "us" is never overlooked by Calvin in this connection.[64]

Our study has been structured by the thesis that for Calvin love is the chief defining characteristic of God the Father and is the foundation of the church. The high estimate Calvin places upon prayer is due in part to the

[58] III,20.4f., 16.29.
[59] III,20.1.
[60] III,20.7-9.
[61] III,20.11.
[62] III,20.13,29.
[63] III,20.31-33.
[64] III,20.38f., 44f., 47.

fact that through prayer we must fully realize and benefit from the love of the Father. Calvin's stress at the beginning of his chapter and at the beginning of his discussion of the Lord's Prayer is upon God's love, especially as manifest in his election and providential care of his beloved children.[65] God's love is the foundation of our being as Christians. But our life is a life of constant becoming because, as we learn from the definition of our life as one of prayer, it must be a life of constant repentance (regeneration) and forgiveness of sins (free reconciliation). If God's love is his gift to us, then constant repentance for sin is his mandate upon us—our vocation in this world.

A subordinate thesis of our study was that, concerning life in this world, the love of God is manifested as order and is achieved by the proper exercise of justice and freedom, according to Calvin. Calvin closes his chapter by considering prayer not in terms of a separate act but as a lifelong discipline or vocation. He speaks of perseverance. Only the power of the Holy Spirit affords us the interior freedom from the world, the freedom by which we are able to endure its trials. And it is via experience of the onslaughts of this world that we gain the true interior sense of the righteousness or justice of Christ.

2. IN A REAL SENSE it would be correct to say that according to Calvin, the proper preaching of the Word and administration of the sacraments may be the most important but are not the only external means by which we are invited into and sustained within the holy community. Calvin began his chapter on prayer, that most intimate commerce of the invisible church with God, with an emphasis upon God's providential care of the world as a reason for our confidence in prayer. And he concluded the chapter with an emphasis upon the equally providential tribulations of the world as a reason for the need to persevere in prayer. Not only the agencies of the visible church, but also the events, institutions, and orders of "this world" are means by which the body of Christ is sanctified.

The question of this concluding part of our study of Calvin is, what is the place or function of the worldly realm in the life of the church?

The differences among Luther, Simons, and Calvin on this question are quite definite but extremely hard to document with explicit references. They are differences of general mood, feeling, and esthetics, and can be grasped only as a by-product of extended study of many specific themes. Adequate generalization is for a scholar the most useful of achievements, but also the most difficult of tasks. Let us, however, try to do this in the interests of our closing themes of prayer and perseverance.

Because of the functional absence of ontological rootage in his theology, his consequently sharp distinction between the children of light and the children of darkness, and the egregious personal afflictions he endured as an evangelical Christian, Menno Simons could give no positive significance to the worldy realm. At the very best it was neutral with regard to the life of the church. Normally, in spite of his rare, rather *pro forma* assertions that it was a gift of God, worldly life appeared to Simons as the

[65]Cf. particularly III,20.2f., 11f., 36f.

instrument of the Devil. It was the instrument by which, save for the rescuing efforts of the Spirit of Christ, all men would be stripped of hope for salvation. The world was a kind of hell.

Luther's mature evaluation—official if not personal—was to a degree opposite that of Simons. Luther's growing interests in the "orders of creation" (his last major work was the commentary on the book of Genesis) either effected or reflected a sense that God's unlimited power realized itself in a variety of forms, of which created forms, or orders, the church was only one. Hence all the worldly orders—government, family, labor and economic life, the world of nature itself, and the church— were equally good expressions, equally "masks" of God's creative will. The obligation upon all the orders was to recognize, nourish, and defend the specific and unique functions of each order within the over-all expression of God's creativity. The world was not heaven to Luther. But it was natural, and hence was to be accepted as it was created.

Calvin's sense of things was not merely a sterile compromise of the two positions described above, but a real third alternative. Calvin both affirms the goodness of the world, like Luther, and also appreciates its threat to salvation, like Simons. The difference that makes Calvin's position a real alternative is this. Luther and Simons, though evaluating it differently, looked at the world as a fact, as a fact of being; Calvin looked at the world and saw it as an instrument of becoming. He saw it, if we might hazard the word, as a purgatory, as a good means by which the people of God, wholly by the power of the Spirit, might complete the goal of holiness which is the object of their election in Christ.

Calvin, like Luther, insisted that Christ ruled both the worldly and the spiritual realm.[66] But unlike the German reformer, Calvin looked at the realms from the point of view of God's general sovereignty and providence, and his special election. Hence for Calvin the two realms were much more fully integrated than for Luther. As the above references indicate, Calvin saw the worldly realm not only as a co-ordinate entity whose basic functions were internally self-defined, but also as an instrument, like the visible church, whereby God sustains his spiritual kingdom. The world and all therein, Calvin stressed particularly in his discussions of providence and election, was created for the benefit of the children of God. The worldly realm always is a present being, we heard Calvin say earlier, while the spiritual realm always lives from its future, as a becoming. The kingdom of God, according to Calvin, was "the forgiveness of sins, salvation, life, and utterly everything that we obtain in Christ."[67] The chief function for which God in his providence created the worldly realm, therefore, was to assist the achievement of these things.

How does the worldly life contribute to these ends? Here Calvin, having given the worldly realm a more dynamic function vis-à-vis the true church than Luther, also evaluated it more positively in the same dynamic

---

[66]I,4.2; II,2.13,15; III,19.15; 2S0.41ff.; cf. 1541 Catechism, q. 268; *Com. on John* 1:5, p. 34.   [67]III,3.19.

context than Simons. For the world through all of its trials and tribulations disciplines the children of God in perseverance and accordingly in the appreciation of divine justice.

Calvin took numerous occasions in the *Institutes* for meditation upon the trials, the miseries, and the dangers with which life tempted the Christian soul.[68] In the face of such dangers, Christians are not expected to remain unmoved or to exhibit the "iron philosophy" of the Stoics. Life is a good, not a neutral thing, and we legitimately grieve at its diminution. But we are trained by its adversities to resist loving it inordinately, trained to endure it as a preparation for the future life which, by comparison, makes this life seem hateful to us.[69] The cross that we live under while on earth, Calvin says, must be understood as a sign of God's love. By means of that *vita crucis* we gain a deeper knowledge of ourselves, i.e., of our sinfulness and weakness. And so by means of the world, Christians are trained to "advance toward humility and so, sloughing off perverse confidence in the flesh, betake themselves to God's grace."[70]

We are back where we began our study of Calvin: true knowledge of man, and true knowledge of God! Yet Calvin becomes even more specific in his discussion of the object of worldly trouble. Not only must we see adversity as a sign of God's love, but we must understand it as a sign of God's will. That is, unlike the philosophers and their "fate," Christians in tribulation look to scripture, which

> bids us contemplate in the will of God something far different: namely, first *righteousness* and *equity*, then concern for our own salvation. Of this sort, then, are Christian exhortations to patience. Whether poverty or exile, or prison, or insult, or disease, or bereavement, or anything like them torture us, we must think that none of these things happens except by the will and providence of God, that He does nothing except with a *well-ordered justice*.[71]

God in his love creates worldly adversity in order that we might learn to contemplate his justice. And only by the power of the Holy Spirit may we develop the perseverance required in that school for character, the world.

God's election of us is the reason why we may persevere with confidence.[72] Faith cannot be faith unless it endures. God's work in us, via the agency of Christ, the Holy Spirit, and the church, is the perfection of our perseverance.[73]

[68]Cf. I,17.10; III,2.40, and the chapters on providence, prayer, and crossbearing.
[69]III,8.8f.; 9.2ff.
[70]III,8.2; cf. 8.6.
[71]III,8.11, emphasis mine. Cf. Wallace, *Christian Life*, p. 69ff.
[72]III,21.1; 22.10; 24.6; Hunter, p. 102f.
[73]II,15.3; II,3.6,14; 5.3; *Com. on Rom.* 5:2, p. 189; on 8:29, p. 318; *Com. on John* 14:16, p. 92; *Com. on Eph.* 1:13, p. 208. For other references to Christian perseverance, cf. *Institutes* I,15.8; II,3.9f.; III,20.51.

****

If self-denial is the vocation of Christian man, then perseverance—perseverance in work and especially in prayer—is the standard by which that vocation is judged successfully accomplished. Calvin's personal history is a good illustration of this theology of perseverance. Unlike Luther, who ultimately resigned the fray, and unlike Simons, who chose not to enter it, Calvin kept his soul, his body, and all his energies engaged with the trials and tribulations the worldly realm provided him. Though he would have personally preferred the life of the retiring scholar, Calvin had his heart "subdued to teacheableness"—constantly. He had to learn humility—constantly. That was how he saw the challenges posed to him by the world in the form of Geneva. God in his providential care, wisdom, and power trained Calvin, like an English bulldog, never to let go. He trained him in perseverance.

If history provides any basis for judgment about these matters, Calvin's vocation would have to be judged successfully completed.

Such a biographical evaluation, however, would not have pleased Calvin. The object of the discipline which God's world forces upon us, Calvin would remind us, is that we learn God's righteousness and justice, and our nothingness apart from him. "We are not our own. . . . We are God's: let his wisdom and will therefore rule all our actions. We are God's: let all the parts of our life accordingly strive toward him as our only lawful goal."

Soli deo gloria.

CHAPTER EIGHT

Conclusion: The View from Trent

Even though he knows that the circumstances of the times and the characters of the reformers studied make such wishes fanciful, the historian of Christian thought nevertheless might wish that Luther, Simons, and Calvin had had more direct theological contact with each other. Or failing that, that they had considered each other's mature writings, responding to them fairly, open-mindedly, and without undue polemics. Had any of these things been possible, the historian speculates, the theological, political, and ecclesiastical relationships among the major reforming groups would have been different. An improved intercommunication might not have succeeded in bringing the parties into closer theological accord, although one might have hoped for this. It might rather have sharpened the various chasms among them. But in that case the contemporary differences might have more nearly approximated the distinct pattern which the modern theological analyst thinks differentiate the positions of his subjects. At least the comparative historian would find his work easier.

The brute fact, however, is that Luther and Calvin had little direct contact with each other and none with Simons. Both Simons and Calvin were significantly influenced by Luther's early reformed writings, but apparently neither had much time, opportunity, or perhaps inclination to consider the later works. Language barriers were only partly responsible. It was in the interests of ecumenism that his church left many of Luther's later, harsher, more truculent writings untranslated. Luther appears to be unread in any of Simons' works, and evidence that he had read Calvin is very weak.[1] Neither Simons nor Calvin appears to have had any direct acquaintance with each other's work.

The mediated communication was best between Luther and Calvin, chiefly via Melanchthon. But Luther never got much beyond his early experiences with Carlstadt, the "Schwermerei," and the Peasants' Revolt—hardly fair bases from which to cast a generalization over Simons and his friends. The mediated connections between Simons and Calvin were the controversialists, Martin Micron and John à Lasco. Simons may have gained a reasonably approximate estimate of Calvinism via these contacts. But Calvin, made aware of only the 1554-58 disputes over Simons' peculiar christology, and his views more affected by Servetus and the libertines in his own city, cannot have formed a much more accurate picture of Simons than did his Wittenberg colleague. Simons appears to respond only to the antinomians and contented hypocrites in the Lutheran establishment.

---

[1] Cf. John T. McNeill, *Unitive Protestantism* (Richmond, Va.: John Knox Press, 1964), p. 195.

In view of the circumstances described above, we cannot view fairly the position of any reformer through the eyes of any other. There is relatively less distortion of impression between Luther and Calvin, but not enough information from Luther on Calvin to make that joint comparison useful. Simons' experience with the agents of Luther and Calvin was somewhat more distorted, especially with respect to Luther, but the paucity of reference, especially to Calvin, and the radically different bases from which he viewed things make his evaluation unuseful.

It is, however, Simons and his friends who suffer most. Formidable language barriers; minimal access to the press; the gross prejudice and willful ignorance of others; compromising if completely unjust association in the public mind with everyone from Münsterites to Jews to Italian freethinkers—all this and more prevents us from considering an evaluation of Simons through the eyes of his contemporary opposite numbers.

It would be expected that in this closing chapter we would repeat in summary fashion the specific contrasts developed throughout the preceding chapters. Yet there is another approach which will be much more stimulating, more useful, and somewhat fairer to the larger context of sixteenth-century Reformation theology. Though it has not been the focus of attention, Roman Catholic thought has occasionally surfaced in this study, largely as the system of positions against which Luther, Simons, and Calvin developed their own views on specific themes. But need it be noted that even relative to the issues posed for investigation by the hypothesis of the present study, there were not three basically new sixteenth-century constructions, but four?

The reforming, constructive decisions of the Council of Trent will provide an interesting and relevant vantage-point for assessing the results of our investigations. The Council fathers were finally able to get to the heart of the basic theological issues. And the major issues that the fathers addressed were just those posed by our hypothesis—including the functional trinitarian relationships. The Council formalized positions on Christian life very similar to some of those of the Protestant reformers studied (chiefly Simons). And it may have introduced an understanding of functional trinitarian relationships completely different from that held in common by Luther, Simons, and Calvin. It is thus to be expected that the Tridentine understanding of the church will reveal interesting convergences and divergences from that held by the Protestant reformers.

A thorough internal analysis of the canons and decrees of the Council of Trent is beyond the scope of this concluding chapter. Rather, we shall consider only the more obvious features of the published documents bearing on our subjects of Trinity, church, and ethics among the Protestant reformers studied. The Tridentine decrees will serve as a viewpoint external to the positions of Luther, Simons, and Calvin, from which the convergences and divergences of their positions might be seen more clearly. We begin with the trinitarian issue, continue with the matter of Christian life, and end with the understanding of the church.

A. *Revelation and the Trinitarian Functions*

Like the major Protestant reformers, the fathers of Trent did not believe that the doctrines of the Trinity or of creation were at issue in the Reformation theological crisis.[2] But perceptions of trinitarian relations and functions emerge from one's understanding of the nature and contents of revelation and of the relationship of the church to that revelation. It is at this point that the canons and decrees of the Third and Fourth Sessions of the Council of Trent become directly relevant to our summary.

A fundamental breach between Trent and the Protestant reformers can be seen in the very order in which the subjects of the first sessions are treated. The purpose of the Council's efforts being "the extirpating of heresies, and the reforming of manners," the fathers begin in Session Three not with a presentation of the scripture as the formal principle by which all subsequent issues are to be decided, but with the tradition of the church, i.e., the creed.[3] Neither Luther nor Calvin disputed the creed. They, and even Simons, had acknowledged that the creeds of the early church were inspired by the Spirit and were therefore useful though necessarily subordinate instruments by which the correct interpretation of the scriptures could be insured. But its placement, and the fact that the fathers both consider it the first most necessary tool to their desired ends, and also assert that a creed by itself has been able to effect those ends,[4] caused the reformers to throw up their hands in despair, convinced that nothing had changed in Rome's basic understanding of revelation.

The Protestant reformers were, however, wrong about that, as the results of the Fourth Session, "Decree Concerning the Canonical Scriptures and Traditions,"[5] indicate.

We have seen that while Luther effectively identified the terms "Gospel" and "Christ" or rather "Christ *pro me*," Simons and Calvin like nearly all second-generation reformers tended to understand "Gospel" as the teaching or doctrine which Christ brought and which is recorded exclusively in the Bible. The fathers of Trent share with Calvin and Simons this understanding of the Gospel as something distinguishable from Christ himself. But that is all they share.

The history of the Gospel, yet undefined, exceeds the limits of Christ. It is something first "promised through the prophets in the holy Scriptures," then "first promulgated with [Christ's] own mouth," "then commanded to be preached by His Apostles to every creature. . . ."

---

[2] Hubert Jedin, *A History of the Council of Trent*, trans. Dom Ernest Graf, 2 vols. (Edinburgh: Thomas Nelson & Sons, 1957-1961), 2:63.

[3] Ibid. Jedin is somewhat misleading when he says the "formal dogmatic principle" herein is "Creed, Holy Scripture, and Apostolic Tradition." Creeds *are* part of the apostolic tradition.

[4] *Canons and Decrees of the Council of Trent*, ed. and trans. H. J. Schroeder (St. Louis, Mo.: B. Herder Book Co., 1941), Sessio Tertia, p. 294: ". . . quo solo aliquando et infideles ad fidem traxerunt, haereticos expugnarunt et fideles confirmarunt."

[5] Schaff's title in his translation of this text wrongly omits "and Traditions" and hence is deceptively incomplete.

The Gospel is not to be identified with scripture (Simons' tendency of thought) and is not identified with Christ himself (Luther's tendency of thought). Then how is the Gospel to be defined? The statement proceeds with its only near-definition. It is not a true definition but, as before, rather states how the Gospel is used in the church's life. The Gospel is something which was commanded by Christ "to be *preached . . . as the foundation of all*, both saving truth and moral discipline" (emphasis mine).

The Council's habit of thinking of revelation in terms of both doctrine and discipline is a habit the reformers would affirm, though with different emphases. Luther would stress the importance of the doctrinal aspect, Simons that of the discipline. Calvin's position seems most in line with the evaluation of Trent, in two respects. Calvin would most appreciate the balance of the emphasis. And Calvin's sense of the "Christian philosophy" or "wisdom" which wholly originates in but which is distinguishable from the words of scripture, seems to make this humanist evangelical Christian's position more comparable to Trent's view of the Gospel as source or fount of truth and discipline.

The next phrases of the decree introduce the matter stimulating our immediate interest: trinitarian function. Having defined the Gospel in terms of its use, the fathers of Trent proceed to state wherein that of which the Gospel is the source is recognized, i.e., the instrumental forms available to the church for carrying out its mission to extend saving truth and moral discipline in the world. One must read very carefully here. Not the Gospel, but the truth and discipline are contained "in [*et*] the written books, and [*et*] the unwritten traditions which, received by the Apostles from the mouth of Christ himself, or [*aut*] from the Apostles themselves, the Holy Ghost dictating, have come down even unto us, transmitted as it were from hand to hand. . . ."

Bad as they would appear to the Protestant reformers, these phrases would not invite their deepest rebuke. For all the reformers, even Simons, in fact if not in principle recognized and used the unwritten traditions as a subordinate basis for their decisions vis-à-vis faith and morals. The real issue, however, was on the relative valuation. On this point the Council fathers continued with what to students of the history of Catholic theology was a breathtaking, precipitous advance. The Council "receives and venerates with an equal affection of piety and reverence [*pari pietatis affectu ac reverentia*] both the books of the Bible, as also [*necnon*] the traditions," as having been dictated "either [*vel*] by Christ's own word of mouth, or [*vel*] by the Holy Ghost, and preserved in the Catholic Church by a continuous succession."

The truth and discipline form a broad stream which clearly overflows the single channel of the written books into both the extra-biblical oral tradition of Christ and the continuing traditions dictated by the Spirit. Jedin indicates[6] that the fathers understood the written and unwritten traditions as supplemental, even though the phrase "*partim . . . partim*" was ultimately dropped in favor of the less sharp "*et . . . et*" in the final text. The distributive sense, however, reappears in the "*necnon*" and "*vel . . . vel*"

[6]Jedin, 2:74f.

phrases later in the decree. The most significant feature of the decree, however, is the recognition of parity of valuation between the written and unwritten traditions. Whether it be considered a radical new departure from the medieval theology or a natural culmination of it,[7] parity of traditions was an issue that gravely taxed the Council fathers before it was finally accepted.[8]

This decree at least offers occasion for the idea that the fathers worked from a different understanding of trinitarian functional relationships than did Luther, Simons, or Calvin. The key, as it has been the key to differentiating the positions of the Protestant reformers, is the work of the Holy Spirit.

Though the decree says that God is the author of both the Old and New Testaments, it states that both scripture and the unwritten traditions on faith and morals are venerated as having been dictated either by Christ or by the Spirit. In spite of the initial ambiguity here, the preceding phrases in the decree suggest that the fathers see the "one God," Christ, and the Spirit in distinct functions with regard to revelation. God (the Father) is the author of the books of the Bible. Christ is the dictator of some of the unwritten tradition, and the Holy Spirit is the dictator of some of it. Is there intended a meaningful distinction between "author" and "dictator" corresponding to the distinction between written and unwritten sources? If so, does that mean that Christ and the Spirit are related to revelation in a distinguishably different way than the "one God"? Secondly, it would seem apparent that the relationship of Christ and the Spirit to the unwritten traditions of which they are dictators is also distinct. Christ communicates it with his "own word of mouth" to the Apostles, while the Holy Spirit presumably communicates it via an internal dictation to the heart which only subsequently is expressed physically or orally. Thirdly, while it is clear that the oral tradition from Christ temporally overlaps the written form, it is also clear that the internal teaching of the Spirit must be temporally subsequent to Christ but could also overlap the written tradition. It is these overlaps, combined with the distinct forms of revelation and associated methods of communication, that provide the strongest evidence that the fathers at Trent may have understood the persons of the Trinity to be differentially functional in the transmission of different saving truths and disciplines. This might fairly be concluded, even though we recognize that the Council would insist that the whole Trinity is always involved in all external relations, and that the distinct revelatory sources are fully, mutually supplemental and enhancing, and not at all contradictory.

The internal subtleties and complexities of the decree become mere details, however, in the strong contrast with the positions shared by Luther, Simons, and Calvin. Although all the reformers can ascribe all the functions of love, power, and justice to all the persons of the Trinity, it is, as we have

[7]Cf. Heiko Oberman, *The Harvest of Medieval Theology* (Cambridge, Massachusetts: Harvard University Press, 1963), pp. 361-422, and the subsequent literature stimulated by Oberman's work.

[8]Jedin, 2:74f., 82f., 86f.

seen, the characteristic Protestant emphasis that the form, justice, or teaching function is pre-eminently associated with Christ. The Holy Spirit can be said to be the author of scripture in the sense that he inspired the writers with his power and grace. The Holy Spirit can also be said to certify the Word of Christ in the heart, and in that sense is called our teacher. The Holy Spirit can be said to discern among the new teachings and interpretations with which the church is always confronted, and in that sense is its guide to saving truth. And the Holy Spirit can be said to exercise the Christian in the moral discipline which, as much as true doctrine, is the content of God's revealed will for us. In that sense he is our master. However, these are all functions which but assist the communication of the Word—the Word of which, strictly speaking, Christ alone is the embodiment (Luther) or the teacher (Simons and Calvin). None of the reformers, not even Simons, came close to giving the Holy Spirit the distinct substantive teaching authority that the decree of Trent does.

A related matter will make the contrast above come into still sharper focus. The reformers gave different scope to the work of the Spirit relative to the Word of God. And they all affirmed that the Holy Spirit functioned in the creation and maintenance of the natural world—a function, however, which had little if any perceived direct connection with the Gospel of Christ, and so could provide no grounds of evangelical Christian doctrine. Among the Protestant reformers, Luther allowed greatest room for nonscriptural, traditional, even "rational" usages in the church, since as he said, the Holy Spirit had more important business than deciding matters of church order. Simons, with his principle that what scripture does not explicitly mandate is forbidden, left least room. But whatever the range of opinion, Calvin's view that the acceptable tradition concerns only those external observances that pertain to decency and discipline, and not to doctrine,[9] is common to the Protestants. The reformers agreed: regarding the saving knowledge of God's will toward us, the Spirit strictly speaking has no substantive teaching or doctrinal function at all outside of, beyond, or in addition to that which is taught by Christ.

It would be completely wrong to infer from the above that the basic difference between the Protestant and Catholic reformers on the matter of trinitarian function is that the former adhered to the rule that the Trinity operates *ad extra* as one, while the latter did not. The basic difference must be sought not in the trinitarian relationships but in the functional relationships asserted. Let us restrict attention for the moment to the teaching function.

The Protestant reformers defined the content, form, and locus of dogmatic authority much more narrowly than did the Council of Trent. In terms of content, only those materials directly relevant to faith, to what Trent called "saving truth," were considered binding. Within this restriction there was some room for variation among the Protestants. Calvin's sense of "progressive" revelation in scripture allowed differential emphasis. The

[9]John Calvin, *Antidote to the Council of Trent*, (Edinburgh: Calvin Translation Society, 1851), p. 70.

Protestants could differ somewhat over what was properly included as "saving truth." Luther was most restrictive here, virtually eliminating the scriptural materials on discipline and church order from that which he considered dogmatically binding. Simons by contrast tended to see New Testament patterns of church order and discipline as a most important aspect of doctrine. Calvin's position on this issue was more mediate, although by his decision not to include discipline as a formal mark of the visible church he showed himself nearer his German colleague.

The fathers of Trent, however, defined the content of revelation not univocally in terms of "saving truth," but bivocally in terms of saving truth and moral dicipline. With the theological influence of Thomas Aquinas clearly apparent, the decree of the Fourth Session gives equal dogmatic status to materials distinct as to content. And since there is a much greater variety both in written scripture and in the post-scriptural religious traditions as to what constitutes the God-willed standards of moral discipline, the fathers at Trent were faced with a much more complex problem regarding the unity of revelatory content than were the Protestants.

As to form, a similar contrast appears. Luther, Simons, and Calvin totally rejected all notions that we receive God's will in any other way than via the written Word. Again there is some room for variation. For Luther, the "Word of God" was the product of an encounter between the text of Scripture and the faith (and unfaith) of the hearer. Calvin, though basically sharing this view, gave far less play to the human mind and would not at all have admitted human unfaith into the exegetical and hermeneutic process. Simons did not emphasize faith by hearing, and appears to give no function at all to human contribution. The Word of God equals the written text, and as such is available for reading and obedience by any who choose.

On the closely related matter of locus, again the Protestants agree, with variations. "By scripture alone," of course, but not "by scripture exclusively," except in the normative sense. The usages of the early church, the views of the orthodox Fathers, and the creeds were accepted in at least a *de facto* way by Luther, Simons, and Calvin as legitimate though subordinate loci of teaching. The reformers differed among themselves, however, over how much of, and for how long, that tradition could be acknowledged.

Regarding form and locus, the Roman position is enormously more inclusive, and hence much more complex and more difficult to express in terms of the unity of revelation. One must speak not of "form and locus" but of "forms and loci" distinct and of equal appropriateness. The fact that the Roman position is far more inclusive, more catholic, in what is recognized as the contents, forms, and loci of revelation than the Protestant position, is related to a basic difference in the understanding of trinitarian functions vis-à-vis revelation. Defining revelation much more simply and narrowly, the Protestants were much better able to sustain the position that the revelatory functions of the three persons were wholly, mutually inclusive. The Roman position, though asserting that the Trinity operates as one in this matter, could not assert a mutual inclusiveness of function, but had to acknowledge a variety of overlapping, distinct, though mutually qualifying functions.

Wherein, then, does the unity of our knowledge of God's will lie? Or to put it in a way more useful to our considerations in this section, wherein lies the basis for the authority of Christian doctrine? The answer is as clear as it is classic. For Luther, Simons, and Calvin, the unity and authority of Christian doctrine rests in God alone as he revealed himself in the biblical word. For Trent, the unity and authority of Christian teachings rests in God alone as he indwells the living church.

The more the decrees of the Third and Fourth Sessions are studied, the more apparent it becomes that the understanding of the church is the single most important factor differentiating Catholic and Protestant views on the question of revelation and its sources. Reference to the church has in fact been a constant, insistent theme throughout these decrees. We must now pick up these references in order to understand how, via the doctrine of the church, the fathers of Trent were able to maintain the unity among the diverse contents and forms of what they considered revelation. In addition, we shall gain another clue in answer to the question of how the Roman view of the Trinity may differ in basic ways from the views of Luther, Simons, and Calvin.

The decree of the Third Session gives the initial impression that a new creed is to be set forth. But the fathers recur to traditional use. The creed offered is that "which the holy Roman Church makes use of. . . ." and which will be expressed ". . . in the very same words in which it is read in all the churches."

In the decree of Session Four it is said first that it is "in the Church" that the purity of the Gospel is preserved. Then traditional usage is again appealed to: the synod will follow "the examples of the orthodox Fathers" in the assessment of that which has "come down even unto us, transmitted as it were from hand to hand. . . ." And then it is stated—we must read very carefully here—that the [equal] veneration of the written and unwritten materials stems not only from the belief that they were dictated by Christ or the Spirit but also from the belief that they "are preserved in the Catholic Church by a continuous succession."

Now Luther, Simons, and Calvin had a high respect for what they considered the authentic traditions of the church. But none of them, nor any Protestant, could possibly have included the preserving function of the church as one of the grounds for his estimation of the normative value of scripture. For the fathers of Trent, however, inclusion of the church's role is necessary in order to maintain unity among the revelatory traditions.

Following a listing of the accepted canon, the decree asserts the importance of the church even over the divinely written sources. For the canon of scripture is acceptable only in a certain form: ". . . as they have been used to be read in the Catholic church, and as they are contained in the old Latin vulgate edition. . . ." On the latter point the fathers, knowing very well the weaknesses of the vulgate, nevertheless approve it, for the interim, because of "the lengthened usage of so many ages. . . ."

Finally it is asserted that the church functions as the sole definitive interpreter of the meaning of these written sources, not only in matters of faith but also in matters of Christian morality.

* * * * * *

What are we to make of all these statements? One conclusion is clear. The cumulative effect is to grant the church a vastly more important position in the theology of revelation than any Protestant formulation could possibly grant. So great is the difference of estimation concerning the church's function vis-à-vis revelation that we question whether there may be a corresponding difference in the prior assumptions concerning the nature of the church to explain it. Assuming that decisions on trinitarian issues are the primary ones, our object in this section is to investigate the extent to which the decrees of the Third and Fourth Sessions suggest a position on trinitarian functioning significantly different from the positions of Luther, Simons, and Calvin. Observing the evidentiary limits imposed by the specific subject matters addressed in these decrees, and granting that the Council fathers did not assume that trinitarian issues were involved in their deliberations, we nevertheless submit that the language and emphases of these decrees afford evidence relevant to our objective.

First of all is the matter of the status of tradition. On this subject the position of Trent is clear. Saving truth and moral discipline apprehended in the form of the *traditio* of the living church are considered equal in normative status to saving truth and moral discipline apprehended in the form of the *scriptio* of the living God. The key words have been left in Latin to remind us that what we tend to interpret in English-from-Latin translation as simple nouns are in fact derived from verbs: it is the specific activity that is given name in the Latin words. The point: "tradition" must be understood to refer not merely to a content but also to the process and means of transmission—an emphasis explicit in the decrees. The importance of this reference to our question is this: whatever valuation be given to the content can and must obtain, though perhaps with some qualifications, for the process and means of transmission as well. And what is that process and means? It is the Catholic Church, which transmits from hand to hand, as it were, and preserves by its continuous succession. In a very real sense it is true to say that the living church not only has its written and unwritten *traditio*, but also *is* itself that *traditio*. The revelatory authority of the saving truth and moral discipline under each form cannot be separated from the revelatory authority of the church. And that is why the church can claim the absolute right to determine canon, edition, interpretation, and the use of even the written forms of its truth and discipline.

Can we take the argument one step further? The above functions, to the Protestant mind, must be attributed to the Holy Spirit and not to the church. Earlier we maintained that differences concerning the role of the Holy Spirit were the key factors in comparing the positions of Luther, Simons, Calvin, and Trent. But now it appears that differences concerning the role of the church are the key. The fathers consistently begin the decrees with the phrase, "The sacred and holy, ecumenical, and general Synod of Trent—lawfully assembled in the Holy Ghost, the same three legates of the Apostolic See preciding therein. . . ." This is more than a perfunctory formula. We have seen evidence in the decrees of the near identification of *traditio* and church relative to revelatory function. Can we also see at least a high degree of correspondence between the authority of the deliberating, lawfully assembled Synod and the authority of the Holy Spirit?

To conclude this line of argument for the moment: one can see that while the Protestants spoke of the roles of Father, Son, and Holy Spirit in the matter of revelation, the fathers of Trent increasingly speak of the roles of Father, Son, and Church (*traditio*) in this matter. We have here a hint at a basic difference in trinitarian understanding. In the following section we shall be led to the same conclusion by means of a different association.

B. *Justification and Sacrament*

After lengthy negotiations with both Rome and the Catholic rulers, the fathers of Trent decided to consider simultaneously issues arising under the two heads of "extirpating of heresies" and "reforming of mores." The individual reform decrees, however, bear no direct relationship to the dogmatic decrees with which they were jointly published. This does not mean the Council saw no relationship between doctrine and ethics. Rather, they considered "reform of mores" to refer to the structure and operation of the church and its officials. It would not, accordingly, be useful to study the content of these technical, administrative and statutory reforms as a means of contrasting the positions of the Protestant reformers on the matter of Christian ethics.

One may see this rather sharp distinction between the structure and operation of the church, and the "saving truth and moral discipline" which it preserves and administers, as a basic feature differentiating the Roman approach from that of the Protestants. Among the latter, Luther appears closest to the Roman view with his position that, within the general patterns of New Testament ecclesiology, specific adaptations of church structure and operation are matters relatively external to faith and can be decided on the basis of appropriateness to circumstances, efficiency, and traditional usage. For Calvin and Simons, however, matters of church order were most certainly not *adiaphora* only marginally related to issues of faith and ethics. Simons in particular held that the structures and operations of the church were the key factors for the nurture, extension, and completion of the regenerate life which is the substance of Christ's teaching. And yet, though Simons would thus seem farthest removed from the Roman position, from another point of view he seems closest to it.

Questions of the scriptural or traditional justification for its organizational system aside, the elaborate hierarchical structures of the Catholic Church can be seen to have a very definite and direct connection with Christian ethics at the layman's level. Its function as a "preserver" of the "purity" of the Gospel is a major element in the church's self-understanding, of course. Yet while Luther and Calvin effectively if not formally subordinated the sacramental to the doctrinal role in their definitions of the church, such is not the case with Rome. For if we look at its structural rationale from the point of view of what is considered needful in the daily moral life of its members, the Roman ecclesiastical apparatus appears as an extensive support facility for the discharge of its sacramental ministry. That is the point of view most fully shared by Menno Simons, even though he does not construe "discipline" as "sacrament." And in spite of the few basic (and the many only apparent) sharp contrasts between his ecclesiology and sacramental theory and that of Rome, Simons shares with Rome the effective if not formal superordination of "moral discipline" over "doctrine" in the definition of the church.

The question of the self-understanding of the church will occupy us more fully in the following section. But we already have before us one of the keys by which, from the viewpoint of the Trent decrees, we may relevantly asssess the Protestant reformers' positions on Christian ethics. For the Protestant positions on the Christian life are addressed directly in the dogmatic section of the Tridentine decrees—the sections bearing on the issues of original sin, justification, and the sacraments. The fathers of Trent were quite conscious of their decision to formulate "moral dicipline" in terms of sacramental life. That is the most eminent habit of thought distinguishing Catholic from Protestant theology on the matter of Christian ethics.

The canons of the Fifth Session, on original sin, most sharply reveal the contrasts between Simons on the one hand and Luther and Calvin on the other. The first three canons, directed against extreme Pelagian views, evoke no basic objection from the Protestants, if Calvin's comments can be taken as representative.[10] Simons would object only to the phrase "and to infants" in the third canon concerning the applicability of the baptismal merits of Christ. Canon four, however, specifically anathematizes those who deny the need and validity of infant baptism and would be denounced by Simons but approved by Luther and Calvin. By contrast canon five, which excludes views denying that in baptism not only the guilt but also the "true and proper nature" of sin is removed, would eliminate the views of Luther and Calvin, but—could we ignore the vastly different sacramental theory informing the language of the canon—would be acceptable to Simons.

The canons on original sin merely state the thinking of the church on the initial circumstances or preconditions of Christian ethics. The subsequent dogmatic decrees, however, strike to the heart of the differences between Catholic and Protestant. Except for the decree on Scripture and tradition, the decree on justification was the most negatively defining position of the Roman church for the initiating Protestant reformers of the sixteenth century.

Calvin alone published a significant response to the initial work of Trent. And Calvin was the most classically educated, sophisticated, judicious churchman among the major Protestant reformers. And yet

[10]*Antidote*, p. 85.

Calvin apparently was unwilling ("unable" is an adjective that cannot be made to apply here) to address himself to basic differentiating features of the decree that even a twentieth-century student in historical theology would recognize upon a careful first reading. The political, polemical, public-relations, life-and-death religious circumstances of the mid-sixteenth century are understandable but nevertheless unacceptable excuses for the failure, even in a technical treatise, to address the rather obvious and basic differences of assumption.

For a variety of reasons, some legitimate, the fathers of Trent were not able to complete detailed work on their constitutions on the Christian life until October 11, 1551 (Thirteenth Session). By this time the four-year hiatus had buried any remaining Protestant speculation that more was to be gained from addressing the work of the Council, even if the second founders of the Protestant movements had been willing to listen.

The first three chapters on justification bridge the preceding anthropological canons. They stirred no particular objections from Calvin, although the concluding phrase of Chapter One, on the continued existence of free will, goes against the views of Luther and Calvin but would be affirmed by Simons.

The next six chapters, however, expose the heart of the dispute between Catholic and Protestant, and among Protestants, very clearly. The brief Chapter Four in itself contains a number of differentiating elements. First of all, justification is described not as a static relationship but as an activity, a *translatio* (note the verbal root) from the state of original sin as *terminus a quo* to the state of grace as *terminus ad quem*. Now Luther and Calvin would have given more emphasis to justification as a changed relationship between God and man, the locus of the change being in God. Chapter Four, however, assumes that justification is a process of change happening within man. As Jedin remarks, the fathers all assumed justification to be "an entitative, supernatural elevation, through sanctifying grace and the meritoriousness of good works performed in a state of grace."[11] Only Menno Simons among the Protestant reformers would have completely shared this assumption, if not the language and conceptions in which it is expressed.

Secondly, Chapter Four indicates that the processs required, "since the promulgation of the Gospel," the "laver of regeneration, or the desire thereof." The statement that justification necessarily includes regeneration would be strongly affirmed by Calvin and even more strongly emphasized by Simons. But what of the last clause, "or the desire thereof"? The clause does not weaken the assertion that regeneration is necessary: it refers rather to the "laver" of regeneration, i.e., the sacrament of baptism.

That is the third point. The process which the fathers have summarized in Chapter Four by way of introducing the analysis to follow is a process which can be termed "first justification" and whose end is baptism. Luther and Calvin, who viewed justification as a changed relationship of God to man covering man's entire life of faith, could never have restricted the

[11]Jedin, 2:248.

discussion of first justification to so narrow a substantive matter. Nor would they have undertaken so exhaustive an analysis of it as do the fathers in Chapters Five through Nine. That such differentiations and analyses are possible is due to the distinct factors and changes involved in an entitative process. Simons, however, though he would not engage in so vigorous an analysis, would be very much at home with the restricted discussion in Chapters Four through Nine. For although he rarely disscussed justification in any detail, that which the fathers here call the justification terminating in baptism is approximately what Simons means by conversion.

Fourthly, we see in Chapter Four the first indication that the Catholic position much more fully integrates and appreciates the church's sacramental life in its understanding of Christian life than do Luther and Calvin, all their defenses of the need for the sacraments notwithstanding. Once again Simons' theology, though vastly contrasting on the meaning and function of the sacraments, shares this emphasis on the church's instrumentality most fully with Rome.

Chapters Five through Nine present a detailed analysis of the process of justification culminating in baptism. Luther and Calvin (but Simons much less) would object to the assertion in these chapters of free human co-operation in the preparatory process. The heart of the matter appears in Chapter Seven, which finally offers a definition of justification. Calvin attacked the Tridentine decrees most heavily at this locus.[12] A number of points stand out in this chapter, each developing the summary points noted in Chapter Four.

According to the fathers, justification includes not only remission of sins "but also the sanctification and renewal of the inward man. . . . " Calvin objects to the formal inclusion of sanctification under the head of justification, insisting that these matters, though intimately and necessarily related, are nevertheless to be kept distinct in our theology. What he apparently chose not to see, however, was that what he considered sanctification is distinguished from first justification in the decrees. It is considered in the post-baptismal chapters commencing with Chapter Ten, "On the increase of justification received." In part, these are only terminological differences. But to that degree, since they are fairly obvious, they could and should have been recognized by Calvin. The fathers of Trent were well aware of them. For in Chapter Seven they decline to define the righteousness of Christ, and by implication, faith in Christ, as the "formal cause" of justification (Calvin had so defined it in the *Institutes* III,14.17). Canons 10-14 specifically anathematize those who would restrict justification to a merely formal or forensic decision based upon the presence of faith. The formal cause is rather

> The justice of God . . . whereby he makes us just . . . that, to wit, with which . . . we are not only reputed but are truly

[12]*Antidote*, pp. 114ff.

called, and are just, receiving justice within us, each according to his own measure which the Holy Ghost distributes as he wills, and according to each one's proper dispositon and co-operation.

The last phrases in particular sharpen the differences between Rome and the reformers. It could not be clearer that the fathers do not understand justification as a putative, relational change the locus of which is the divine decision. Rather, they see justice as a quality which inheres the soul, a quality proportionate to the degree of presence, within the forgiven soul, of the gifts of faith, hope, and love. That justice can be qualitatively differentiated in this way is due precisely to the fact that it is strictly related to the differential degrees of sanctification and renewal present in those preparing for baptism. And it is the increase of this sanctification and renewal, with the corresponding justice, from the state of original sin to the state of baptismal grace, that the fathers mean by justification. The locus of the change is not God's decision, but the human soul.

Our consideration of the decrees on original sin and justification to this point has had the effect of pointing out very sharply the differences between Luther and Calvin on the one hand, and Menno Simons on the other. But Chapter Seven once again reveals itself as the heart of this decree in that the position taken defines the views of Simons as well. Those whom Trent says are justified are, in their differentiated degrees of sanctification and renewal, admitted into full status in the church by means of the grace conferred in the sacrament of baptism. For Simons, the parallel conversion process is likewise preparatory. But however many differentiations he may be willing to recognize in this process, Simons would allow none to be reflected in the church's acceptance via the rite of baptism. The process must be fully complete prior to the request to enter the church. For Simons, conversion does not exist until it exists as a completed, perfected change in man. In rhis way Simons, though from a different point of departure, in effect arrives at about the same understanding concerning conversion that Luther and Calvin did concerning justification: it indicates an absolute change in the relationship between God and man. And baptism by no means confers any special grace, as though by this means supposed qualitative differences among petitioners could be effaced. For Simons, baptism is but the recognition by the community that the absolute change in relationship has been effected.

The concluding two chapters of the first section[13] pick up the question of the interpretation of the Pauline phrase that we are justified by faith, freely (Ch. 8), and condemn the view that believers can and must be certain of their salvation (Ch. 9). This latter matter was most troublesome to the fathers, and their decisions were attacked furiously by Calvin, as we might expect. Even though the issue by its placement appears to be peripheral to

---

[13]Following the arrangement of Jedin, 2:307f.

the central concerns of the first section of the decree, Chapter Nine in fact offers materials very germane to the hypotheses of the present study. The matter of the certainty of salvation appears both to Calvin and to Trent as a direct consequence for moral discipline of a prior decision about saving truth. For Calvin and Luther, as we have seen, justification is based wholly in Christ, and that fact is therefore grounds for at least Christian confidence—a term to which the fathers of Trent have no objection. But for Calvin justification is ultimately based wholly upon God's eternal election in Christ, and therefore the faithful may, indeed must, be certain of their status before God. The position is mandatory because the point of contact of the Trinity with the world, as we argued in Chapter Six of this study, is for Calvin wholly on the divine side: the elective love of the Father. Calvin's attack upon Chapter Nine of the decree on justification recurs constantly to the Father's love, which makes our prayer life possible, as the grounds of this certainty.[14]

The Trent decrees, however, begin from the assumption that justification is an activity which partially inheres the worldly order. It is a reality the constitutive elements of which are the created soul in all its qualitative differentiation as well as in the corresponding divine grace. Therefore because of the relativizing conditions of finitude, ignorance, and insensitivity obtaining for all created entities, no such absolute certainty with regard to the adequate presence of grace, hence justice before God, is possible.

Our study has suggested that the eminent point of contact between God and the world was for Luther the righteousness of the incarnate Christ; for Simons the power of Christ's Spirit; and for Calvin the elective love of the Father. It has not been the burden of our study to investigate the Roman position on this matter. Yet our consideration of the decree on justification has necessarily touched upon that question. It was suggested above that in contrast to Calvin, the Tridentine view is that the locus of the justification process is partially inherent in the created order, i.e., in the status of the human soul. The question now is: what, where, and in what form is that justifying grace which is the other constitutive element in the process?

The fathers were well aware that the position taken in Chapter Nine could be mistaken as undermining the soul's confidence appropriate in the light of ". . .the promises of God, and of the efficacy of the death and resurrection of Christ." Yet on that basis alone, there obviously can be no lack of certainty: the trustworthiness of God's promises and the efficacy of Christ's work are not to be doubted in the least. But we cannot judge the present question on that basis alone. What is missing from the above appeal is any reference to the function of the Holy Spirit. It therefore seems that Trent's position, at least on the question of the certainty of justification, is significantly conditioned by what it assumes concerning the Third Person of the Trinity. Do the fathers of Trent, like Menno Simons, see the Spirit functoning as the eminent point of connection between God and the world?

[14]*Antidote*, p. 125. The same intimate relationship between election, love, prayer, and certainty is of course amply demonstrated in the *Institutes*, particularly III,20-24.

Once again the position of Menno Simons appears to be the critical demarcation point between Protestant and Catholic. The answer to the question, on the basis of Chapter Nine, at least, is "yes" and "no." The statement giving occasion to each answer is strikingly clear.

There appears to be only one locus in the decrees where there can be found a complete, informal statement of trinitarian function, beyond the *pro forma* scriptural quotations regarding baptism and the more problematic assertions in the decree on Scripture and traditions. That statement occurs in Chapter Nine, immediately following the reference to "the promises of God and the efficacy of Christ," quoted above.

> For even as no pious person ought to doubt of the mercy of God, of the merit of Christ, and of the virtue and efficacy of the sacraments, so each one, when he regards himself, and his own weakness and indisposition, may have fear and apprehension touching his own grace; seeing that no one can know with a certainty of faith, which cannot be subject to error, that he has obtained the grace of God.

This statement names the constitutive factors in the justification process in an excellent double trinitarian phrase, its balanced contrast of the perfection of God with the imperfections of man suggesting to us the style of Calvin. Let us concentrate attention, however, on the first side of the statement.

The earlier reference to God's mercy and Christ's merit suggests that, like Simons and Calvin, the fathers of Trent ascribe the function of love preeminently to the Father, and justice to the Son. Unlike Calvin, but like Simons, the statement does not locate the point of connection ("efficacy") between God and the world in the Father's love, but elsewhere. Where? For Simons the efficacy lay, not in the Third Person of the Trinity as distinct from the Second Person, but in what he termed the "Spirit of Christ." This way of putting it made it difficult for us to arrive at a clear distinction between Simons and the magisterial reformers over the functions of Christ and the Spirit.

The Trent statement is strikingly parallel to Simons' view in this regard. In the last phrase before the trinitarian statement, efficacy is ascribed to Christ; but then it is merit (justice or form) which is ascribed to Christ, and "virtue and efficacy" to the third element. And thus, for reasons similar to those obtaining for Simons' views, the position of Trent is equally difficult to compare with those of Luther and Calvin over the function of the second and third trinitarian elements.

The phrase now being considered not only has revealed the close proximity of the positions of Simons and the fathers of Trent, however; it also reveals the profound differences of these views. For Simons, the third element was the Spirit. It is the Spirit, invisible, working powerfully in the heart of the community and of the individual, who is the efficacious presence of God in the world. The Trent statement, however, moves with what to a Protestant seems a baffling ease from Father to Son to—sacraments.

Let us assume, in the interests of the theses pursued in this study, that the apparent substitution of "sacrament" for "Holy Spirit" in this functional trinitarian ascriptive pattern is an accurate expression of the Roman view in contrast to those of the Protestants. At once a number of admittedly speculative but highly fruitful and potentially significant comparisons emerge. Let us focus now on the basic comparison relevant to the placement of Luther, Calvin, and Simons relative to the position of Trent, as a means of concluding our preliminary assessment of Protestant Christian ethics as seen from the latter perspective.

As noted throughout this study, the issue which by its underdeveloped nature most sharply divided the general views of Luther, Simons, Calvin, and now (as we see) of Trent as well, was the issue of the Holy Spirit in his functional relationship to immanent Christian life in all its aspects. In many respects the differences of opinion may reflect prior, perhaps only semi-conscious esthetic valuations concerning the possibility and—to the extent that this is admitted—the locus and form of the connection between things of the Spirit and things of the flesh. We have tried to distinguish these decisions among the Protestant theologians studied. The decisions have vast consequences in the comparison of the trinitarian theory, ecclesiology, and ethics of the Protestant reformers.

In contrast, the Roman assumptions about the relationship of Spirit and flesh, if the Trent decrees can be taken as representative here, are so distinct that the Protestant views appear no more than subtle variations on a common theme.

Though differing on what they considered the eminent locus of contact between the Trinity and the world, none of the Protestant reformers was able or willing to fuse completely the gap between the transcendent Trinity and the immanent order. Luther came closest to doing so with his position that Christ's body and blood really existed efficaciously "in, with, and under" the physical elements in the Supper. Simons' complete elimination of "the flesh" from all considerations of spiritual efficacy left the gap widest. Yet in all instances there continues to exist a hiatus between the transcendent God and the immanent world—the "strange hiatus" which Regin Prenter, in his comments on Luther's understanding of Word and sacrament relative to the work of the Spirit,[15] evaluates as the chief mark differentiating Protestant evangelical theology from Roman Catholic theology on the matter of the Spirit.

The fusion is made in the Trent decrees. It was possible to make it because when the fathers defined the functional or efficacious trinitarian relationships, the third element is not said to be the Holy Spirit, but the sacraments. It is the sacrament that is God's efficacious presence in the world. The relationship between God and world, though finally not patent of full specification, is nevertheless asserted to be direct. The relationship is

---

[15]Regin Prenter, *Spiritus Creator*, trans. John M. Jensen (Philadelphia: Muhlenberg Press, 1963), pp. 166f.

that of substance to form; transcendent divine essence apparent through immanent physical accident.

Since it is functionally definable as the agency of the sacraments, and since it is by its liturgical function that the sacraments gain their efficacy, the church becomes in the Tridentine view the critical locus between God and world, Spirit and flesh. Would it be going too far to say that in terms of functional trinitarian ascriptive patterns, the implications of Trent are that we may speak of the Father as love, the Son as justice, and the church as efficacious power?

C. *Church and Spirit*

Although the narrow evidence upon which it is based renders the above statement speculative, it was made chiefly to underscore what is a basic and unmistakable difference of opinion between Rome and all the Protestant reformers. The subtitle of this study, "Trinity, Church, and Ethics in Reformation Theologies," suggests that ecclesiology was but one of the factors to be considered in differentiating Reformation views. The general thesis was that the doctrines of church and ethics were conditioned by prior decisions regarding the functions of the Trinity and the trinitarian functions held to be most intimately connected with the world.

From the point of view of Trent, however, the assumed subordination of ecclesiology to "trinitarian theology" appears to give our hypothesis a decidedly Protestant bias. And that estimation is correct. Each of the Protestant reformers took the position that the authentic Christian church could be said to exist only to the degree that it conformed to the doctrine, sacraments, and (in the case of Simons) the discipline instituted by Christ and revealed in the scripture. Throughout the Trent decrees, however, we are confronted with the fact that this evaluative pattern is not shared by Rome. In fact it frequently appears to be reversed. The church is not conditioned by the trinitarian and moral theologies considered to be legitimately deduced from the scripture alone; rather, it is the church which determines the legitimacy of Biblically-derived positions on faith and morals.

In Section A we first assumed that the matter of tradition was the most important factor differentiating Catholic from Protestant. Our consideration led us to the conclusion that the fathers of Trent understood the role of the Holy Spirit relative to the teaching function of Christ quite differently than did the Protestants. On this basis we could entertain the possibility that there may have been basic differences in trinitarian understanding involved. And we were led to the idea that because of the intimacy of association, the term "the church" could replace "Holy Spirit" as one agency of revelation.

In Section B we began by assuming basic differences in understanding "justification" and "sanctification" relative to Christian ethics. But we were led to another term which, by the context in which it is used, very clearly required us to shift attention back to trinitarian issues again: not tradition here, but sacrament. And then to the extent it can be understood as its sacramental life, the church once again emerges as the named third element in the trinitarian ascriptive pattern.

The question to which both lines of investigation lead is, what do the fathers of Trent see to be the relationship between church and Holy Spirit? The continued investigation in this concluding section of our study will be pointed to this question.

Once Trent affirmed the parity of tradition, it is understandable that the interest of Protestant commentators in the subsequent work of the Council of Trent flagged. To the Protestant mind this decree gave the Catholic Church *carte blanche* to confirm or formulate virtually any teaching it wished. Yet because the issue had become the signal issue of the Reformation crisis, the subsequent decree on justification was fully responded to by Calvin. With the published work of the Seventh Session, however, even Calvin's *Antidote* very quickly exhausts its applicability. For the *Antidote* was concerned with what Calvin considered poisonous doctrine. Beginning with Session Seven, however, the Trent decrees concern themselves with the sacraments, which Calvin considered, for all their value, merely "appendages of doctrine" (*Antidote*, p. 172; cf., however, p. 174).

Nothing more clearly indicates the profound difference between Catholic and Protestant than this different evaluation of the place of the sacraments. For the fathers of Trent the matter of revelation and its sources was an important prolegomenon, and the titled decrees on original sin and justification important but partial formulations necessitated by Protestant criticism. It is only with the work of the Seventh Session that Trent begins to concentrate on matters most intimate to its own view of the life of the Christian church. And it is in the subsequent decrees that we find the basic features differentiating Catholic from Protestant, not only on the matter of Christian ethics but also on the matters of ecclesiology and the function of the Holy Spirit.

The fathers of Trent do not see the sacraments as "appendages of doctrine." The prologue to the decrees of the Seventh Session begins: "For the completion of the salutary doctrine on Justification, . . . it hath seemed suitable to treat of the most holy Sacraments of the Church, through which all true justice either begins, or being begun is increased, or being lost is repaired."

At least two very basic differentiating points are evident in the prologue. If we could substitute the phrase "spiritual dicipline" for the term "sacraments" here, the evaluative position would be most compatible with the position of Menno Simons. But as it stands, the decree gives the sacraments a much more important function in the process of justification than do the Protestant reformers. The reformers could assert that the preaching of the word was a mediate but necessary function in the beginning of the process of justification. For as Luther in particular emphasized, the faith which alone justifies is a faith originating *ex auditu*. But whatever functional value they they might attribute to the sacrament, none of the Protestant reformers would allow that whatever was meant by justice before God could be increased or repaired, much less originated, through the sacraments. For Rome, however—and here the opinion of Simons is shared—there is no justice or justification until and except insofar as it is actualized in Christian discipline. For Simons, that meant actual conformity to the discipline instituted by Christ in scripture. For Rome, however—and this is the point of demarcation from Simons and hence from all the reformers—it meant in addition the full participation in the sacramental ministry of the church.

That is the second main differentiating emphasis of the prologue. A Protestant hand would have written ". . . the most holy sacraments of Christ," or ". . . the most holy sacraments instituted in the Scripture." The decree, however, speaks of the most holy sacraments of the church as being the locus of the origin, increase, or repair of Christian justice. The role of the church in the process of justification is given a valuation, corresponding to the valuation of sacrament, that none of the Protestant reformers could give.

There is more than a "correspondence" of emphasis regarding church and sacrament, however. For the prologue goes on to state that in the view of Trent, the Protestant heresies vis-à-vis the sacraments are ". . . exceedingly prejudicial to the purity of the Catholic Church, and to the salvation of souls . . ." (note the order). And then occurs the first subtle shift in the authoritative justification for the forthcoming canons. The fathers will recur not, as we might have expected from the decree of the Fourth Session, to scripture and tradition equally valuated, but ". . . to the doctrine of the holy Scriptures, to the apostolic traditions, and to the consent of other councils and of the Fathers . . . ." In the absence of further specifications, one can conclude that the scripture theoretically can have a relatively diminished role in the authentic bases of sacramental doctrine. For our thesis, however, the most important aspect of the prologue to the decrees of the Seventh Session is the close identification of interests between sacramental doctrine and the doctrine of the church. We are investigating the possibility of a basic difference between Catholic and Protestant concerning trinitarian functions, and have wondered about the relations Trent perceives between the church and the Holy Spirit. What we see is that the relation will be specified by reference to the sacramental function Trent sees so basic to Christian ethics.

1. SACRAMENT AND CHURCH. The reason why the fathers of Trent give such importance to the role of the church in Christian life is that in their view the process of justification is actualized only via faithful participation in the sacraments. The focus on the sacramental aspect of justification with which the decrees of the Seventh Session begin cannot come as a surprise to us, for already in the decree of the Sixth Session the fathers carefully integrated the sacraments of baptism and penance (Chs. 7 and 14) into their theoretical consideration of the doctrine of justification. The latter sacrament is what chiefly concerns us here. For not only does what Protestants discuss as the process of sanctification or the life of discipline appear to

Trent as the regular participation in the sacrament of penance, but this sacrament also involves indirectly the sacraments of baptism, confirmation, eucharist, extreme unction, and orders. Of these, the relationship of penance to baptism, eucharist, and orders is most important for our consideration in this concluding section.

The relation seen by Trent between baptism and penance affords a useful viewpoint for the comparison of the Protestant reformers on the relationship of both sacrament and church to Christian life.

Unlike Luther and Calvin, the fathers of Trent took "justification" to refer not to an absolute, changed relationship between God and man, but to a process whereby a virtue which could be qualitatively and quantitatively differentiated, i.e., "justice," was infused in the soul. Trent could accordingly speak of the "increase," "loss," or "repair" of justice, and its understanding of the relation and effects of the sacraments relevant to this process was modulated correspondingly. Both penance and baptism have as their chief effect the remission of sins (14, on penance, Ch. 1) and thereby reconciliation with God. But not only is the sacrament of penance held necessary to salvation, assuming a post-baptismal fall (Ch. 2, cf. Ch. 4), but just because of that assumption, penance becomes much more important to the actual Christian life than baptism. For the saving graces imparted through baptism are lost in the subsequent theoretically unnecessary but practically inevitable commission of mortal sins. Penance was then the repeatable but "laborious" (Ch. 2) kind of baptism which could be applied against effects of whatever sins had been committed since the last participation in the sacrament. The sacrament of extreme unction, though formally differentiated by Rome, is functionally the last act of penance.

Luther and Calvin's view of the relation between baptism and penance is exactly reversed, though gradations are apparent. Luther held penance in higher regard than Calvin, but their common opinion is expressed in Luther's view that our life of repentance is a daily creeping back into baptism, and in Calvin's view (*Institutes* IV,15.4; 19.17) that baptism is the only and true sacrament of penance. Since no notion of justice as a quality of soul which can be gained or lost informed their positions, baptismal repentance is not sacramentally repeatable.

Simons' position, on the other hand, though informed by a vastly different sacramental theory, is functionally closer to that of Trent. He distinguishes baptism and penance in function much more than do Luther and Calvin, but also more than does Trent. For Simons, baptism is the non-repeatable sign of admittance into the community on the basis of a completed conversion. The practice most relevant to Mennonite discipline, however, was for Simons, as for Rome, the repeatable penitential practice—not in the Catholic cycle of confession-absolution-satisfaction, but in the nearly parallel Mennonite cycle of ban-repentance-readmission.[16]

The second aspect of Simons' views which reveals his greater proximity to Rome is the importance of the church in penitential praxis. All the

---

[16]Cf. George H. Williams, *The Radical Reformation* (Philadelphia: The Westminster Press, 1962), p. 499. Williams, however, has confused the order of the Roman penitential system.

reformers of course tied baptism very closely to the church. But only Trent and Simons saw a necessary systematic relationship between their doctrines of the church and the efficacy of their penitential systems. Luther and Calvin vented their wrath more fully against the Catholic penitential system than against any other aspect of Catholic teaching. Much of that wrath was directed against what Calvin particularly is sharply aware of: what he took to be the unwarranted intrusion of church organization into the purely spiritual matter of repentance.[17] The key decisions of the Council on this matter—decisions from which follow all the specific teachings incurring the wrath of Calvin—come in Chapter One of the decree on penance.

> But the Lord then principally instituted the sacrament of penance, when, being raised from the dead, he breathed upon his disciples, saying: Receive ye the Holy Ghost: whose sins you shall forgive, they are forgiven them, and whose sins you shall retain, they are retained. By which action so signal, and words so clear, the consent of all the Fathers has ever understood that the power of forgiving and retaining sins was communicated to the apostles and their lawful successsors, for the reconciling of the faithful who have fallen after baptism.

In this passage, however, only the power of the keys is stressed in relation to the church's ministry. The church's formal, exclusive, judicial role in the exercise of this sacramental function is simply stated but not defended here. But soon that lack is more than made good. For in Chapter Five, the fathers state, with a logic baffling to the Protestant mind,

> From the institution of the sacrament of penance, as already explained, the universal Church has always understood that the entire confession of sins was also instituted by the Lord, and is of divine right necessary for all who have fallen after baptism; because that our Lord Jesus Christ, when about to ascend from earth to heaven, left priests his own vicars, as presidents and judges, unto whom all the mortal crimes, into which the faithful of Christ may have fallen, should be carried, in order that, in accordance with the power of the keys, they may pronounce the sentence of forgiveness or retention of sins.

Confession was instituted and is held necessary because Christ instituted the priesthood! For Protestants, the relation between the church and penitential practice is formulated as a question: what limited role therein does the church play, given the true doctrine of repentance instituted by Christ? Calvin and Luther saw no necessary role, and insisted that the minister could at most only declare or pronounce a forgivenss of

---

[17] Cf. *Institutes* III,3-5 and IV,12.19, for the general discussion.

sins assumed to have already and actually been granted by God. To the fathers of Trent, however, the issue is reversed. The question is, what are the characteristics of the sacrament of penance, given the true doctrine of the church? Here it is stated that confession is necessary, and that the effect of the corresponding decisions regarding absolution or retention is not merely declaratory, but judicial (canon 9)—because of the ecclesiology assumed.

There is one more step to this Tridentine logic connecting sacrament and church. With what to Catholic ears is a baffling logic, Calvin had argued that there could be no doctrinally juridical character to the pronouncement of a confessor. Why? Because in view of the history of errors of pronouncement, it must be concluded that the church does not "have" the Holy Spirit, who of course cannot err in judgement (*Institutes* III,4.20). To put it differently, there is nothing about the exercise of the church's ministry in the matter of penance that could give the practice the status of a sacrament or the minister any juridical authority.

We have seen that for Trent what is said about penance is significantly determined by what is said about the church. Regarding the question of the place of the church in the Christian life of discipline, the important issue between Rome and Geneva is not so much whether penance itself is or is not a sacrament. It is whether or not there is any juridical authority to the decisions of the confessor. The arguments only appear to miss each other. Calvin argues that there is no juridical authority because history has shown the decisions to have been wrong in many cases; Rome argues that the decisions are correct if—because—they are rendered by one with juridical authority! The head-to-head difference of opinion concerns the nature of the church. For Calvin, the hearer of confession is but a human minister of God's Word and ordinances. Church offices and officers are defined by administrative function only. And all such human functions are shot through with error, hence of no juridical authority. For Trent, however, the exercise of the keys does have juridical status because the status of the confessor is not adequately defined in terms of function, in terms of "minister." The one who "ministers" in this particular way is the one who offers that most holy of sacraments, the Sacrifice of the Mass. The status of the one fit to do this cannot be defined merely in terms of function. He must be a priest—an ontological status, not merely a function. The conferring of priesthood—order—is therefore given the status of a sacrament.

> Sacrifice and priesthood are, by the ordinance of God, in such wise conjoined, as that both have existed in every law. Whereas, therefore, in the New Testament, the Catholic Church has received, from the institution of Christ, the holy visible sacrifice of the Eucharist; it must needs also be confessed, that there is, in that Church, a new, visible, and external priesthood, into which the old has been translated. And the sacred Scriptures show, and the tradition of the Catholic Church has always taught,

that this priesthood was instituted by the same Lord our Savior, and that to the Apostles, and their successors in the priesthood, was the power delivered of consecrating, offering, and administering his body and blood, as also of forgiving and of retaining sins (23, Ch. 1).

There is a systematic connection between the Protestants' relative diminution, compared to Rome, of both sacrament and church in the life of Christian discipline. For the Protestants, whatever sacramental or disciplinary efficacy is held to exist is due to the direct influence of the Word and the Holy Spirit of Christ alone. The church is but a human order. As such, its functions are always to be critically evaluated against the standards of the Word. And to the extent the sacramental functions it assumes for itself are seen to rest in no specific institution of Christ, the church must be relativized like any other human institution. For Trent, however, the importance of the sacraments cannot be diminished by appeal to the merely human character of the church. For the priesthood, in terms of which the church is defined, is itself a sacramental status. Therefore all the functions exercised in that status are of sacramental import. This belief is stated in the opening phrase of Chapter Two of Session 23, immediately following the passage quoted above, "And whereas the ministry of so holy a priesthood is a divine thing. . . ."

In terms of its relevance to Christian discipline, the importance of penance, both its sacramental and (in part also) its juridical status, is due to the sacramental status of those who administer it. The priesthood not only has the power of the Holy Spirit (Ch. 2) to forgive and retain sins; it has the Holy Spirit himself (canon 4, on orders). Calvin's argument that the Roman penitential praxis is shot through with errors of decisions, and accordingly cannot be said to reflect the discerning presence of the Holy Spirit, and hence is not binding, remains to be considered, however. The question is, what is the relationship, as Trent sees it in contrast to the Protestants, of the Holy Spirit to the administration of the sacraments?

2.SPIRIT AND SACRAMENT. As suggested earlier, it is in terms of its sacramental theory that Catholic theology can complete the fusion of things human and divine. Since Simons' theology is effectively without transcendental reference, his sacramental theory is not particularly relevant to the question now before us. Calvin's criticisms of Roman sacramental theory, however, are very relevant. The Trent decrees on the sacraments basically reconfirmed the church's doctrine, and Calvin's *Antidote* offers no new critical insights on the matter. For he had fully responded in the *Institutes*.

In his sacramental doctrine, as elsewhere, Calvin was very concerned to maintain God's "distance" from things of the flesh. To him, the Roman view threatened the glory of God by too close an identification of God with the sacrament. Even though Calvin argued that it is in the Spirit and by the Spirit alone that the sacramental union is achieved, he was concerned even here to avoid too close a relationship between Spirit and sacrament.

In the Roman view, reconfirmed at Trent, the sacraments are of course said to have effects for faith and the remission of sins. But it is also insisted that faith is not the only object of sacramental action (cf. canon 5 to the general decree on sacraments). For Calvin, however, the sacraments are defined wholly in relation to their effects on faith (IV, 14.1-8). Conversely, Calvin refuses to permit any sacramental implication in the exercise of the keys. The exercise of the keys does not imply a power separate from that of the preaching of the Gospel (III,4.14). The use of the keys is wholly for the purpose of discipline (IV,12.1). Calvin seems particularly incensed that Rome sees any efficacy to lie in the sacramental acts themselves. To him, the sacraments do not justify or confer grace. Christ is the "matter" of all the sacraments; it is God's mercy, and not our penance, which is the cause of forgiveness; and the sacrament of baptism is not an instrumental cause of anything (III,4.3; IV,14.14,16; *Antidote*, p. 116f.).

The position of Calvin against Rome is, however, but a consequence of a much more basic difference of opinion. The differences noted above arise partially in the context of the issue of sacramental administration. All parties agreed that it is the Holy Spirit who gives efficacy to the sacramental acts. The basic question, however, is the relationship held to exist between the work of the Holy Spirit and the administration of the sacraments. Calvin is well aware that this is a critical issue: he devotes considerable time to it in the opening pages of discussion of the meaning of sacrament.

Calvin insists on keeping Word, Spirit, and sacrament quite distinct. The sacrament is but an "outward sign" (IV,14.1) or "appendix" of the Word. Its function is actually not even to confirm the Word, but is to establish us in faith (3). But is not that function to be attributed to the Holy Spirit? Calvin admits this, but by making a distinction refuses to fuse even the functions of Spirit and sacrament.

"For first, the Lord teaches and instructs us by his Word. Secondly, he confirms it by the sacraments. Finally, he illumines our minds by the light of his Holy Spirit and opens our hearts for the Word and sacraments to enter in . . ."(8). The functions of the Word and Spirit clearly distinguished, Calvin feels he needs to elaborate on the distinction of Spirit and sacrament. The Spirit is required for the efficacy of the sacrament, but efficacy lies in the Spirit.

> Therefore, I make such a division between Spirit and sacraments that the power to act rests with the former, and the ministry alone is left to the latter—a ministry empty and trifling, apart from the action of the Spirit, but charged with great effect when the Spirit works within and manifests his power. (9)

Sections 10-12 continue to elaborate the relationship, Calvin ending characteristically:

> . . . Neither ought our confidence to inhere in the sacraments, nor the glory of God be transferred to them.

> Rather, laying aside all things, both our faith and our confession ought to rise up to him who is the author of the sacraments and of all things.

Calvin is clearly very concerned to keep God and the world sharply distinct by radically subordinating the function of the sacrament to that of the Spirit. In the Roman view, the functions of the sacramental administration and of the Holy Spirit are fused. We have seen some indirect evidence of this in the claim that the decisions of the confessor in the sacrament of penance have juridical status. More direct evidence emerged in regard to the sacramental status of order. Exercise of the keys has juridical status because the confessor is a priest or shares in the priesthood. Why is that fact important to our question? Because the sacramental status of order appears to be necessitated by the chief function for which the priesthood was instituted: the Sacrifice of the Mass. The Sacrifice of the Mass is the sacramental function which stands behind all other sacramental functions and which is the basis for the claims of efficacy of those other sacramental functions. And it is in what the Council of Trent says about the Sacrifice of the Mass that we have unmistakable evidence of the identification, in function at least, of God and the world, the work of the Holy Spirit and the sacramental administration.

The eucharist is, of course, the center of sacramental (i.e., moral) life. The objections of Luther and Calvin to Roman sacramental theory were directed most extensively against the Mass, and the Trent decrees concern themselves more fully with this than with any other aspect of sacramental doctrine. Although it is considered a distinct sacrament, penance (and extreme unction) is treated by the fathers within the general context of the decree on the eucharist. Conversely, the Sacrifice of the Mass, though not a separate sacrament, is given extensive separate consideration. Thus it may be seen that there are three basic elements in the doctrine of the eucharist which impinge upon the question of the relationship between God and the world as seen by Trent: 1) the objective relationship, in terms of Christ's presence in the bread and wine (decree of the 13th Session); 2) the sacramental efficacy *ad nos* (14, on penance); and 3) the sacramental efficacy *in deum* (22, on the Sacrifice of the Mass).

We have already considered the first element. None of the Protestants could go so far as Rome in the identification of divine and human sacramental presence. Relative to the matter of penance, Chapter Three of the decree on the eucharist does offer relevant data. Though it shares many characteristics with the other sacraments, ". . . there is found in the Eucharist this excellent and peculiar thing, that the other sacraments have then first the power of sanctifying when one uses them, whereas in the Eucharist, before being used, there is the Author himself of sanctity." Efficacy and presence are clearly distinguished here in a way neither Luther nor Calvin could accept. The issue is the locus of efficacy. For Luther and Calvin it is wholly in Christ's presence, however that presence be conceived. For Trent, however, efficacy is not co-extensive with presence: all the sacraments are equally efficacious, but Christ is not equally present, nor present in the same way, in all of them. Efficacy is co-extensive in locus with the sacramental act itself. Grace is contained in and conferred by the sacramental action itself (*ex opere operato*). It is with the sacramental action that we are now concerned.

Above we saw that for Calvin there is a very sharp subordination of the "outward" physical signs and acts to the role of the Holy Spirit vis-à-vis sacramental efficacy. The Spirit is not bound to any instrumental signs or acts; hence, the performance of these signs and acts cannot have any necessary or direct connection with, for example, the judgments of the Spirit in the matter of the exercise of the keys. Since efficacy is wholly the act of the Spirit, Calvin went out of his way to insist that the object or direction of efficacy in the sacramental administration was exclusively God to us. For Trent, however, there are two directions of efficacy involved in the full celebration of the eucharist: God-to-man, in the penitential praxis and in the reception of the Lord's Supper, and man-to-God in the Sacrifice of the Mass.

We have seen that the order of priesthood is intimately related to the Sacrifice of the Mass. The question now is what makes possible the assertion of efficacy Godward? Two elements are involved: the quality of the actor and the quality of the act. In principle, the quality of the actor was determined by the assertion that the order of priesthood is a sacramental order. We shall return to this below. The closely related matter of the quality of the act is the subject of the decree of the 23rd Session.

Quite simply, the issue is one of the perfection of the act. This is indicated in the first chapter of the decree. Everything said subsequently about the Sacrifice of the Mass depends upon the determination of this matter. In Chapter Four, the determination is made.

> And whereas it beseemeth that holy things be administered in a holy manner, and of all holy things this sacrifice is the most holy; to the end that it might be worthily and reverently offered and received, the Catholic church instituted, many years ago, the sacred Canon, so pure from every error, that nothing is contained therein which does not in the highest degree savor of a certain holiness and piety, and raise up unto God the minds of those that offer. For it is composed out of the very words of the Lord, the traditions of the Apostles, and the pious institutions also of the holy Pontiffs.

We cannot let the Catholic argument that the phrase "pure from every error" is different in meaning from the phrase "completely true" distract us, whether that argument be in reference to the canon of the Mass or to papal decisions on matters of faith and morals. Completion of truth is not an issue in either case; only very delimited functions are characterized by the phrase. And in the present context what is asserted is that there is, as far as human perception grants, a perfection to its end of the signs and acts constituting the administration of the Sacrifice of the Mass. That is the only characteristic allowing the assertion that there is an efficacy Godward in the eucharistic administration. And that perfection of function is based, necessarily though perhaps only partially, on the claim that the administration of the sacrament reflects a complete fusion of divine and human agency. That is the ultimate force of *ex opere operato*.

Is there a comparable fusion between the agency of the Spirit and that of the priest?

3.SPIRIT AND CHURCH. One of the regular themes apparent in the decrees and canons on the sacraments is the close relationship asserted between the sacraments of penance and eucharist. The grounds for the relationship are more basic, and more specific, than the church's disciplinary requirement that participation in the sacrament of penance is ordinarily necessary for participation in the eucharist (13, Ch. 7). We have seen in the general canons on the sacraments that the fathers anathematized those who insisted that sacramental efficacy was in regard to faith alone (13, canon 5). Sacramental efficacy is in two directions, manward and Godward. The penultimate ground for the relationship of the two sacraments has to do with those functions within the sacraments wherein the two efficacies are exercised, i.e., in penance with the forgiveness or retention of sins, and in the eucharist with the Sacrifice of the Mass and the reception of the Lord's Supper. The efficacy and the relationship of the functions is clearly stated in the canon on order:

> If any one saith, that there is not in the New Testament a visible and external priesthood; or, that there is not any power of consecrating and offering the true body and blood of the Lord, and of forgiving and retaining sins, but only an office and bare ministry of preaching the Gospel . . . (23, canon 1).

It is by virtue of the sacrament of order that there is efficacy in the administration of the other sacraments. But what is it that provides this power and authority for the priesthood in reference to the two sacraments? There are only two places in the material on the sacraments where John 20:23 is quoted with significant purpose: "Receive ye the Holy Ghost . . ." is the ultimate basis for the juridical exercise of the keys (14, Ch. 1) and—not the efficacy of the Sacrifice of the Mass, as we might expect—for the validity of order as a sacrament (23, Ch. 4).

Note that although Christ's granting of the Spirit is the ultimate basis for the relationships among the subjects of the keys, sacrifice, and priesthood, these subjects stand in different relationships to each other and hence in different relationships to the Holy Spirit.

The power of the keys is most removed from the Holy Spirit. It is described wholly as an exercise, and both the legitimacy and the efficacy of that sacramental exercise is based directly on the existence of the priesthood (14, Ch. 5), which is defined not merely as an exercise, but as a sacramental status (23, Ch. 3 and related canons). This difference is further indicated, and in more direct manner, when the fathers say that a power of the Holy Spirit exists in the administration of the sacrament of penance (14, Ch. 1) but that the Holy Spirit himself is present in the sacrament of order (23, Ch. 4). The effective subordination of penance to eucharistic sacrifice is also reasonably clear. The material on penance occurs mainly within the context of the discussion of eucharist. Ordinarily penitential discipline is in preparation for eucharistic participation. And the efficacy of the adminsitration of the keys is due to their exercise by the one who alone is fit to offer sacrifice, the priest.

On this latter matter—the relationship between order and sacrifice—the decrees are at first less clear. The opening chapter on the Sacrifice of the Mass—if we can decipher the inordinately long and complicated second sentence—suggests that Christ offered sacrifice in order that among other things the priesthood might be continued after his death. It seems that sacrifice is the legitimating basis of priesthood. But the sentence goes on to state that after the institution of the sacrifice, Christ in a separate act (*tunc*) constituted the priesthood.

The opening chapter of the decree on order is likewise unclear. It begins by saying that sacrifice and priesthood are so conjoined (*ita . . . conjuncta sunt*) as to co-exist in every law. The conjunctive relationship, however, is not clearly specified. Once again it seems as though it is the sacrificial function (*cum igitur . . .*) which authorizes the priesthood (*. . . fateri etiam*). But a careful reading indicates that it is the church which has received Christ's institution (*institutione*, a verbal noun) of the sacrifice. And what is the church which exercises this instititution but the sacramental order of priesthood? The chapter then goes on to state that Christ instituted (*institutum esse*) the priesthood. But it does not say it was instituted in order to offer sacrifice. The nature of the conjunction of sacrifice and priesthood is left unstated. What we have is *atque*; the church affirms that the priesthood was instituted, and that the power (note the shift to function) of sacrifice was delivered to it, as also (note the subordinate sense) the power of the keys.

We can answer the question posed if we get past the details to the general picture presented by Trent's decrees on the sacraments. The power of the keys, subordinate to sacrifice, is a function, the sacramental character of which is authorized by the sacramental status of the priest. The Sacrifice of the Mass, though the most important part of the eucharistic function and though its canon is said to be pure of every error, has no sacramental status separate from that of the eucharist in which it is embedded. It too is a power, not a status.

Penance and eucharist involve four functions. In each there is an efficacy manward (forgiveness of sins, reception of the Lord's body), and Godward (retention of sins, Sacrifice of the Mass). But these four functions, each noted in the closing lines of 23, Ch. 1, are all called in the opening line of 23, Ch. 2, the divine ministry of the priesthood. Priesthood is the sacramental status; the specific functions are not sacraments themselves, but receive sacramental efficacy from the sacramental status of their administrator.

****

The primary object of this concluding chapter to our study was to see the contrasts between Luther, Calvin, and Simons on the issues of Trinity, church, and ethics as these contrasts are exposed from the viewpoint of Trent. Consideration of the Tridentine positions on revelation and justification not only confirmed the differences we established among the Protestants, but also revealed a more basic contrast—that between Catholic and Protestant—which thereby reveals the unity among the Protestant positions. The expression of this fundamental contrast is the relatively greater role of the church in the formulation of doctrines concerning the above issues which Catholic theology expresses. So great is this difference of evaluation that we began to suspect a basic difference in trinitarian understanding between Catholic and Protestant. The issue began to crystallize in terms of the question: what is the relationship between the Third Person of the Trinity and the church? We found that in order to begin to formulate the answer in terms relevant to the decrees of Trent, we had to speak in terms of sacrament. The matter then finally became formulated as the question: what do the decrees on the sacraments of penance and eucharist reveal or imply about the relationship of church and Spirit asserted by Trent? In Section C we have been sketching all three relationships. What has emerged is a pattern of assertion which has three basic features. 1)Trent sees a much closer relationship among sacrament, church, and Spirit than do the Protestant reformers. So close do these relationships appear that one is sorely tempted to overstate the case and say that there is a virtual identification of the three subjects. 2)The proximity of relationship, however, appears only in terms of function, and not in terms of being or status. Throughout the analysis, the verbal or functional sense of the important nouns kept coming to our attention. 3)The key functional element is the church. But the church is not simply defined in terms of function. It is itself asserted to be an holy order, and it is that status which gives efficacy to the critical functions in both the sacrament of penance (the keys) and the sacrament of eucharist (the sacrifice). Tha status asserted for the church in each of these critical functions is based on its possession of the Holy Spirit (John 20.23).

We should now be able to answer the original question: what is the relationship between church and Holy Spirit, insofar as that relationship suggests a significantly different trinitarian understanding than is shared by the Protestant reformers?

Although occasionally the language of Trent suggests that "church" can replace "Holy Spirit" in trinitarian formulations, we of course cannot conclude that "church" is a term univocal with the Third Person of the Holy Trinity. The Holy Spirit is divine being, fully God, and his nature is exclusively, purely, eternally spiritual—characterizations that cannot be applied in the same way even to the Second Person, much less to the church. Even though the church be defined in terms of the sacramental order of priesthood, and associated most intimately with the Holy Spirit, theologically there is a world of difference between "divine being" and "holy order." As emphasized from the earliest pages of this study, the orthodox doctrine of the being of God in his inner-trinitarian relationships was not a divisive issue among Luther, Simons, and Calvin, or between the three of them and Trent, and accordingly was not the focus of our investigation. Our focus was exclusively upon trinitarian functions *ad extra*. On this issue we could see real differences among the Protestants. The fathers of Trent, like Simons and Calvin, appear to ascribe the power function primarily to the Holy Spirit. And somewhat like Simons but unlike Calvin, the fathers of Trent base the authority of the church on its possession of the powers and presence of the Spirit. It seems thus that Simons and Trent are closest in trinitarian functioning. But we cannot conclude from the language of the above summary that Trent's position is but one particular though extreme variation (Luther being the opposite extreme) of solution to the general problems posed for investigation in this study. There is a combination of two positions, one an assumptive metaphysical position and one a theological or doctrinal position, that produces a basic categorical difference between Catholic and Protestant relative to the general issue of the study. As appeared to be the case so often in our study, the decisions of Menno Simons function as the clearest line of demarcation between Catholic and Protestant.

Luther and Calvin assumed, with Roman theology, the "vertical" or ontological world-view in which the things of "this world" of mere appearance were theologically valuated in terms of their perceived degree of participation in the "really real" spiritual reality above mere appearance. Menno Simons appears at least actually if not assumptively to deny this metaphysical view. For him theological reality is wholly spiritual, but on a single existential plane. Things of this physical world are not theologically subordinate or dependent: they are irrelevant.

On the other hand, only Simons shares with Rome both the trinitarian functional ascriptive pattern and the selection of the function of the Holy Spirit as the basis of the authority of the church. These decisions basically explain why in the comparison of specific Catholic and Protestant theological positions, Simons almost always appeared closest to Rome.

Had Luther and Calvin, assuming Roman metaphysics, made the same theological decisions as Simons, their position could be categorized, in terms of the issues posed in this study, as Catholic. Had the fathers of Trent, making the same theological decisions as Simons, also assumed Simons' metaphysical position, their position could be categorized, relative to the issues of our study, as Protestant. We are not saying that one or the other of either the metaphysical decision or the theological decision is the basic demarcation line between Catholic and Protestant. We are suggesting that the consequence of the combination of these decisions is a categorical difference between Catholic and Protestant relative to the issues posed by the study. We submit that in virtue of the different combinations of metaphysical and theological decisions, there eventuates a categorical difference between Catholic and Protestant on the issue of trinitarian function. That categorical difference is expressed in terms of the functional relationship asserted between the church and the Holy Spirit. Assertions of identity of function and assertions of difference of function cannot be viewed as merely qualitative or quantitative gradations. Such a difference amounts to a categorical difference.

Although they made different combinations of metaphysical and theological decisions, Luther, Simons, and Calvin all agreed that there is and remains an unbridgeable "gap" between the work of the Third Person of the Trinity and the ministrations of the church relative to both doctrine and discipline. It is because they recognize this gap that the Protestant reformers consistently subordinate the church to the Spirit, evaluate the church against the standards of the Spirit, and assert the freedom of the Spirit beyond even the correct determinations of the church.

The effect of their combination of metaphysical and theological decisions, however, is that the fathers of Trent assume an identity of function between the Holy Spirit and the church. The church "has" or "possesses" the Spirit. The words in quotation do not of themselves indicate the basis upon which that identity is asserted. But we have shown that the Tridentine statements have, in terms of sacramental administration, asserted that identification in terms of function.

We need not review the data or the interpretation of the data bearing on this conclusion. The hour is late, and the reader, like the writer, has other necessary things to do before he sleeps. Let me, however, conjoin two questions for further reflection.

Did not all the Protestant reformers say, in their discussions on prayer, that the functions of the Holy Spirit were to comfort us and to intercede for us? The former function is a manward efficacy, the latter a Godward efficacy. Each functional efficacy of the spirit is legitimated by Christ's institution: the Spirit is called Comforter and Advocate.

By virtue of his sacramental status, perhaps equally legitimated in the scripture by Christ, is not the function of the priest, in the administration of the sacraments of penance and eucharist, to be identified with those functions of the Spirit?

The question of what the degree of identification of function between the office of the priest and the office of the Holy Spirit implies relative to the question of the identity of being of priesthood and Spirit, is a matter that we may leave to another day.

John R. Loeschen
July 1980

APPENDIX

Statistical Analysis of Frequency of Associations Among Trinitarian Terms and Related Concepts in Menno Simons' *The Foundation of Christian Doctrine*

In the following six tables, terms or phrases listed at the top of the numbered files were tabulated according to selected verbal associations, listed in the lettered ranks. A pair of terms or phrases was considered associated when each member occurred in the same "meaning unit." The meaning unit might be a sentence, a clause, a phrase, or a series of individual terms or phrases in sequence. In Table Two, for example, by far the most frequent kinds of linkages were the conjunctions "and," as in "Spirit and Word of Christ," and "of," as in "Spirit of Christ" or "Spirit of God"; and simple enumerations such as "Spirit, Christ, love, peace . . . ." It would be better, of course, if a more objective means of identifying associations were possible. but perhaps the lack of such means is compensated for by a practised theological eye. Further notes on the method of identifying associations will be given in the individual tables.

Since these tables contain all the linguistic occasions in the text of the *Foundation Book*, they do not represent a data sample but an entire data universe. It would therefore be possible to attribute significance to differences between the absolute numbers of studied occurrences. I have decided, however, to be extremely conservative in statistical interpretation, especially in view of the limits of the method of data collection. I shall appeal only to those differences which are significant when the data from the *Foundation Book* are analyzed as a sample of a larger potential data source, i.e., the entire corpus. The statistical instrument used is a formula for "significance of difference of two proportions." Ranks and files, singly, partially, or in combination, are compared in the formula

$$S = (P_1 - .50) \times 2\sqrt{T}$$

Where S = confidence level, and
P_1 = rank or file of larger frequency, divided by the total (T) of all ranks or files considered.

A confidence level of 2.58 or higher means the probable degree of error over a larger sample is .01 or less; a confidence level of 1.96 to 2.57 means the probable degree of error over a larger sample is .05 to .01.

In adddition, the method of data collection required that a single occurrence of a term often be tabulated at least twice, as in "Spirit of God and Christ," where "Spirit" would be tabulated both under the rank, "God" and the rank, "Christ." This means the total in the calculation is somewhat inflated. The total occurs in the denominator of the studied proportion, however, and therefore the achieved figures for level of confidence will be lower than would actually be the case. In other words, the statistical results err on the conservative side.

Since a large variety of words is useful to suggest one or the other of the concepts "love," "power," and "justice," and since assignment of these words to a concept category might be subjective, I have listed all the different words or phrases occurring in the text of the *Foundation Book* in the categories to which I assigned them. The same listing occurs for cognates of "church" in Table Six. Most phrases occurred only once or twice. In only a few cases was the choice of a category somewhat difficult. But the statistical patterns were so strongly marked that a shift in category of a few cases would not affect the conclusion.

I wish to thank Dr. Raphael Hanson, Professor of Psychology at California State University, Long Beach, for his assistance in the preparation of this analysis.

Table One

Association of some major theological terms with terms naming God, Christ, or the Trinity

Rank   *File*

		1 Word	2 Grace	3 Love	4 Faith	5 Church	T
A.	No specific association or other	55	31	60	64	15	225
B.	God, Father, Lord*	140	40	12	4	9	205
C.	Christ, Jesus, Lord*	82	25	19	5	23	154
D.	Lord (not specific to Christ)*	112	16	2	2	8	140
E.	Trinity named	—	1	—	—	—	1
T		389	113	93	75	55	725

Proportions analyzed	Confidence level	Probability of error
1. Rank B vs. Rank C	2.65	< .01
2. Ranks of C+D (File 1) vs. Rank B (File 1)	2.92	< .01
3. Rank B (File 1) vs. Rank C (File 1)	3.87	< .01
4. Ranks C+D vs. Rank B	4.02	< .01

*Many references to the Second Person contained explicit mention of the term "Lord"; many other cases in which "Lord" occurred demanded ascription to Christ because of the context. While Simons almost always uses the term "Lord" in reference to Christ, I have separated those cases where the explicit or contextual association is lacking. The ascription of "Lord" to Christ in all cases where the references are not explicitly or contextually to "God" is analyzed in the second and fourth proportions.

Table Two

Association of names for the Third Person of the Trinity, and cognates, with terms naming the First or Second Person of the Trinity, and cognates

Rank   *File*

		1 Spirit	2 Holy Spirit	3 spirit†	T
A.	No specific trinitarian reference, or other	8	31	25	64
B.	Word of Christ	47	2	3	52
C.	Christ	24	6	8	38
D.	God, Father	15	2	1	18
E.	Word of God	14	2	1	17
F.	Lord*	10	—	2	12
G.	Fully Trinitarian	1	12	—	13
T		119	56	40	214

Proportions analyzed	Confidence level	Probability of error
1. Rank A vs. Rank G	4.04	< .01
2. Ranks B+C vs. Ranks D+E+F+G	2.46	< .01
3. File 1 vs. File 2	4.76	< .01

† "spirit," though a cognate, is almost always used by Simons in lower case, to designate man's psychological faculty. Hence it does not figure in our trinitarian analysis. In a few cases "spirit" is associated with Christ or God. I take these instances of lower case printing as simple lapses of consistency in Simons' script.

* All references, regardless of other associations. Cf. note to Table One.

Table Three

Association of "Spirit" and cognate terms with functionally trinitarian component terms, and cognates*

Rank   *File*

		1 Holy Spirit	2 Spirit	3 Spirit of Christ	4 Spirit of God	5 Spirit of the Lord	T
A.	power, and cognates	12	13	6	7	7	45
B.	form, and cognates	7	5	12	9	9	42
C.	love, and cognates	11	7	3	2	2	25
D.	sacraments and church institutions	13	2	2	2	1	20
T		43	27	23	20	19	132

Proportions analyzed	Confidence level	Probability of error
1. Rank B vs. Rank C	2.13	> .01
2. Rank A vs. Rank C	2.35	> .01

*Terms taken to be the theologically related to "power," as occurring in the text:
"sword of, through the, led by the, resist the, constrained by, ruled by, impulsion of, driven by, renewing of the, moving of the, spark of the, motivated by the, truimph by the, quench the, freedom of the, liberty of the, threatened by the, inspiration of the"

Terms related to "form":
"illumination of the, taught by the, learned from the, reproved by the, walk in the, witnessed by the, weigh with the, conduct according to the, examine by the, speak the word of the, admonition of the, foretold by the, light of the, council of the, contrary to the,

conform to the, forbidden by the, enlighten by the, requires of, follow the, law of the, judge by the, reproved by the, true, false, understand scripture by the, prove by the"

Terms related to "love":
"joy in the, grieving the, seal of the, assured by the, grasped in the, fed by the, children of the, despise the, keep the, preserve the, life in the, indwelling, death in the, reject the, unity of the"

Table Four

Association of "Word" and cognate terms with functionally trinitarian component terms, and cognates*

Rank		File				T
		1 Word of God	2 Word of the Lord	3 Word	4 Word of Christ	
A.	Form, and cognates	76	79	22	26	203
B.	Power, and cognates	19	14	17	11	61
C.	Love, and cognates	7	7	12	5	31
T		102	100	51	42	295

Proportions analyzed	Confidence level	Probability of error
1. Rank A (Files 2+4) vs. Ranks B+C (Files 2+4)	5.76	< .01
2. Rank A vs. Ranks B+C	6.58	< .01
3. Rank A vs. Rank B	8.79	< .01

*Terms taken to be theologically related to "form," as occurring in the text: "obscure, light of, teaches, followers of, intent upon, judge, proclaim, know, preach, obedient to, speak, instruct, will of, covenant of, commandment of, office of, doubt, heed, hear, believe, live by, doctrine of, abuse, listen to, pervert, knife of, lamp of, reject, confess, weigh by, gospel of"

Terms related to "power":
"commanded by, fear, rule by, abide, new birth from, obey, submit to, regenerated by, constrained by, broken by, rebel against, born of, stands firm in, seed of, calling by, war against, spirit of, oppose"

Terms related to "love:"
"abide in, despise, cross of, peace of, salvation, bound with, bread of, sanctified by, trust, serve, remedy of, feed, children of, delight in"

Table Five

Association of "Love" and "Holy Spirit" with various subjects.

Rank		File 1 Love (Lord's Supper Section)*	File 2 Love	File 3 Holy Spirit	T
A.	Church†	17	16	20	53
B.	Christ□	17	16	4	37
C.	no specific association, or other	8	10	13	31
D.	power, grace✓	—	—	15	15
E.	God	5	4	—	9
T		47	46	52	145

Proportions analyzed	Confidence level	Probability of error
1. Files 1+2 vs. File 3	3.37	< .01
2. Ranks A+B (Files 1+2) vs. Ranks C+D+E (Files 1+2)	4.05	< .01

* The relatively largest number of references to love comes in the brief (10 pages) section on the Supper, which I have separated for special reference.
† Included in this rank are specific references to the church, and other terms referring either to institutions of the church or to "fraternal" or "brotherly" love.
□ Included in this rank are specific references to Christ by title (Jesus, Savior, Lord), and also references to his teaching, example, life, atonement, and to faith in Christ.
✓ Included in this rank are the associations for power, listed in the notes to Tables Three and Four, plus specific mentionings of "grace."

Table Six

Association of "Church" and cognates with trinitarian terms and cognates

Rank   File

		1 Church	2 Christians	3 Children of	4 Members of	5 Other*	T
A.	Christ, Lord	33	17	8	11	29	98
B.	no specific reference, or other	11	20	—	—	7	38
C.	God	4	5	9	—	10	28
D.	Spirit	2	2	2	—	2	8
E.	Word	3	2	—	—	2	7
F.	Holy Spirit	1	—	—	—	2	3
G.	Word and Spirit	1	—	—	—	1	2
H.	Spirit of Christ	—	1	—	—	1	2
T		55	47	19	11	54	186

Proportions analyzed	Confidence level	Probability of error
1. Rank A vs. Ranks B-H	3.89	< .01
2. Files 1-4 vs. File 5	5.73	< .01

*The following cognates for church occurred in the text:
"household of, elect of, people of, heirs to, followers of, those born of, the righteous, the poor ones, friends of, those of, Anabaptist, congregation, fellowship, school of, the regenerated, disciples of"

BIBLIOGRAPHY

Primary Sources

Calvin, John. *Institutes of the Christian Religion.* Edited by John T. McNeill, translated by Ford Lewis Battles. 2 vols. Library of Christian Classics, vols. 20-21. Philadelphia: The Westminster Press, 1960.
___. *Instruction in Faith.* Translated by Paul. T. Fuhrman. Philadelphia: The Westminster Press, 1959.
___. *Works.* 51 vols. Edinburgh: Calvin Translation Society, 1844-1856.
Grebel, Conrad. *Conrad Grebel's Programmatic Letters of 1524.* Translated by John C. Wenger. Scottdale, Pa.: Herald Press, 1970.
Hubmaier, Balthasar. *On Free Will.* In *Spiritual and Anabaptist Writers.* Edited by George H. Williams. Library of Christian Classics, vol. 25. Philadelphia: The Westminster Press, 1957.
Luther, Martin. *Luther: Early Theological Works.* Edited and translated by James Atkinson. Library of Christian Classics, vol. 16. Philadelphia: The Westminster Press, 1962.
___. *Luther and Erasmus: Free Will and Salvation.* Edited and translated by E. Gordon Rupp and Philip S. Watson. Library of Christian Classics, vol. 17. Philadelphia: The Westminster Press, 1969.
___. *Luther: Lectures on Romans.* Edited and translated by Wilhelm Pauck. The Library of Christian Classics, vol. 15. Philadelphia: The Westminster Press, 1961.
___. *Werke: Kritische Gesamtausgabe.* Weimar: H. Böhlau, 1883—.
___. *Luther's Works.* 55 vols. American Edition, edited by Jaroslav Pelikan and Helmut T. Lehmann. St. Louis: Concordia Publishing House, 1955—.
Melanchthon, Philip. *Melanchthon on Christian Doctrine. Loci Communes 1555.* Translated and edited by Clyde L. Manschreck. Library of Protestant Thought. New York: Oxford University Press, 1965.
Phillips, Dirk. *Enchiridion.* In *Spiritual and Anabaptist Writers.* Edited by George H. Williams. The Library of Christian Classics, vol. 25. Philadelphia: The Westminster Press, 1957.
Ridemann, Peter. *Account of Our Religion, Doctrine, and Faith.* Translated by Kathleen Hasenberg. London: n.p., 1950.
Simons, Menno. *The Complete Writings of Menno Simons.* Edited by John C. Wenger, translated by Leonard Verduin. Scottdale, Pa.: Herald Press, 1956.
Stadler, Ulrich. *Cherished Instructions.* In *Spiritual and Anabaptist Writers.* Edited by George Williams. The Library of Christian Classics, vol. 25. Philadelphia: The Westminster Press, 1957.
Trent, Council of. *Canons and Decrees.* In *The Creeds of Christendom.* Vol. II: *The Greek and Latin Creeds, with Translations.* Edited by Philip Schaff. New York: Harper & Brothers, 1919.

___. *Canons and Decrees*. Edited and translated by H. J. Schroeder. St. Louis: B. Herder Book Co., 1941
Zwingli, Ulrich. *Zwingli and Bullinger*. Translated by G. W. Bromiley. The Library of Christian Classics, vol. 24. Philadelphia: The Westminster Press, 1953.

Secondary Sources

Althaus, Paul. *The Ethics of Martin Luther*. Translated by Robert Schultz. Philadelphia: Fortress Press, 1972.
___. *Die Theologie Martin Luthers*. Gütersloh: Gerd Mohn, 1963.
Bauman, Clarence. "The Theology of the Two Kingdoms: A Comparison of Luther and the Anabaptists," *Mennonite Quarterly Review* 38 (January 1964): 37-49.
Beachy, Alvin, J. "The Grace of God as Understood by Five Major Anabaptist Writers," *Mennonite Quarterly Review* 37 (January 1963): 5-33.
Bonhoeffer, Dietrich, *Ethics*. Edited by Eberhard Bethge, translated by Neville Horton Smith. New York: The Macmillan Co., 1962.
Burkhart, Irvin E. "Menno Simons on the Incarnation," *Mennonite Quarterly Review* 4 (1930): 113-139, 178-207, and 6 (1932): 122-123.
Burkholder, J. Lawrence. "The Anabaptist Vision of Discipleship." In Guy F. Hershberger, ed. *The Recovery of the Anabaptist Vision*. Scottdale, Pa.: Herald Press, 1957.
Davis, Kenneth R. "Erasmus as Progenitor of Anabaptist Theology and Piety," *Mennonite Quarterly Review* 47 (July 1973): 163-178.
Dyck, Cornelius J. "The Christology of Dirk Philips," *Mennonite Quarterly Review* 31 (July 1957): 147-155.
Ebeling, Gerhard. *Luther: Einführung in sein Denken*. Tübingen: J. C. B. Mohr, 1964.
___. *Word and Faith*. Translated by James W. Leitch. Philadelphia: Fortress Press, 1963.
Fast, Heinold. "The Dependence of the First Anabaptists on Luther, Erasmus, and Zwingli," *Mennonite Quarterly Review* 30 (April 1956): 104-119.
Fortman, Edmund. *The Triune God: A Historical Study of the Doctrine of the Trinity*. Philadelphia: The Westminster Press, 1972.
Friedmann, Robert. "The Encounter of Anabaptists and Mennonites with Anti-Trinitarianism," *Mennonite Quarterly Review* 22 (1948): 139-162.
Hall, Thor. "Possibilities of Erasmian Influence on Denck and Hubmaier in Their Views on the Freedom of the Will," *Mennonite Quarterly Review* 35 (April 1961): 149-170.
Harding, Vincent. "Menno Simons and the Role of Baptism in the Christian Life," *Mennonite Quarterly Review* 33 (October 1959): 323-334.
Hillerbrand, Hans J. "Anabaptism and History," *Mennonite Quarterly Review* 45 (April 1971): 110-117.

___. "Anabaptism and Protestantism: Another Look," *Church History* 29 (December 1960): 404-423.

___. *Christendom Divided*. Philadelphia: The Westminster Press, 1971.

___. "The Origin of Sixteenth-Century Anabaptism: Another Look," *Archiv für Reformationsgeschichte* 53 (1962): 152-180.

Hunter, A. M. *The Teaching of Calvin*. London: James Clarke and Co., 1950.

Jacobs, Paul, *Prädestination und Verantwortlichkeit bei Calvin*. Neukirchen: Buchhandlung des Erziehungsvereins, 1937.

Jedin, Hubert. *A History of the Council of Trent*. 2 vols. Translated by Dom Ernest Graf, O.S.B. Edinburgh: Thomas Nelson & Sons, 1961.

Keeney, William E. "Basic Beliefs of the Dutch Anabaptists." In Walter A. Klaassen *et al.*, eds. *No Other Foundation*. North Newton, Kansas: Bethel College, 1962.

___. *The Development of Dutch Anabaptist Thought and Practice from 1539 to 1564*. Nieuwkoop: B. de Graaf, 1968.

Krahn, Cornelius. *Dutch Anabaptism: Origin, Spread, Life and Thought, 1450-1600*. The Hague: Martinus Nijhoff, 1968.

Kreider, Robert S. "Anabaptism and Humanism: An Inquiry into the Relationship of Humanism and Evangelical Anabaptism," *Mennonite Quarterly Review* 26 (April 1952): 123-141.

Krusche, Werner. *Das Wirken des Heiligen Geistes nach Calvin*. Göttingen: Vandenhoeck & Ruprecht, 1957.

Littell, Franklin H. *The Anabaptist View of the Church*. 2nd ed. Boston: Starr King Press, 1958.

___. *The Free Church*. Boston: Starr King Press, 1957.

___. *The Origins of Sectarian Protestantism*. New York: Macmillan Co., 1964.

___. "Spiritualizers, Anabaptists, and the Church," *Mennonite Quarterly Review* 29 (January 1955): 34-43.

___. *A Tribute to Menno Simons*. Scottdale, Pa.: Herald Press, 1961.

Loeschen, John R. *Wrestling with Luther: An Introduction to the Study of His Thought*. St. Louis: Concordia Publishing House, 1976.

Löfgren, David. *Die Theologie der Schöpfung bei Luther*. Forschungen zur Kirchen- und Dogmengeschichte, Bd. 10. Göttingen: Vandenhoeck & Ruprecht, 1960.

MacGregor, Geddes. *Corpus Christi: The Nature of the Church According to the Reformed Tradition*. Philadelphia: The Westminster Press, 1958.

McNeill, John T. *The History and Character of Calvinism*. New York: Oxford University Press, 1954.

___. *Unitive Protestantism*. Richmond, Va.: John Knox Press, 1964.

Metzke, Erwin. *Sakrament und Metaphysik: Eine Lutherstudie über das Verhältnis des christlichen Denkens zum Leiblich-Materiellen.* Stuttgart: Kreuz-Verlag, 1948.
Niebuhr, H. Richard. *Christ and Culture.* New York: Harper & Row, 1951.
___. *The Social Sources of Denominationalism.* New York: Henry Holt, 1929.
Niesel, Wilhelm. *The Theology of Calvin.* Translated by Harold Knight. Philadelphia: The Westminster Press, 1956.
Nygren, Anders. *Agape and Eros.* Translated by Philip Watson. Philadelphia: The Westminster Press, 1953.
Oberman, Heiko. *The Harvest of Medieval Theology.* Cambridge: Harvard University Press, 1963.
Oosterbaan, J. A. "The Theology of Menno Simons," *Mennonite Quarterly Review* 35 (July 1961): 191-192.
Ozment, Steven. *Homo Spiritualis.* Leiden: E. J. Brill, 1969.
___. *Mysticism and Dissent: Religious Ideology and Social Protest in the Sixteenth Century.* New Haven: Yale University Press, 1973.
Oyer, John. "The Reformers Oppose the Anabaptist Theology." In Guy F. Hershberger, ed. *The Recovery of the Anabaptist Vision.* Scottdale, Pa.: Herald Press, 1957.
Parker, T. H. L. *Calvin's Doctrine of the Knowledge of God.* 2nd. ed. Edinburgh: Oliver & Boyd, 1969.
Prenter, Regin. *Spiritus Creator.* Translated by John Jensen. Philadelphia: Muhlenberg Press, 1953.
Schroeder, W. Widick. *Cognitive Structures and Religious Research: Essays in Sociology and Theology.* East Lansing: Michigan State University Press, 1970.
Stephens, W. P. *The Holy Spirit in the Theology of Martin Bucer.* Cambridge: Cambridge University Press, 1970.
Stoesz, Willis M. "The New Creature: Menno Simons' Understanding of the Christian Faith," *Mennonite Quarterly Review* 39 (January 1965): 5-24.
Tillich, Paul. *Love, Power, and Justice.* New York: Oxford University Press, 1954.
___. *Systematic Theology.* Vol. 1. Chicago: University of Chicago Press, 1951.
Troeltsch, Ernst. *The Social Teaching of the Christian Churches.* 2 vols. Translated by Olive Wyon. New York: The Macmillan Co., 1931.
Verduin, Leonhard. "Menno Simons' Theology Reviewed," *Mennonite Quarterly Review* 24 (January 1950): 53-64.
Wallace, Ronald S. *Calvin's Doctrine of the Christian Life.* Edinburgh: Oliver & Boyd, 1959.
___. *Calvin's Doctrine of the Word and Sacrament.* Edinburgh: Oliver & Boyd, 1953.
Weingart, Richard E. "The Meaning of Sin in the Theology of Menno Simons," *Mennonite Quarterly Review* 44 (January 1970): 25-39.

Wendel, François. *Calvin: The Origins and Development of His Religious Thought.* Translated by Philip Mairet. New York: Harper & Row, 1963.

Wenger, John. "The Biblicism of the Anabaptists." In Guy F. Hershberger, ed. *The Recovery of the Anabaptist Vision.* Scottdale, Pa.: Herald Press, 1957.

Williams, George H. *The Radical Reformation.* Philadelphia: The Westminster Press, 1962.

Willis, E. David. *Calvin's Catholic Christology: The Function of the So-Called Extra Calvinisticum in Calvin's Theology.* Leiden: E. J. Brill, 1966.

Wingren, Gustaf. *Luther on Vocation.* Translated by Carl Rasmussen. Philadelphia: Fortress Press, 1957.

Wray, Frank J. "The Anabaptist Doctrine of the Restitution of the Church," *Mennonite Quarterly Review* 28 (July 1954): 186-196.

Yoder, John H. "The Prophetic Dissent of the Anabaptists." In Guy F. Hershberger, ed. *The Recovery of the Anabaptist Vision.* Scottdale, Pa.: Herald Press, 1957.

Zijpp, N. van der. "The Conception of Our Fathers Regarding the Church," *Mennonite Quarterly Review* 27 (April 1953): 91-99.

INDEX

This study is wholly concerned with 1) the systematic interrelations among the themes of Trinity, Church, and Ethics; 2) with the internal interrelations of all the sub-topics involved in each of the above main themes, and 3) with the relationships of all the above as they compare with, differentiate, and influence the four major reforming groups of the sixteenth century.

Needless to say, a highly-refined subject index to this sort of study is not only nearly impossible, but would reflect a way of thinking just exactly opposite to that taken in the text. Yet an index is an extremely useful reference tool. The index developed herewith is intended to provide the reader an instrument which is at once a general subject register and a highly detailed outline.

Only significant *discussion*, rather than mere *mentioning*, of a term or subject will be included herein. The level of refinement has been intentionally kept very low. And I have tried to emphasize, via the strictly parallel organization of topics, the need for the reader to follow through with the task of cross-referencing as he pursues his research in the text.

The cross-referencing is critical: the Triune God, we recall, relates *ad extra* as One. So does his true church, and so do his unprofitable servants.

I. *General Organization of the Study*
   A. General hypothesis, 8-11
   B. Limits upon conclusions, 6, 12f.
   C. Methods of research, 45ff.
      See also: Appendix 11-14

II. *Luther*
   A. General Characteristics of
      1. approach to biblical interpretation, 16, 19ff., 28f.
      2. systematic and speculative character, 15f., 28, 34f., 47, 60f.
      3. writing style, 12, 14f., 29f.
   B. Trinitarian theology, General
      1. conservative nature, 4f., 13f., 20, 51
      2. early writings, 19f., 24, 33
      3. relation to Augustine, 21
      4. relation to Calvin, 30, 33, 39, 191f.
      5. relation to Simons, 26f., 30, 32f., 39, 191f.
   C. Trinitarian Ascriptive Patterns
      1. *vis.* Father (power), 23ff., 58
      2. *vis.* Son (form), 24, 26, 30f., 34, 38
      3. *vis.* Holy Spirit (love), 19f., 24, 26ff., 36f., 58f.

D. Understanding of Church
  1. *vis.* Christ, 32, 34
  2. formal definitions, 32f., 35
  3. *vis.* the Keys, 47ff., 53f.
  4. *vis.* worldly orders, 59ff.
E. Understanding of Ethics
  1. *vis.* Christ and Church, 39ff., 53
  2. *vis.* freedom and order, 49f., 60ff.
  3. *vis.* peace, 51f., 63
  4. *vis.* the Two Realms, 54ff.

III. *Simons*
  A. General Characteristics of
    1. approach to biblical interpretation, 73
    2. understanding of history, 67
    3. writing style, 12, 67ff.
  B. Trinitarian Theology, General
    1. conservative nature, 4f., 13f., 73
    2. non-transcendental character, 10, 74f., 80f., 100, 106f.
    3. relation to Calvin, 39, 67, 73ff., 78, 92, 104, 191f.
    4. relation to Luther, 39, 73ff., 88f., 9l2ff., 104, 191f.
    5. relation to Council of Trent, 87, 95, 98
    6. summary, 93f.
  C. Trinitarian Ascriptive Patterns
    1. *vis.* Christ's nature, etc., 77, 80, 87ff., 98f., 108f.
    2. *vis.* Christ's word, 73, 76ff., 91f.
    3. *vis.* Christ's Spirit, 73f., 76ff., 82, 86f.
  D. Understanding of Church
    1. conversion by Holy Spirit, 84
    2. creation by Holy Spirit, 82f.
    3. perfection, 81f.
    4. separation from world, 83, 104f., 108f., 111, 121ff.
    5. tradition, 100ff., 110
    6. visible-invisible, 106f.
    7. summary, 79, 85, 97, 106f.
  E. Understanding of Ethics
    1. ban and shunning, 109, 111ff.
    2. general principles relative to Bible, 92f., 98f.
    3. law, 110f.
    4. pacifism and mission, 118ff.
    5. two kingdoms, 107, 116f.

IV. *Calvin*
  A. General Characteristics of
    1. approach to biblical interpretation, 131f., 134ff., 140, 143ff.
    2. systematic character, 125ff., 143ff., 161
    3. writing style, 12

    B.   Trinitarian Theology, General
          1. conservative nature, 4f., 14
          2. creation-redemption tension, 130, 150, 168
          3. relation to Augustine, 21, 133
          4. relation to Council of Trent, 176
          5. relation to Luther, 39, 125, 129, 133, 136, 141, 147, 171, 181, 186, 189f.
          6. relation to Simons, 39, 125, 159, 171, 176ff., 185f., 191f.
          7. summary, 129f., 133ff.
    C.   Trinitarian Ascriptive Patterns
          1. *vis.* Father (elective love), 136ff., 141, 149, 151ff., 164
          2. *vis.* Christ, as logos, gospel, 139, 141, 149; as order, 141f., 145f.; in union with man 140, 147ff., 166, 168ff.
          3. *vis.* Holy Spirit, and Christ, 139, 142, 167; as power, 142f., 146, 167
    D.   Understanding of Church
          1. justification, forgiveness, repentance, 162ff., 181f.
          2. perfection, 162, 168ff.
          3. visible, and invisible, 159f., 165, 178ff.
    E.   Understanding of Ethics
          1. Discipline, 171ff., 182
          2. law, 173ff.
          3. prayer, 182ff.
          4. two realms, 176ff., 180, 185ff.

V.   *Council of Trent*
    A.   1. General relation to Protestantism, 189ff., 211f.
          2. relation to Calvin, 194f., 197f., 212ff.
          3. relation to Simons, 194f., 201, 204f., 207, 209f.
    B.   Trinitarian Functions, 192f., 197f., 204ff., 216ff.
    C.   Church and Sacraments, 206, 209ff., 214ff.
    D.   Church and Ethics, 198ff., 207ff.

John Richard Loeschen graduated in 1962 from the University of Illinois, Urbana, where he received Phi Beta Kappa honors, with an A.B. in Psychology. He received a B.D. from Chicago Theological Seminary in 1965. He received a Ph.D. in Historical Theology from The Graduate Theological Union, Berkeley, California, in 1968, upon completion of the thesis "Eschatological Themes in Luther's Theology." The thesis year was made possible by a fellowship from the Rockefeller Foundation.

He taught briefly at Mills College, Oakland, California, during his dissertation year. He became assistant professor of history at the School of Divinity, St. Louis University, from 1968 to 1971. Following post-doctoral research at the GTU from 1971 to 1973, he resumed teaching in the department of religious studies, California State University, Long Beach, until 1978.

Dr. Loeschen has contributed articles on medieval and reformation subjects to various scholarly journals, and in 1976 published *Wrestling With Luther: an introduction to the study of his thought* (Concordia Publishing House).

Since 1979 he has been employed as Sales and Service Manager for a furniture manufacturer in Los Angeles. During this time he has continued private research in the history of theology. The present book is the first fruits of that private study.